# Physical Best

## ACTIVITY GUIDE

### Elementary Level

American Alliance
for Health, Physical Education,
Recreation and Dance

Human Kinetics

**Library of Congress Cataloging-in-Publication Data**

Physical Best (Program)
    Physical Best activity guide—elementary level / American
Alliance for Health, Physical Education, Recreation and Dance.
       p.    cm.
    Includes bibliographical references (p.   ).
    ISBN 0-88011-962-4
    1. Physical education--Study and teaching (Elementary)--United
States.  I. American Alliance for Health, Physical Education, Recreation and Dance.  II. Title.
Recreation and Dance.  II. Title.
GV365.P5   1999
372.86--dc21

                                  98-39291
                                      CIP

ISBN: 0-88011-962-4

**Acquisitions Editor:** Scott Wikgren; **Developmental Editor:** C.E. Petit, JD; **Assistant Editor:** Phil Natividad; **Copyeditor:** Bonnie Pettifor and Anne Mischakoff Heiles; **Proofreader:** Erin Cler; **Graphic Designer:** Nancy Rasmus; **Graphic Artist:** Kathleen Boudreau-Fuoss; **Photo Editor:** Boyd LaFoon; **Cover Designer:** Jack Davis; **Photographer (cover):** Tom Roberts; **Photographer (interior):** Tom Roberts, except where otherwise noted. Photos on pages 159 and 233 by Karen Maier. Photo on page 51 courtesy of Instructional Media Services, Cleveland State University, Cleveland, OH and Shaker Heights City School District, Shaker Heights, OH. Photos on pages 39 and 121 by An Noë (FLOK, KULeuven, Belgium); **Illustrators:** Mary Yemma Long, Joe Bellis, and Kathleen Boudreau-Fuoss; **Medical Illustrator:** Beth Young; **Printer:** United Graphics

Printed in the United States of America    10 9 8 7 6 5 4 3 2 1

**Human Kinetics**
Web site: http://www.humankinetics.com/

*United States:* Human Kinetics, P.O. Box 5076, Champaign, IL 61825-5076
1-800-747-4457
e-mail: humank@hkusa.com

*Canada:* Human Kinetics, 475 Devonshire Road Unit 100, Windsor, ON N8Y 2L5
1-800-465-7301 (in Canada only)
e-mail: humank@hkcanada.com

*Europe:* Human Kinetics, P.O. Box IW14, Leeds LS16 6TR, United Kingdom
(44) 1132 781708
e-mail: humank@hkeurope.com

*Australia:* Human Kinetics, 57A Price Avenue, Lower Mitcham, South Australia 5062
(088) 277 1555
e-mail: humank@hkaustralia.com

*New Zealand:* Human Kinetics, P.O. Box 105-231, Auckland 1
(09) 523 3462
e-mail: humank@hknewz.com

# Contents

# About Physical Best

Physical Best is the educational component of a comprehensive health-related physical education program. Additional program resources include:

- *Physical Best Activity Guide—Secondary Level*
- The companion teacher's guide, *Physical Education for Lifelong Fitness*
- *FITNESSGRAM* test for evaluating students' physical fitness, developed by the Cooper Institute for Aerobics Research (CIAR)
- Brockport Physical Fitness Test (developed specifically for students with disabilities)
- Educational workshops for teachers available through AAHPERD which enable teachers to become certified as health-related physical education specialists

The Physical Best program is offered through The American Fitness Alliance (AFA), a collaborative effort of AAHPERD, CIAR, and Human Kinetics.

## Achnowledgments

AAHPERD gratefully acknowledges the contributions of the following teachers to the *Physical Best Activity Guides*: Ellen Abbadessa (Arizona), Carolyn Masterson (New Jersey), Aleita Hass-Holcombe (Oregon), Jennifer Reeves (Arizona), Marion Franck (Pennsylvania), John Kading (Wisconsin), Suzann Schiemer (Pennsylvania), Ron Feingold (New York), W. Larry Bruce (Cuba), Barbara Cusimano (Oregon), Deborah Loper (Nebraska), Laura Borsdorf (Pennsylvania), Jeff Carpenter (Washington), Larry Cain (Wisconsin), Nancy Raso-Eklund (Wyoming), Kathleen Thorton (Maryland), Nannette Wolford (Missouri), and Lawrence Rohner (New Mexico).

AAHPERD would also like to thank Dr. Paul Saltman of the University of California at San Diego for his guidance on nutrition issues, and Gopher Sport and Mars, Incorporated for their financial support of the Physical Best program.

# Preface

> "I hear and I forget. I see and I remember.
> I do and I understand."—Chinese proverb

Welcome to the *Physical Best Activity Guide—Elementary Level*. The activities we are sharing in this book have been designed and successfully used by physical educators from around the country to help their students "do and understand." They are designed to help students gain the the knowledge, skills, appreciation, and confidence needed to lead physically active, healthy lives and are part of Physical Best.

Physical Best is the educational component of a comprehensive health-related physical education program. It complements and supports—not necessarily replaces—existing physical education curriculums, and helps teachers assist students in meeting the NASPE National Physical Education Standards related to health-related fitness.

All Physical Best materials, resources, and workshops will:

- Emphasize enjoyable participation in physical activities that are relevant to students.
- Offer a diverse range of noncompetitive and competitive activities appropriate for different ages and abilities, allowing students to successfully participate.
- Emphasize the personal nature of participation in lifelong physical activity.
- Provide appropriate and authentic assessment as part of the learning process, designed so students take on increasing responsibility for their own assessment.
- Follow proven educational progressions that lead to students taking increasing responsibility for their own health-related fitness.
- Enable students to meet the NASPE National Physical Education Standards for health-related fitness.

## The History of Physical Best

In 1987 the American Alliance for Health, Physical Education, Recreation and Dance (AAHPERD) challenged the nation's youth to become more physically fit. One path to achieving this objective involved tapping our own resources, our physical educators. Physical Best was envisioned as a program to enhance an existing curriculum, supplement daily plans or act as a total package.

Physical Best is a total curriculum package designed to assist youths in understanding the importance of a lifetime of physical activity. Yet this total package can be geared up or down for your school's particular needs/demands.

This program does not cater to the 10% or so that are athletically talented, but focuses on educating *all* children, regardless of their abilities, from a health-related viewpoint. Many health-minded organizations (including the American Academy of Pediatrics, American Medical Association, President's Council on Physical Fitness and Sports, the allied health community, and the US Department of Health and Human Services) emphasize the importance of physical activity to our children. Even top athletes must understand the health aspects of lifelong physical activity so they do not become sedentary after completing their competitive athletic careers.

Based on these concepts, scholars and practitioners at AAHPERD developed Physical Best. First and foremost, Physical Best is educational. The elementary and secondary activity guides provide ideas for quick, easy activities and learning station ideas. You can easily include them in your existing plans or use them on their own. Through these activity guides and in combination with your own curriculum, you'll help your students understand why physical activity is important to their health.

Physical Best is individualized—students compete only with themselves, not against others. This philosophy complements the various authors of today's physical education textbooks. However, Physical Best differs from some in that it does not claim to stand alone, thus eliminating all other aspects of our discipline. The motivation, the test procedures, and the goal setting program are all designed to work on self-improvement regardless of the student's level of skill and fitness. The *FITNESSGRAM* test battery is criterion-referenced. This inspires students to achieve goals, not strive to meet unrealistic standards, and to include physical activity in their lives outside of school. This Physical Best philosophy will remain the focus of the program as it expands and evolves.

Physical Best is a total package. It is not designed as an instructional unit. It becomes a part of the "branching off" of other activities. It was designed so that instructors could use all or part of the package. It does not tie instructors down to day-to-day lesson plans. It encourages creativity and makes it easy for you to include elements of Physical Best in your existing program.

## Inclusion in Health-Related Fitness

Everyone can benefit from a health-related fitness program, regardless of gender, culture, or ability. Inactivity and poor diet cause more preventable deaths each year in the United States than illicit use of drugs, firearms, sexual behavior, microbial agents, and alcohol *combined* (McGinnis 1993)! While not every student can equally benefit from, or even participate in, every activity, including everyone in your health-related fitness program isn't just a good idea—it's the law.

Including all of your students should not be an afterthought, but an important part of your planning and teaching process. We'll discuss some of the most significant inclusion issues in sidebars like this one throughout Part I of this *Activity Guide*. We've also designed the activities for easy adaptation to a wide variety of special circumstances.

# Physical Best Activity Guides

The *Physical Best Activity Guides* will help you bring the theory behind health-related fitness into your school with a variety of fun, developmentally appropriate activities that combine physical activity with other aspects of learning. Each *Activity Guide* begins with a review of the health and teaching principles behind an effective health-related fitness curriculum. The *Activity Guides* then present a variety of activities that focus on the four elements of health-related fitness:

aerobic fitness, muscular strength and endurance, flexibility, and body composition. These activities stress class management, keep group instruction and demonstration to a minimum, maximize the number of practice trials, and provide frequent individual feedback, instruction, and encouragement.

The *Activity Guides* are designed to facilitate a health-related fitness program at your school. You'll find further information in *Physical Education for Lifelong Fitness: The Physical Best Teacher's Guide*. This book, forthcoming in early 1999, will provide a strong theoretical background for health-related fitness programs, including specific advice on integrating The Cooper Institute's *FITNESSGRAM* into a complete program. We're developing other Physical Best resources, including workshops with certification from AAHPERD.

We should be teaching children what they need to know to become healthier. This can be accomplished by incorporating Physical Best into our existing lesson plans. Therefore, we can teach children how to become fit for life through fun, basic skill development and participation. Physical Best can help accomplish this goal via its developmentally appropriate activities and concepts. Let's put the education back into physical education. Join us in using the new Physical Best.

# PART I  Teaching Health-Related Fitness

# Chapter 1
# Health-Related Fitness

Fitness is defined as a condition in which an individual has sufficient energy to avoid fatigue and enjoy life. It is also defined as the capacity of the lungs and muscles to function at optimum efficiency (Pate 1983). The content area of physical fitness includes learning experiences associated with achieving optimum health through the components of cardiovascular endurance, muscular strength and endurance, flexibility, and body composition.

Physical fitness can be divided into health- and skill-related components. Health-related fitness focuses on factors that promote optimum health and prevent the onset of disease and problems associated with inactivity. Health-related fitness includes cardiorespiratory (aerobic) fitness, muscular strength and endurance, flexibility, and body composition. Skill-related fitness includes balance, agility, coordination, power, reaction time, and speed. To help children develop active lifestyles, health- and skill-related fitness must be taught equally.

The components of health-related fitness can be measured separately, and exercises have been designed to improve each specific area. The most important point in physical education is to teach *total fitness* in ways that develop each of the areas of health-related fitness. Research demonstrates that individuals who engage in regular physical activities to improve the four components of health-related fitness better their basic energy levels and lower their risk for heart disease, cancer, diabetes, osteoporosis, and other chronic diseases.

# Components of Health-Related Fitness

A health-related fitness curriculum integrates physical fitness testing and education. A good physical-fitness curriculum emphasizes the four components of the health-related fitness: cardiovascular endurance, muscular strength and endurance, flexibility, and body composition (CDC 1997).

## Cardiorespiratory Fitness

Cardiorespiratory endurance involves the ability of the heart and lungs to supply oxygen to the working muscles for an extended period of time. Also called aerobic endurance or fitness, it is the ability of the circulatory and respiratory systems to adjust to and recover from the effects of moderate to vigorous activity, such as brisk walking, running, swimming, or biking. Cardiorespiratory endurance is determined by a concept called maximum oxygen uptake ($\dot{V}O_2$ max), in other words, how well one consumes oxygen during moderate to vigorous physical activity.

There are four techniques to help students improve their cardiovascular endurance: continuous, interval, Fartlek, and circuit-course activity. Continuous activity may include both anaerobic and aerobic activities. *Aerobic* activities, meaning "with oxygen," are done continuously, are longer in duration, and can be sustained over a period of time. *Anaerobic* activities are short blasts of activity done in the "absence of oxygen." Interval activity includes physical activity that alternates in intensity levels. Fartlek is similar to interval activity, but with it the terrain (such as hills) controls the intensity levels. Circuit training (circuit-course activity) combines continuous activity with flexibility and muscular strength-endurance activities, providing more variety.

## Muscular Strength and Endurance

*Muscular strength* is a measure of the greatest force that can be produced by a muscle or group of muscles. *Dynamic strength* is the force exerted by a muscle group as the body moves, such as in a push-up. *Static strength* is the force exerted against an immovable object, such as pushing against a wall. The benefits of increasing muscular strength include a reduced risk of injury as well as improved posture, physical performance, and body composition. Developing strength requires working against a resistance in a progressive manner. Muscular strength can be improved in children, although they are incapable of producing large muscle masses.

*Muscular endurance* is the ability to contract a muscle or group of muscles repeatedly without incurring fatigue. The longer a muscle is used, the greater its endurance becomes. In children, locomotor activities help develop muscle endurance. The primary objective of developing muscular endurance in children is their being able to participate in activity for longer periods of time before feeling muscle fatigue.

Basic guidelines have been established for resistance training and exercise progression in children (see Kraemer and Fleck 1992). In the primary levels (youngsters 7 years and younger) children should be introduced to basic exercises with little or no weight at all. Aim to develop the *concept* of a training session at this age. Teach the exercise techniques and progress from body-weight calisthenics to partner exercises and on to lightly-resisted exercise. Keep the volume low. In the intermediate levels (among youngsters of 8 to 10 years of age) gradually increase the number of exercises. Practice the techniques of exercise in all lifts; start gradually loading the exercises. The training volume should be *gradually* increased and carefully monitored for toleration to the exercise stress.

## Flexibility

Flexibility is the ability of a joint to move freely in every direction or, more specifically, through a full and normal range of motion. Several factors can limit joint mobility, including genetic inheritance, the joint's structure, the amount of fatty tissue around the joint, and the body's temperature. Flexibility can be improved, however, with stretching.

The two most common types of stretching for primary and intermediate level children are static and ballistic stretching. *Static stretching* involves slow, gradual, and controlled elongation through a full range of motion. *Ballistic stretching* employs rapid, uncontrolled, and bouncing or bobbing motions. Ballistic technique is not recommended for the general population whose control may be compromised and whose risk of injury may be increased.

## Body Composition

Body composition refers to the quality or makeup of total body mass. *Total body mass* is composed of lean body mass and fat mass. Lean body mass includes a person's bones, muscles, organs, and water. Fat mass is fat, adipose tissue. The assessment of body composition determines the relative percentages of the individual's lean body mass and fat mass. The skinfold caliper test is the most popular method for measuring body composition.

# Principles of FITT

The Physical Best program follows the FITT principles for improving and maintaining physical fitness. The principles of frequency (F), intensity (I), time (T), and type (T), along with overload and progression, are taught in each health-related concept. We outline them in this section.

## Frequency

Frequency refers to the number of times a person engages in physical activity that is moderate to vigorous in nature. The frequency depends on the intensity and duration of the activity session. There are various standards as to how often one should exercise to improve or maintain physical fitness. According to the *U.S. Surgeon General's Report on Physical Activity and Health*, physical activity that is moderate to vigorous in nature should be done most days of the week.

## Intensity

Intensity refers to the speed or workload used in a given exercise period. Intensity depends on the fitness goals of the exerciser and the type of training method being used. Aerobic intensity is the speed of the activity, and it is measured by checking one's heart rate. Primary grade students should be able to identify where to take the heart rate and understand the relationship between the heart rate (pulse) they feel and the heart's beating. At the intermediate levels students should be able to monitor their own heart rates. Including a higher percentage of moderate-to-vigorous activities helps you match the needs of the students. Intensity with activities for muscular strength and endurance is the workload or resistance of the exercise. With flexibility, intensity is the range of motion the joint can achieve.

Intensity is directly related to how long one can sustain activity. Understanding intensity is one of the hardest notions to teach children, since they do everything fast. Intensity may have to be taught several times to instill safety precautions and to maximize the quality of the activity.

## Time (Duration)

Duration refers to the number of minutes of physical activity. In cardiovascular endurance activities, duration is the amount of time spent doing the activity. For students in the primary levels you should limit the duration to shorter bouts of 6 to 8 minutes, with rest periods lasting at least 1 to 2 minutes between activity bouts. For intermediate-level students you can safely prolong physical activity for 10 to 20 minutes at a time.

Time is how many repetitions and sets one performs in muscular strength and endurance activities. In flexibility exercise, on the other hand, time relates to how long a stretch is held before it is released. The recommended time for children to be physically active is 30 minutes most days of the week.

## Type (Specificity)

What type of exercise you select is related to the principle of specificity. Specificity of training is the physiological adaptation to exercise that is specific to the system being worked or stressed during exercise. For example, the specific training exercises a child does for flexibility do not increase his or her cardiovascular endurance. For maximum effectiveness, aerobic exercises must be rhythmic and continuous and involve the large-muscle groups.

## Overload

Overload is the amount of exercise that is needed to improve fitness levels. The body must perform harder than normal to improve. The overload principle is the basis for considering the variables of frequency, intensity, time, and type. To best explain overload to children, let them experience it firsthand—through vigorous activity and by keeping track of how long they sustain activity or how many repetitions they perform.

## Progression

Progression is *how* overload should take place. An increase in the level of exercise, whether it be to run farther or to add more resistance, must be done in a particular progression. This enables the body to adapt slowly to the overload; thus, it eventually makes the overload normal. Children need to understand that improving their level of fitness is an ongoing process. To help children better understand progression and see that they are improving, give them opportunities to track their progress. You can effectively help them achieve this understanding through pretests and posttests.

# Fitness Is for Everyone

Physical activity, its assessment, and the opportunity to benefit from a health-related fitness education program are important to the well-being of all people in society, regardless of their gender, ethnicity, physical competence, or having particular disabilities. The concept of inclusion provides students with positive relationships through their interactions, and these interactions should carry the concepts through to adulthood. The overall mission of the physical educator is to help *all* students enjoy and learn about physical activity so that they will continue to be active the rest of their lives.

### Individuals With Disabilities

Including individuals with disabilities in the physical education setting shows that physical activity is for everyone. It is the responsibility of every professional conducting physical activity programs to explore all options for including people with disabilities in their programs.

All people have equal rights to the health-related benefits of physical activity programs, and the values of these programs accrue equally to all. Participation in physical activity contributes to human growth and development. Emotional and social development flourishes through interaction with peers in play activities, but such opportunities often elude individuals with disabilities. By conducting properly planned and integrated programs, however, trained professionals can provide opportunities for people with disabilities to participate in developmentally appropriate activities.

As a professional conducting the program, you are responsible for successfully including all participants. A leader shapes the attitudes of an entire group. Providing inclusive programs requires your gaining the necessary knowledge and skills to include individuals with disabilities, being accountable for a positive attitude, ensuring equal treatment across all lines of diversity, and effectively communicating, both verbally and nonverbally.

It is possible that regular physical education may not be an appropriate placement for some individuals with disabilities. Having support from parents, other teachers, a peer tutor, or a teacher assistant can sometimes alleviate disruptive behaviors (which often result in safety risks). However, if a student is not receiving any benefit from regular physical education, continues to be disruptive to others, or continues to pose a severe safety risk, an alternative placement is appropriate. Ongoing evaluation determines whether the alternative placement is effective for a particular student or whether participation in regular physical education one or more days a week would be more beneficial.

Students with disabilities shouldn't be placed in physical education classes solely for their social development or to have only passive roles, such as being a scorekeeper. The major purpose of participation in the physical education is to help students become active, efficient, and healthy movers. Physical education goals as defined by IDEA, Part B, include the development of gross motor skills, development of fundamental motor patterns, development of health-related fitness, and development of skills needed to participate in lifetime leisure pursuits, including individual and team sports.

**Fitness for Individuals With Disabilities.**   Fitness education and testing programs for individuals without special disabilities have traditionally emphasized a balanced approach, with expectations of achievement in all four physical fitness components. This approach represents the ideal—to maintain health-related standards of fitness in every way, including an active lifestyle.

Some individuals with disabilities, however, may have different lifestyles. For example, some may have great amounts of leisure time, others may have occupations demanding physical labor, still others, sedentary occupations or limited ambulating abilities. The health-related fitness profile for individuals with disabilities needs to be personalized according to disability, daily-living needs, current activities, and the person's potential.

**Programming for Individuals With Disabilities.**   To plan physical fitness activities that are appropriate for people with disabilities, you must consider the individual's initial or present level of performance. You can determine their present level of performance through a careful assessment of the person's physical fitness needs. The *Physical Best and Individuals with Disabilities Manual*, as well as other resources, provides tools for assessing the fitness level of someone with disabilities.

## Gender Inclusion

Physical education and sport are often gender-based, which can perpetuate stereotypical beliefs and attitudes. Females, in general, have had fewer opportunities and less encouragement than males to be physically active. Physical activity is often more valued in the male domain. However, by eliminating systemic barriers and ensuring all individuals the freedom to develop their own interests and abilities, individuals, groups, and society all will benefit.

Gender-equitable education involves including the experiences, perceptions, and perspectives of girls as well as boys in all aspects of education. The inclusive strategies that promote girls' participating also reach boys, who are excluded from the girls' experiences, perceptions, and perspectives by more traditional styles of teaching and curricular content.

Physical educators, interacting daily with students, are in an ideal position to promote and affect desirable attitudinal changes in students. In providing a gender-equitable learning environment, you have opportunities to enhance students' sensitivity to gender considerations. Inequity can surface in the general physical education program, in access to resources such as equipment, and in the attention and

> ### Principles of Gender Equity in Education
>
> - All students have the right to a learning environment that is gender-equitable.
> - All education programs should be based on the students' abilities and interests.
> - Gender equity incorporates a consideration of social class, culture, ethnicity, religion, sexual orientation, and age.
> - Gender equity requires sensitivity, determination, commitment, and vigilance over time.
> - The foundation of gender equity is cooperation and collaboration among students, educators, educational organizations, families, and members of communities.

interactions that teachers and coaches give or have with students. Equipment availability should reflect equal value placed on female and male participation. How educators and coaches organize for activity, assign responsibilities, and speak can either detract from or inspire gender sensitivity.

The National Girls and Women in Sports Association has initiated guidelines to ensure attention and interaction free of gender bias. These include the following:

- Distributing leadership and demonstration roles among all students
- Assigning nonstereotypical responsibilities to both genders
- Modifying rule games to involve all students, without losing the essence of the game, and explaining why modifications are desirable
- Handling behavior problems consistently among both females and males, not using gender-based assumptions as punishments
- Using nonsexist language
- Avoiding the use of gender as the sole criteria for grouping
- Not tolerating or allowing inequitable student-to-student interactions of a verbal or physical nature
- Incorporating several learning styles

Gender equity is important at all age levels. In the primary and intermediate grades, the most commonly used equity strategies are language cues and student-to-student interactions. Educators should ensure that the student-to-student interactions are positive. Avoid making or tolerating negative statements, such as calling girls "sissy" or "tomboy." Language cues that are respectful and nonsexist should be the norm at this age group. Choosing females as leaders of groups and as demonstrators can help eliminate gender bias.

To promote gender equity, you can include activities that promote a wide movement repertoire for all students. You can provide students with curricular choices to ensure that assessments and intramural activities are not gender-biased.

### Cultural Sensitivity

Cultural variables may significantly affect the delivery and learning of health information, and you should consider them when designing a physical education

*Culture is learned and shared by a group of people. It teaches what to fear, what to respect, what to value, and what to regard as relevant in life. It encompasses many variables, including values, beliefs, and perceptions that given people exhibit. Cultural variables include the group of people in one's life who are considered to be family members and the relationships these people have to one another. Culture is symbolically represented in language and the different ways in which people communicate and interact socially. Cultural variables do not include situational and environmental conditions. Culture is a continuous and cumulative process, rather, a continuum that individuals move along throughout their lives. Experiences over time contribute to movement along the continuum. Teachers, students, and families can be found at different points along their culture's continuum.*

program. Although some similarities do exist within or between groups, differences do, too, and you should examine them for their potential impact on the design and implementation of a health education program.

From culture to culture, the perception of physical activity will differ. In some cultures thinness is perceived to be a desirable health goal; in others, thin people may be considered in poor health, whereas fat people are thought to be healthy and happy. Natural body odors may be acceptable and desirable in some cultures, but offensive to others, especially in physical activity.

Bias in physical education instruction can affect students' self-images, philosophies of life, interpersonal sensitivities, opinions about different cultural groups, and opinions about social problems. Studies have shown that students who feel they are portrayed in stereotypical ways will internalize these notions and fail to develop their own unique abilities, interests, and full potentials. If teachers become aware of their own uncomfortable feelings, they may find it easier to recognize uncomfortable feelings among their students. Once teachers become comfortable with the differences, they can move on to create pleasant experiences that build comfort, acceptance, and respect for diversity in their students and others.

Effective communication with a student is the teacher's most powerful tool for overcoming cultural barriers. It is best that messages about physical activity and health not conflict with existing cultural beliefs, values, and perceptions. When appropriate, messages can acknowledge existing cultural practices, building on cultural strengths and pride.

## Benefits of Fitness

Regular moderate physical activity results in many health benefits for adults. Physical activity has been proved in adults to decrease the risks of diseases that cause mortality and morbidity. Although more research is needed on the association of physical activity and health among young people, evidence already shows that physical activity brings some health benefits for children and adolescents. It improves aerobic endurance as well as muscular strength and endurance, and it decreases the risk factors that lead to cardiovascular disease. Physical activity among adolescents is consistently related to higher levels of self-esteem and self-concept and with lower levels of anxiety and stress.

When you explain the benefits of physical fitness to children, you must explain the concepts at a cognitive level appropriate to their age. At the primary and intermediate levels, you can explain exercise benefits in these ways: Physical activity

- makes the heart pump more strongly;
- helps lower blood pressure and resting heart rates;
- reduces the risks of heart disease;
- strengthens the bones and muscles;
- gives you more energy to do school work, daily chores, and play;
- helps maintain a healthy body weight; and
- reduces stress.

It is important to keep in step with the constant changes in our lives. Modern machines, computers, and other conveniences have made it possible to avoid physical activity. Substantial evidence links the adulthood problems of obesity, high blood pressure, and stroke to failure to develop a physical activity habit during childhood.

## *Process or Product?*

The goal of teaching fitness to children is helping them acquire the skills, knowledge, and attitudes that lead to a lifetime of physical activity. Teaching fitness should be viewed as a long-term process of educating students about physical fitness and the importance of regular activity. The process starts out with achieving lower-order objectives, and it gradually moves to more complex, higher-order objectives that guide students toward valuing fitness and becoming self-directed. Corbin (1987) refers to this process as the "Stairway to Lifetime Fitness."

The Stairway to Lifetime Fitness is a description of hierarchical objectives for a fitness education program. Students move from a level of dependence to independence as they progress educationally through life. As students grow older, they move up each of the five steps toward lifetime fitness. The focus on a particular objective will change as the learner proceeds up the stairway.

**Step 1:**  *Doing regular exercise.* At this stage fitness scores are not important. Children learn what is fun and learn to love exercise. They will develop personal habits of doing exercise regularly.

**Step 2:**  *Achieving physical fitness.* Fitness is temporary. If children achieve fitness goals without obtaining a love for fitness, they will not maintain fitness for life.

**Step 3:**  *Personal exercise patterns.* At this level students learn what activities they personally enjoy doing and can make decisions about personal exercise patterns that are best for them. What is best for one child is not necessarily best for another. Educators begin to relinquish the decision-making process to the students. The role of the educator is to guide the students in making personal activity choices that are sound and realistic.

**Step 4:**  *Self-evaluation.* By this stage students realize what activities they enjoy the most. They begin to establish personal habits and patterns of lifetime exercise. To be fully educated, the older students must be able to assess their own fitness, having a basis for making informed decisions about lifetime fitness. By learning self-evaluation, they can revise their fitness programs as needed.

**Step 5:**  *Problem solving.* Students know the facts about each of the essential components of health-related fitness and are able to plan their own programs. The students essentially become informed consumers in fitness.

Corbin points out that it is the process of exercise that is important when teaching fitness education. If people can do the correct exercises for a lifetime (i.e., as a process) then the product (i.e., physical fitness) will follow. The objectives of teaching health-related fitness are met when the process becomes a regular, permanent part of a person's lifestyle.

## Lifetime Implications for Health and Well-Being

There is little doubt that regular exercise is an important part of a healthy lifestyle. Most experts feel that children and youths need daily physical activity to keep fit and healthy. We have some information already about the effects of physical activity on improving the health of children and how it can carry over into adulthood. Researchers note that when children engage in physical activity, they mix very short bursts of intense activity with easy to moderate activity. Children have difficulty in exercising at one pace for 20 minutes or longer.

Most researchers have reported that the cardiorespiratory systems of children and youths respond to regular aerobic exercise in a way similar to adults. Dr. Thomas Rowland has shown that children can improve aerobic fitness after training, but that the increase is far less in youngsters than in adults. As a result of his findings, Dr. Rowland concluded that children often have high aerobic fitness levels to begin with, that adults may train more effectively than children, and that the bodies of children may lack the ability to adapt and respond fully to regular exercise (Rowland 1990).

Most studies suggest that obese children and youths are less physically active than their peers. Long-term inactivity on the part of children increases the likelihood of being overly fat. Children who are active and lean have less chance of being overly fat later in adulthood. Obesity during childhood has been linked to other risk factors for disease, such as high blood pressure and cholesterol. Studies show that heart disease, cancer, and other chronic diseases are linked to the lifestyles of people and that these behaviors are learned in childhood and adolescence.

Physically inactive children and youths who exercise regularly have lower resting blood pressures and more favorable blood-lipid profiles. In addition, body fat decreases when exercise programs are initiated among children. One of the most valuable health benefits in youth is that when vigorous activity occurs early in life, a higher bone-mineral density is achieved. Most bone buildup occurs during adolescence, so vigorous activity in the earlier years reduces the risk of osteoporosis later in life. Weight-bearing exercises are better for building stronger bones in children than are weight-supported exercises. All of the body's muscles should be exercised to build strong bones.

People begin to acquire and establish patterns of health-related behaviors during childhood and adolescence. Thus, we should encourage young people to engage in physical activity. Schools and communities can improve the health of youngsters by providing instruction, programs, and services that promote enjoyable, lifelong physical activity (CDC 1997).

# Chapter 2 ——————————
# Physical Activity Behavior and Motivation

Over the past 20 years a lot has been learned about the various health benefits of regular activity. Recently, with the release of the *U.S. Surgeon General's Report on Physical Activity and Health,* we have seen that research has demonstrated the health benefits of moderate to vigorous physical activity and, more important, the positive preventive health effects that activity has on adults and children. The task now is to promote healthful physical activity among the population. The important issue for promoting activity is to understand the reasons and behavioral changes underlying a person's level of activity.

Research on physical activity and behavior has examined what influences physical activity and what effect intervention programs have on the activity level of individuals. Half the adult population is mainly sedentary. The problem is how to get them active and, once they are active, to keep them going. It is much easier for people to start an exercise program than to continue it on a regular basis. Adults cite as reasons for exercising achieving better weight control, reducing blood pressure, relieving stress and depression, finding enjoyment, increasing self-esteem, and improving their social life. Many people choose *not* to be active, despite the social, health, and personal benefits of exercising. The reasons these people cite for their inactivity are a lack of time, a lack of knowledge about fitness, inadequate facilities, and their feeling fatigued.

Personal, situational, behavioral, and programmatic factors determine whether someone adheres to a program of physical activity and exercise. These determinants influence both children and adult participation in physical activity. Studies have shown that influences in childhood also play a major role in the adherence to activity in adulthood.

Among the personal factors that influence and determine physical activity are an individual's exercise history, knowledge of or beliefs in health benefits, and personality. People who participate in sports and activity as youngsters have similar adherence patterns. Active children who receive parental encouragement for physical activity will become more active adults than will the children who received no such encouragement. Studies show that high school and college experiences with sport increase the likelihood of exercise adherence in adulthood.

Knowing about the health benefits of physical activity is not enough, however, to inspire activity adherence. Some adults fail to adhere to exercise programs because of negative attitudes they acquired about physical activity when they were younger, and some adults are impeded by a lack of knowledge about the appropriate activity. It is important that knowledge about health-related fitness be an integral part of a fitness education program for adherence to occur later in life.

Self-motivation is consistently related to exercise behaviors and adherence. Individuals who are intrinsically motivated tend to adhere to exercise plans than those who rely on external reasons to exercise.

Situational factors can help or hinder regular participation in physical activity. Social support is critical to enhancing adherence rates among people in exercise programs. When children participate in activities, they seek out approval from teachers, parents, and peers. Like children, adults can also utilize positive social reinforcement. Time is the primary reason that adults give for not pursuing physical activity. Many sedentary people who lack motivation may rationalize that they lack time. It becomes an excuse for not exercising.

Sport psychologists have studied different techniques to enhance adherence to exercise. The different techniques they develop fall into five non-exclusive categories: environmental, reinforcement, goal setting and cognition, decision making, and social support. As environmental approaches they have used prompts, such as signs or bulletin boards for reinforcing the behavior. Having a choice of activities to choose from appears to promote adherence. Reinforcement techniques in exercise adherence must promote self-motivation. These techniques might include occasional rewards, positive feedback, and methods for self-monitoring. Goal-setting techniques should be self-set, rather than having an instructor set them; flexible, rather than fixed; and time-based, rather than distance-based. Using decision-making to enhance adherence involves the participants in the program's structure. Social support, however, is the most important approach with children and adults who are participating in physical activity.

School physical education is probably the most important intervention for promoting children's physical activity and fitness. School physical education is only part of an overall effort to promote desirable physical activity patterns in children. As in adults, other personal factors figure in the mix with children, such as biological and psychological influences. Gender is an important determinant in physical activity. From preschool through adolescence and often into adulthood, boys tend to be more active than girls (Sallis 1991). Positive trends among girls must be encouraged and accelerated to provide them with equal access to and support for healthful physical activity. The decline in physical activity participation is the steepest from childhood to adolescence, and it continues into adulthood.

Knowing *how* to be healthy and physically active is probably more important than knowing why (Desmond et al. 1986). Some knowledge may be helpful to start a child exercising, but it is rarely enough to keep a student active. The positive social and emotional effects of physical activity are powerful motivators for children, so they are what you should stress.

Social and physical environmental factors influence levels of physical activity not only in adults, but also in children. Social influence in elementary and intermediate levels includes peer modeling and support. Peers are very important determinants of children's physical activity patterns. The physical environment is more important in determining physical activity levels outside the school, because physical education programs are usually designed for a particular local climate and the community's resources. Children do most of their activity in the context of organized programs such as after-school programs, youth sports leagues, and clubs. When the goal of an organization is to promote *lifelong* physical activity among children, the levels of adherence to physical activity increase. Television and technology also affect children's activity levels.

All these factors are associated with children's physical activity levels, so effective intervention must operate at many levels. No single approach is likely to be effective. Children's needs change with age. Special attention should be devoted to girls and to adolescents since their activity levels are relatively low. But it is vital that physical education should prepare all children for a lifetime of physical activity, just as other teachers prepare children for a lifetime of learning and work. Children should seek other avenues for physical activity and not rely solely on physical education classes.

## Motivation

The importance of physical activity in a healthy lifestyle has been recognized for years. Data about the benefits of physical activity to children and youth are scarce. Debates continue, for example, about the extent to which children are active, with some of the data's problems reflecting difficulties in measurement. What seems to be emerging, however, is that children's activity levels decline through the teenage years and that boys are more active than girls.

Whatever explanations account for a decrease in activity levels in children, it seems desirable to encourage children's activity for health and developmental reasons. Theorists and researchers have attempted to support determination to exercise but little is yet known about the possible determinants of physical activity in children. One explanation is given by *social-cognitive theory*. This approach to motivation in physical activity involves constructs of self-efficacy (self-perceptions of worth or competence) and, more recently, perceptions of success and definitions of achievement goals (Biddle and Goudas 1996).

Physical education must aim to maintain lifetime exercise (a process) rather than to improve short-term fitness (a product). Adults tend to talk mostly about the product of physical activity, whereas most children discuss physical activity as a process. Youngsters emphasize being included in activities, being wanted by friends, and participating in "fun." In most cases, children learn to value fitness as an end product rather than an ongoing process. Sport psychologists know this "product" as extrinsic motivation.

Motivation takes two general forms: extrinsic and intrinsic. *Extrinsic motivation* involves factors outside the individual, unrelated to the task being performed (Ormrod 1995). Extrinsic motivators can be rewards that encourage participation, help children work to full potential, and recognize success. Although these extrinsic rewards do promote achieving activity goals to some extent, they also have numerous drawbacks. Children view the extrinsic rewards, which are used to control or manipulate children into participating, as the reason to participate in events, activities that they might otherwise have chosen to do on their own (Raffini 1993). In relation to physical activity, if a child participates in activity knowing there is a reward at the end, then the child focuses solely on participating for the reward and not for personal satisfaction or accomplishment. Extrinsic rewards, thus, do not promote lifetime physical activity patterns. If children are given extrinsic rewards they tend to focus on the product (the reward) instead of on the process, and they may stop working once the reward has been received. When children choose to participate on their own, however, and experience feelings of competence, then extrinsic rewards may help reinforce those feelings. This in turn enhances their intrinsic motivation to participate in physical activity. The key is to introduce extrinsic rewards in a correct manner at ideal times.

*Intrinsic motivation* is an individual's internal desire to perform a particular task (Ormrod 1995). Unlike extrinsic rewards, intrinsic motivations promote long-term behavioral changes more effectively. Children working in environments that emphasize intrinsic motivation tend to view physical activity as a process. This ongoing process can lead them to personal satisfaction and competence.

"Fun" is the primary reason, in terms of the experience of intrinsic pleasure, that students give for participating in physical activity. Fun, intrinsically motivating activities involve four characteristics: challenge, curiosity, control, and creativity (Raffini 1993). Teachers must empower children to develop the self-confidence to believe they can accomplish certain tasks, the self-esteem to believe they are worthy, and the self-efficacy to believe they are in control of their lives.

For years, students in physical education have been turned off by exercise. Consider why kids are in physical education: to increase physical activity, improve physical fitness, and improve fitness knowledge. To accomplish these goals and help them develop lifetime habits of physical activity, the key is choosing activities that follow the intrinsic feelings and perceptions kids have. Teachers should invoke children's curiosity. If the activity is too easy, children may become bored. Some bored and frustrated learners may at times need extrinsic motivation to be convinced to exercise. Activities need to be developmentally appropriate for the level and include challenges to spark the curiosity.

As educators, give students a sense of control over the activities. Teach basic skills first. If you take the time to instruct students on the proper form and techniques, they can begin to master these basic skills. The more decisions the students then make in an activity, the more control they have. This type of control teaches them self-responsibility.

You must also provide activities that allow children to be creative and to fantasize about the content of the activity. This gives them a chance to use their creative thinking skills. It has the additional advantage of including students who are not as active or coordinated as well as the more naturally physically adept. By adding new, exciting equipment for classes, you can provide adventure and fun in students' activities. Decorating the gym with posters, charts, and bulletin boards creates a colorful environment.

Students need support and encouragement for their hard work in class. Occasionally provide positive, healthy incentives for active participation. Expressions of motivation are important as well. Some examples of words that connote or promote feelings of intrinsic motivation are *play, excitement, mastery, success, improvement,* and *freedom.* Phrases to encourage students may include *Great job! Way to go! Terrific! Very creative!* and *Much better!* Gestures also are important in encouraging intrinsic motivation. Giving the high five, nodding approvingly, shaking hands, and laughing with a student are all ways to encourage and enhance intrinsic motivation.

Parental support is considered one of the most important determinants of children's involvement in physical activity. Parents can influence their children by modeling physical activity behaviors. Biddle and Goudas (1996) showed clearly the importance of parent and teacher encouragement in strenuous physical activity. Parental encouragement created greater adherence to physical activity through increasing a sense of competence.

In theory and in practice, intrinsic motivation is the key to making physical activity a lifelong habit. A teacher's focus should be to help students internalize motivation and to create opportunities that can give them a sense of accomplishment from within. When intrinsic motivation for physical activity is present, the awards, prizes, and payments become immaterial. Physical education programs should strongly motivate children to maintain their own fitness. Here, in summary, are suggestions for motivating students:

1. Award the *process* of participation, rather than the *product* of fitness.
2. Set goals that are challenging yet attainable.
3. Use visual aids to publicize items of interest in fitness.
4. Emphasize self-testing programs that teach children to evaluate their own fitness levels.
5. Do not use fitness-test results for grading.
6. Involve the parents.

Working toward that happy state in which physical activity sparks the fun, thrill, and excitement in students to carry out continuing fitness activity for a lifetime should be a worthwhile goal for any teacher.

# Goal Setting

According to the *U.S. Surgeon General's Report on Physical Activity and Health*, students should be physically active most days of the week by doing moderate to vigorous activity. The guidelines set by the American College of Sports Medicine recommend a fitness class to be at least 20 minutes in length and to meet at least three times a week. It takes good educational programs, caring instructors, time, facilities, and a desire to improve for students to feel motivated to engage in lifetime healthful behaviors. Most school systems do not allow enough time in physical education to make teaching health skills and fitness a priority for most students. Still, it is vital to encourage students to become active both inside *and* outside of the physical education classroom.

## Foundations for Goal Setting

Attaining fitness benefits often requires several weeks of activity, depending on how frequently your class meets each week and the duration of each exercise period. Formal pre- and posttesting should not occur too soon or too often, although frequent and informal self-testing is helpful to monitor progress. A year-long program will not necessarily result in achieving twice as much fitness as can a semester-long program, but fitness planning should be incorporated into the entire program. If you carefully followed all FITT variables, measurable fitness changes might be noted after only nine weeks of class; however, one entire semester (about 16 weeks) is a more realistic timeframe for inducing measurable fitness changes, provided the frequency and intensity have been adequate. A six- or nine-week retest is useful as a check on whether the initial goals were realistic. The retest or ongoing self-testing and informal testing results can be used to reset and fine-tune the final goals. Scores will naturally change as a student matures, particularly in the elementary years.

The rewards students look for are usually more extrinsic in nature than intrinsic. However, the intrinsic reward of self-improvement brings about behavioral changes that last for a much longer period of time. Goal setting is a mechanism that helps students understand their limits and feel satisfied with their accomplishments. Using goals created from personal assessments establishes their ownership and fosters pride in the process.

Behavior-modification programs are successful because goals are set and action plans are written to help meet those goals. Action plans help to establish a pathway to that destination. Allowing students to write goals based on their performances teaches them the importance of setting goals. They can apply this little teaching technique easily to other areas of their lives. The types of behaviors (goals) students require for improving health fitness can be determined from a pretest. Without goal setting, fitness scores are just data to submit to an administrator or to parents. By incorporating goal setting into the curriculum, fitness scores become much more meaningful. Establishing goals is a good way to encourage changes in behavior leading to improved health and fitness. Goal setting must be done carefully to successfully enhance motivation.

Goal setting takes experience and practice for both the students and educator. You must consider certain factors when setting goals with students. First, students' fitness levels vary widely. Girls and boys differ in certain fitness variables. Growth and maturation also influence fitness levels. The criteria-level charts provided in the *FITNESSGRAM* program reflect both gender and age differences. The teacher should be sure to use the proper charts when setting goals for each child.

The goals for each student should reflect the individual's level of fitness and fitness habits: greater magnitude of goal for less-fit students and lesser magnitude of goal for fitter students. A fit student will have to work hard to make small gains that bring him or her close to personal potential. A less-fit student, expending the same effort, might show dramatic fitness gains but still remain far below his or her potential. Focus not on comparisons but on personal improvement and progress toward personal goals.

Consider also a student's fitness habits. If a youngster has poor flexibility and is already taking part in activities that enhance flexibility in specific joints, then the goal should be set lower than if the same student with poor flexibility rarely does stretching activities. In the second situation, the fact that the student rarely does the appropriate activity opens the possibility that the student might respond well to stretching. In the first situation, on the other hand, where the student already stretches but remains at a low level of ability, factors other than exercise might be affecting that child's ability to improve range of motion. Therefore, goals are always specific to an individual.

Identifying activity habits can also help you find what is likely to motivate a student to participate.

And with habits, remember that exercise is not the only factor contributing to fitness. Regularly consuming a proper diet, maintaining good sleep patterns, and controlling stress are also important. Discovering a student's habits in all these areas will improve your helping the child to individualize and set realistic goals.

Goal setting can be intimidating and time consuming if you are a teacher who has a large class. Having successful strategies beforehand for teaching students goal setting will help you undertake the task.

## Cultural Inclusion

It is important for physical education teachers to know about various cultures because all students are cultural beings. A culture encompasses many of the predisposing, enabling, and reinforcing factors affecting students' health behaviors and status. It affects health and activity decisions. As cultures vary, so do notions of what a human body symbolizes, how it should appear, how it functions most appropriately, and why, when, and how it should be treated. Responses about what is appropriate vary from culture to culture. Cultural values, beliefs, and perceptions influence students' abilities to understand, internalize, and exercise positive health practices that will enhance their quality of life. A culture can help solve problems and conflicts in the school and in the community, making it worth your while to become acquainted with such values. Giving a child messages that invalidate his or her cultural beliefs or values can damage a student's self-esteem. Goal setting should occur based on cultural beliefs. In some cultures, for example, competitive goals are unacceptable for girls, so individualizing goals is better.

Curricular content need not be different when the student population is culturally diverse. Activities that present challenge, risk taking, problem solving, and critical thinking are appropriate at the elementary level. Every child should be encouraged to accept various roles in all physical education activities, at the same time respecting cultural values. At the elementary level the curriculum can include movement education and guided discovery activities that pair words and concepts from several languages in movement tasks, creative dance, rhythmic activities, cooperative tumbling, games, and thematic play. Homework assignments might include studying the contributions to physical education and sport made by individuals (such as Olympians) from various cultures.

The students' ability to integrate their personal and cultural selves is a valuable skill for change. Modeling the integration of content about the contributions of various cultures is vital; it can demonstrate effective ways of using health information within the class.

## Basic Strategies for Successful Goal Setting With Students

First, encourage students to set goals based on their current fitness status rather than on a comparison of their personal status with others'. Motivation is related to competence or perceptions of success in a particular area, so basing success on current physical fitness levels allows each student the potential to improve and thus experience success at goal setting. This positive experience will influence the student's motivation and behavior. Following several goal-setting guidelines will help motivate students maximally and positively influence their behavior and attitude toward physical activity.

**Involve Students in the Goal-Setting Process.**    Involving students enhances their commitment to achieving their goals and encourages self-responsibility for personal fitness. Scores should be their own, not norm-based. Consider the age, maturity level, and knowledge level of each student, which should influence the amount of input you use. And, of course, an individual's interests and needs should be part of establishing the child's fitness goals.

**Start Small and Progress.**    Start with a small class. Begin the goal-setting process with one grade level and continue to set goals with this class as its members progress through the school system. In a few short years, they will be experienced in setting goals in all areas of fitness.

**Focus on Improvements Relative to an Individual's Past Behavior.**    Take into account the student's initial level of performance. The lower the level of performance, the greater the potential for improvement. The higher the level, the less improvement is possible. If a student has problems with motivation, set the individual's goals at lower increments than you might for a student who is already highly motivated. For example, you might need to cajole the less-motivated student more than you would others.

**Set Specific and Measurable Goals.**    Specific and measurable goals are more effective than vague goals (such as "I'll run faster"). For example, if a student wants to run faster and has already completed the mile in 12:05, you can help the student set a more specific, measurable goal of running the mile in 11:50. Students need some instruction, direction, and practice in identifying specific, measurable goals. If the goals are not measurable, it is impossible to determine if the student has been successful at achieving them, which defeats the purpose of goal setting.

**Set Challenging and Realistic Goals.**    When you assist students in setting physical fitness goals, take into consideration the child's initial fitness level. Also plan the time carefully between the pretest (to establish the goal) and the posttest (to measure the achievements). The lower the student's initial fitness level and the longer the time between testing periods, the greater the child's potential for improvement. The higher the student's initial fitness level and the shorter the time between testing periods to work on fitness, the less potential for improvement. It is important that the goal not be so easy that it does not challenge the student. Most students

### Sample Goals for Aerobic Fitness

- I will reduce my mile run by ___ seconds by performing aerobic activity ___ times per week for at least ___ minutes each session.
- I will exercise aerobically ___ times a week, running the one-mile distance at least ___ times a week, timing and logging the results.
- I will perform aerobic activity ___ times a week, recording the amount of time, type of activity, and intensity of the activity.
- I will walk briskly ___ times a week for a total of ___ blocks. Each week I will increase my distance ____ blocks.

make their goals too difficult, and their motivation suffers when they cannot attain their goals. It may be helpful to have students practice setting goals and making intermediate goals until they learn more about themselves and their physical fitness levels.

**Write Down Goals.** Written goals hold more meaning for students and help them focus on what they need to accomplish. If you work with preliterate or dyslexic students, it can help to use alternative methods such as pictures. The Appendix contains a sample contract form for recording specific goals. These are masters that you can use or adapt to fit your program needs. You will also need to spend more time with students who have special health conditions. These students usually need extra guidance or incentives and/or have health concerns.

**Provide Students With Strategies.** Students must understand *how* to change behaviors that are detrimental to improving or maintaining physical fitness. You can suggest examples of strategies, such as having them ride their bike three times a week, do 25 sit-ups each night before bed, or stretch after the day at school by using a series of stretches that you provide. In other words, provide strategies for improvement. It would be better, of course, if the students eventually develop strategies on their own with your guidance. Learning how to develop goals based on FITT and nutrition is a crucial part of the lifelong-fitness process.

**Support and Give Feedback About Progress Toward Goals.** An important aspect of goal setting that many teachers disregard is giving positive reinforcement and encouragement. Verbal encouragement (such as "I see you have been running one mile every other day. Keep up the good work!), written encouragement (such as a note: "John, I was glad to see you practicing modified pull-ups today at recess"), and verbal recognition (such as "Susan has set a great example for all of us by doing her flexibility exercises daily!") can assist in keeping students committed to positive fitness behaviors.

**Create Goal Stations.** Setting up "goal stations" for students helps instill a sense of ownership as the youngsters write their goals. The students can rotate in small groups to work on particular goals. You can group the students according to their receiving similar scores on their assessments. They will likely have similar goals and provide one another extra motivation and encouragement in achieving the goals. As they enter the class, students can also work individually at these stations to improve (instant activity). Allowing them to choose work areas places the responsibility for improvement on them.

**Provide Opportunities for Periodic Evaluation.** Periodic reassessment of fitness behavior helps students assess how they are progressing toward their personal goals. Assessment opportunities should occur regularly throughout the year. These reassessment opportunities can include informal testing and self-testing, both in school and at home. Use the information gained through reassessment to evaluate and adjust existing goals where necessary. You and the students will also have the opportunity after reassessments to change their goals and determine whether the goal was perhaps too difficult or too easy.

## Building a Fitness Program Around Student Goals

The Physical Best program is a model for establishing goals in physical fitness levels, activity participation, and the affective and cognitive domains. The Physical

Best program recognizes the achievement of goals set by students, an important reinforcement for student motivation.

Using goal-setting techniques and strategies helps students have positive experiences through movement activities, feel good about themselves in physical activity, and carry positive fitness habits for a lifetime. Physical educators can support the students' use of goal setting to enhance their lives and fitness abilities.

## Table 2.1    Guidelines for Goal Setting (Amount of Change to Consider a Reasonable Goal)

| Fitness component | Far from criteria levels | Near criteria levels | Equal or better than criteria levels |
|---|---|---|---|
| **Aerobic endurance (1-mile run)** | Decrease time 1-4 min | Decrease time 1-2 min | Decrease time 30-60 s |
| **Flexibility** | Increase reach 2-8 cm | Increase reach 2-5 cm | Increase reach 1-3 cm |
| **Body composition** | Decrease skinfold sum 1-10 mm | Decrease skinfold sum 1-5 mm | Maintain, or possibly decrease 1-2 mm |
| **Upper-body muscular strength and endurance** | Increase by 4-5 reps | Increase by 2-3 reps | Increase by 1 rep |
| **Trunk muscular strength and endurance** | Increase by 5-10 reps | Increase by 3-7 reps | Increase by 2-5 reps |

Table 2.1 provides some guidelines for setting fitness goals, but the numbers in the chart are simply guidelines. Initial level of fitness is already built into the table:

- Low—initial level is far from reaching the criteria levels
- Moderate—initial level is close to the criteria levels
- High—initial level is at or above the criteria levels

Nevertheless, each of the other unique circumstances each student presents must be considered for establishing that student's goals. For example, two moderately fit students might establish upper-body strengths that fall at the extremes of the range. One might have class only two times a week, not get much encouragement at home, and be somewhat overweight. The other student might have an hour-long class five times a week.

Table 2.1 is based on *reasonable estimates*. Pursuing further research will provide more objective informational guidelines, and thus the standards will be adjusted. You and your students will improve in the ability to set goals as you practice setting more goals and observing the outcomes.

# Chapter 3
# The Health-Related Fitness Curriculum

Although the school physical education program is not the only means to develop fitness objectives with youth, it is certainly a primary avenue. At issue is not whether we should have fitness goals in physical education but rather what those fitness goals should be and, more importantly, how we should implement them within the school curriculum. This chapter will review the National Standards for Physical Education and how to implement these recommendations into your program of health-related fitness education.

## National Standards

A national consensus on the foundations of knowledge, skills, and behaviors essential to develop in physical education, adapted physical education, dance, and health education has led to a national standards for these disciplines. The process has helped to update and redefine the disciplines, which subsequently have developed to include more recently identified subdisciplines. As a result of these new subdisciplines, we now have more information about skills and concepts of movement and fitness, motor development, motor learning, and exercise physiology. These are areas not traditionally found in school physical education curricula but essential for all students to enhance their potential and build the habits, attitudes, and skills that will persuade personal choice and participation in physical activity throughout life.

The national physical education standards are based on the definition of the physically educated person as defined by the NASPE *Outcomes of Quality Physical Education Programs* (NASPE 1992). According to this document,

### A physically educated person:

- Has learned skills necessary to perform a variety of physical activities;
- Is physically fit;
- Does participate regularly in physical activity;
- Knows the implications of and the benefits from involvement in physical activities;
- Values physical activity and its contributions to a healthful lifestyle.

The designers intended that all five component parts of the definition not "be separated from each other" (NASPE 1992, p. 6). This definition was further defined in 20 written outcome statements with multiple benchmarks at every other grade level. The writing of the *Moving into the Future: National Standards for Physical Education* (NASPE 1995) began with the intent of developing assessment guidelines for determining achievement of the outcomes. Instead, the result was the compacting of the outcome statements into seven standards to assist in designing pre-K–grade 12 assessments that would determine student achievement toward becoming a "physically educated person." Sample benchmarks, which provide ideas about what might be assessed and achieved, are included to help assess whether the standards are met at specific grade levels.

The standards should be viewed as a whole, regardless of the application or focus on either movement or fitness, the major content areas of physical education. However, to apply the standards in school instructional programs requires some deliberate analysis and isolation of concepts and skills. This analytical application is important to plan for sequential learning, which in turn leads to integrating the parts and then realization of the whole.

The *U.S. Surgeon General's Report on Physical Activity and Health* (1996) reinforces the holistic concept of "a physically educated person." This research-based publication identifies factors that determine the likelihood that physical activity will be initiated and maintained throughout life, including perceived benefit, enjoyment, feelings of competence, safety, access, time, cost, negative consequences (e.g., injury, negative peer pressure, self-identity), and use of labor-saving devices (see p. 46). The report lists "influencing and modifiable determinants" affecting physical activity behaviors among children and adolescents. Some examples of them are self-efficacy, perceptions of sports competence, expected and perceived benefits, negatively associated barriers, intention, enjoyment, favorable attitudes toward physical education, social influences of role models, availability of equipment, and time spent outdoors (p. 234). This report provides a strong message about what school and community programs must do for children to prepare them to live quality lives.

## Inclusion and the Physical Education Curriculum

- No students should have to earn their ways into physical education. It is a school's responsibility to justify why a student with disabilities should be removed from regular physical education.

- Many students with disabilities have unique learning and motor needs. Some students might need modified instruction or goals and might derive different benefits from physical education. A student with mental retardation might need extra verbal cues and demonstrations to understand directions, for example. Another student might work on such individually prescribed skills as improving upper-body strength for pushing, speed, and accuracy in her wheelchair. A blind student might benefit more from the interaction and support of peers during physical education, which can motivate him to try a new skill, such as walking independently. A physical education teacher usually can meet these special needs within typical physical education situations.

- Support staff is needed for both the students with disabilities and the physical educator. Support for students might be providing monthly meetings with an adapted physical education teacher, specialized equipment, or a full-time teacher assistant.

- Removing a student from regular physical education class should be discussed only after attempts made within regular physical education have proved unsuccessful in providing necessary support to the student.

—The National Association for Sport and Physical Education (NASPE) and The American Association for Active Lifestyles and Fitness (AAALF)

Many factors in today's society lure young people from activities that are physical to pursuits that are more sedentary. Less instructional time for physical education, poorly conceived instructional programs, and less direct and inadequately trained curricular supervisors are some factors in the schools. At the same time, greater access to sedentary and technology-based entertainment, leisure activities, and work reflect influences outside the school directly competing with the factors that influence children's developing habits of participation in physical activity.

The Physical Best educational materials have been written to help teachers deliver the essential content identified by the national standards. The materials, presented sequentially, are designed for students to master them in ways that will positively influence their choices for physical activity throughout life. The program resources are related to national standards and identify the factors that link movement, fitness, health, and the aesthetics of leisure activities and the arts.

## National Physical Education Standards

The National Physical Education Standards (NASPE 1995) apply directly to fitness education programs such as Physical Best. Physical education's uniqueness lies in the skills and concepts required for successful performance in all movement forms, including fitness activities for exercise and conditioning programs. Developing movement skills and concepts has multiple purposes and benefits beyond health-related fitness in such arenas as competition, cooperation, and aesthetics. And it is the composite of all these factors that influences participation in physical activity.

The first four standards relate to fitness education in ways that are specifically identified within each instructional idea found in these materials. Some standards have a primary relationship to the unique content of physical education. Others have a secondary relationship, and they affect participation in physical activity but also have similar significance in other disciplines.

**Primary Relationship.**   These are the standards that directly relate to the concepts and movements of good physical education:

*Standard 1.*  Demonstrates competency in many movement forms and proficiency in a few movement forms.

*Standard 2.*  Applies movement concepts and principles to the learning and development of motor skills.

*Standard 3.*  Achieves and maintains a health-enhancing level of physical fitness.

*Standard 4.*  Exhibits a physically active lifestyle.

**Secondary Relationship.**   Standards 5 through 7 have an indirect relationship with physical education in that they justify the mastery of the content defined by Standards 1 through 4. It is not likely that students will achieve Standards 5, 6, and 7 without mastering 1, 2, 3, and 4. Likewise mastering 1, 2, 3, and 4 may not be possible if the learning environment, student behaviors, and affective responses to students do not foster motivation to enhance learning and instill habits. You can relate Standards 5, 6, and 7 generally to all subject areas taught in schools. Attention to them simultaneously with the more specific, content-related standards is essential to counteract factors that often negatively influence participation in physical activity.

*Standard 5.*  Demonstrates responsible personal and social behavior in physical activity settings.

*Standard 6.*  Demonstrates understanding and respect for differences among people in physical activity settings.

*Standard 7.*  Understands that physical activity provides opportunities for enjoyment, challenge, self-expression, and social interaction.

## National Health Education Standards

The National Health Education Standards published in *Achieving Health Literacy* (Joint Committee on National Health Education Standards 1995) are linked to the physical education standards. Health education affords unique knowledge about health, preventing disease, and reducing risk factors in all situations and settings—and it influences behaviors that promote these aims. They include not only physical activity but other areas of personal, family, and community life.

**Primary Relationship.**   Health standards 1, 2, 3, and 4 are most closely related to fitness education. Students will:

*Standard 1.*  Comprehend concepts related to health promotion and disease prevention.

*Standard 2.*  Demonstrate the ability to access valid health information and health-promoting products and services.

*Standard 3.*  Demonstrate the ability to practice health-enhancing behaviors and reduce health risks.

*Standard 4.*  Analyze the influence of culture, media, technology, and other factors on health.

**Secondary Relationship.**  Standards 5, 6, and 7 could be related to any discipline including fitness education within physical education.

*Standard 5.*  Demonstrate the ability to use interpersonal communication skills to enhance health.

*Standard 6.*  Demonstrate the ability to use goal-setting and decision-making skills to enhance health.

*Standard 7.*  Demonstrate the ability to advocate for personal, family, and community health.

## National Standards for Dance Education

The National Standards for Dance Education (NDA 1995) are closely linked to physical education. Dance is both a movement form (as are sports, aquatics, fitness activities, and outdoor recreational activities) and a physical activity providing health and fitness benefits. Its uniqueness as a physical activity, however, is that it also is an art form, affording opportunities to create, communicate meaning, and interpret cultural issues and historical periods. Movement fundamentals found in dance are recognized as the foundations for all other movement forms. They are closely related to the development of all motor skills and movement performances.

**Primary Standards.**  All of the dance standards relate to the understanding of movement forms in general. For purposes of these materials Standards 1 and 6 are of primary importance. Standard 6 relates to the specific fitness needs of dance performers.

*Standard 1.*  Identifying and demonstrating movement elements and skills in performing dance.

*Standard 6.*  Making connections between dance and healthful living.

**Secondary Standards.**  These standards relate closely to the structure of all movement forms. They permit learning in a noncompetitive approach that focuses on structure, critical thinking, creativity, communication, and the integration of multiple disciplines. These factors help build confidence and competence in movement performances, prior to competitive involvement. The *U.S. Surgeon General's Report on Physical Activity and Health* clearly identifies them as critical and modifiable factors that influence participation in physical activity.

*Standard 2.*  Understanding choreographic principles, processes, and structures.

*Standard 3.*  Understanding dance as a way to create and communicate meaning.

*Standard 4.* Applying and demonstrating critical and creative thinking skills in dance.

*Standard 5.* Demonstrating and understanding dance in various cultures and historical periods.

*Standard 7.* Making connections between dance and other disciplines.

Integrating the national standards in physical education, health, and dance provides an important way to promote the effects of physical activity on health and one's personal choice to be physically active. None of these disciplines stands alone. Few student groups are solely focused on just one purpose, whether it be health, competition, or aesthetics. While some students have a greater interest in, more facile learning style for, flair for, or yearning after one of these areas, all youngsters benefit from learning and applying these standards. The recognition of these interdisciplinary links helps us maximize our energies for teaching and learning the essential content of them all.

## Sequential Learning Plan

Each of the standards documents is sequential. The standards you have read here have additional, sequentially written transitional standards from one grade or school level to the next, leading to completion of the program standards. Physical education standards are designated for grades K, 2, 4, 6, 8, 10, and 12; health standards for grades 4, 8, and 11; and dance standards for grades 4, 8, and 12. Regardless of the grade designation, developing the content stepwise will enable mastery of both concepts and knowledge. Teachers should identify even further, smaller chunks of information and skill development. They can use these more detailed bits to plan instruction according to the developmental stage and progress of their individual students. Written instructional courses, units of study, and individual lesson plans provide the details to effectively make these developmental connections. The Physical Best materials provide you with sample ideas of useful activities that assist teachers in delivering these "smaller chunks."

General expectations for each of these levels can be found in other resources as well. For instance, the "Premises," established by the Outcomes Committee to provide direction for the writing and implementation of *Outcomes of Quality Physical Education Programs* (Premise 11, p. 9)—and later for the writing and implementation of the physical education standards—have identified expectations level by level. Various state departments of education also provide direction and a rationale for establishing a sequence of learning, identifying in their curricular and regulatory documents the unique responsibilities particular to each grade or school level. These are general guidelines for grade-level emphases:

| | |
|---|---|
| *All grades* | Physical fitness, movement skills, concepts, and affective development. |
| *Primary grades* | Movement-skill acquisition and awareness of the effect of physical activity on the body. |
| *Intermediate grades* | Movement-skill acquisition and identification and definition of specific fitness factors and their relationship to specific types of activities. |

*Middle school*   Mastery of common physical activity skills and strategies; concepts of physical fitness training and conditioning; skills and fitness development; awareness of personal factors influencing the personal choice of physical activity.

*High school*   Integration of physical fitness concepts and strategies, health fitness status, and needs for physical activity performance.

Teaching any one of the many content areas in isolation from other areas gives you only short amounts of time to spend with it. So, even though teachers do not have expertise in all curricular areas, their basic knowledge of each should stimulate creative ways to make connections between the various areas. Here are a couple of ways to maximize, even making daily, the focus on fitness concepts, skills and activities:

• Seek out teachers in other disciplines within the school, investigating essential content being taught by each, sharing essential content being taught in the physical education class, and providing creative activities that link fitness concepts to other subjects taught in the school.

• Create a fitness corner in the elementary classroom. Think up physical activities that might be used to teach math and science concepts while reinforcing application to movement or encouraging participation in physical activity.

School is the work of children and adolescents, just as a job or career is the work of adults. Whatever their ages, people must become more aware of how they can deliberately include physical activity in their personal daily agendas—in ways that are habit-forming. That will not happen unless the plan to include it is developed and maintained at every stage of our lives, including K-to-12 school programs. Therefore, daily physical activity must be planned for all grades in school (and deliberate attention and access later given to physical activity in the workplace).

## Specific Activities and Activity Modifications

Some of the activity suggestions have been adapted from *Dynamic Physical Education for Elementary School Children* and *Physical Best and Individuals with Disabilities*.

### Aerobic Endurance

• Allow individuals to run or walk for time rather than distance.
• Use peer tutors or buddies to help set the pace for the activity.
• Use equipment that may help motivate individuals to continue to move.
• Engage in activities that encourage individuals to move for as long as possible.
• Modify jump-rope activities.

### Upper-Body Strength and Endurance Activities

• Provide activities that encourage students to pull their own body weight.
• Allow children to lift stuffed animals or bottles filled with colorful rocks.
• Use a parachute and make large and small waves.
• Use bands or terry-cloth wrist weights to increase arm strength.
• Have individuals maintain a crab or push-up position for as long as possible.

### Lower-Body Strength and Endurance Activities

• Practice a variety of abdominal activities.
• Using a parachute, have half the group lie back while the other half sits up.

### Flexibility

• Place objects, such as beanbags, at individuals' feet to encourage their reaching down for them.
• Use lightweight, colorful scarves that can be tossed in front of and to the side of the body; encourage the individual to reach for the scarf.

# State Standards and Curriculum Regulations

Standards and curriculum regulations are written within state government, a political context. These documents may not include enough essential content or provide the conditions necessary to achieve it as identified by national standards. Why? State and local documents must address the understanding, expectations, resources, and needs of many constituent groups—not only those who are professionally trained but also lay persons called upon to support the educational system and its programs. Standards must be achievable by all students. Often the expectations are based on the varied experiences and visions of the lay persons or politicians who approve them.

Local school-district standards usually reflect locally acceptable expectations, cultures, and the unique resources of the community being served. When writers and teachers set up curriculums, they should use national standards to provide a content-inclusive foundation on which local school districts can interpret state standards. For classroom teaching to be effective, it must be directed by knowledgeable, up-to-date professionals who have studied the disciplines and can interpret state and local standards to deliver essential content to all students. Physical activities come in many types, but they may present similar benefits of achieving and maintaining healthful levels of fitness. Students in our classes come from varied backgrounds and with different preferences for physical activity. When these students make decisions about participating in physical activity, they are directly influenced by experiences in physical education classes. "Essential content," therefore, must include developing competence in activity skills and understanding of the concepts common to any physical activity choices students may subsequently make.

Physical and health educators are responsible, therefore, for maintaining a high enough level of expertise to be able to interpret state standards. Through them instructional programs can deliver essential content that represents the totality of the disciplines as identified by national standards. The Physical Best program, focused in fitness education, provides instructional materials to do just that.

# Chapter 4
# Teaching Principles for Health-Related Fitness

Physical education has many purposes, ranging from developing motor (e.g., throwing or catching) and social (e.g., cooperation) skills to learning exercise training principles. All these purposes aim to help children grow up to be physically active adults. Other parts of the physical education curriculum teach students cognitive information about physical fitness concepts, involve them in learning experiences to apply the fitness information, and guide them toward valuing an active, fitness-oriented lifestyle. These activities and concepts taught in class are designed to help children develop into "physically educated" people. The *National Content Standards in Physical Education* (AAHPERD 1996) states that a physically educated person "exhibits a physically active lifestyle" and "achieves and maintains a health-enhancing level of physical fitness."

Physical Best supports the program goals of the National Standards: to instill in children and youths the knowledge, skill, and attitudes that will prepare and encourage them to engage in appropriate physical activities throughout their lifetimes. Using the goals of the National Standards and the Physical Best programs as a guide, teachers can design yearly and daily plans to incorporate appropriate learning activities related to physical fitness.

## Characteristics of a Quality Physical Education Program

Quality physical education programs are structured so that the duration, intensity, and frequency of activities help motivate students and meet their individual needs. When appropriate, students participate in selecting activities from all movement categories. All students have an equal opportunity to participate in a balanced physical education program. A quality physical education program will

- foster the development of positive attitudes;
- foster active participation;
- require problem-solving skills;
- recognize differences in students' interests, potential, and cultures; and
- develop personal and career-planning skills.

A good physical education curriculum also balances health-related physical fitness, motor skills, content knowledge, and personal and social development activities. To develop a quality fitness plan Virgilio (1997) makes these suggestions to physical educators:

- Plan, communicate, and cooperate with classroom teachers, administrators, and health service professionals.
- Choose noncompetitive, developmentally appropriate fitness activities, including a wide variety of exercises and movement experiences for general body development.
- Make sure that children are physically active most days of the week at least 30 minutes a day.
- Teach the benefits of an active lifestyle throughout their lives.
- Include children of all abilities in activities.

- Emphasize rewards, not awards, using positive reinforcement and incentives to motivate the children instead of giving awards for levels of fitness.
- Encourage self-responsibility for fitness programs by teaching the students how to monitor their progress and set goals.
- Make fitness activities fun and enjoyable, allowing children to enjoy activities with friends and the community.
- Integrate fitness education throughout the school year in the classroom and other subject areas.
- Use a variety of teaching strategies and styles by recognizing how your students learn about physical fitness.
- Model positive exercise behaviors.

Through participating in a physical education curriculum, youngsters develop the knowledge, skills, and attitudes necessary to incorporate physical activity into regular routines and leisure pursuits to live active, healthy lifestyles. The curriculum's components involve active living, movement, and personal and social responsibility. Students learn to understand the principles and concepts that support active living, develop and maintain a personal level of functional physical fitness, and develop positive attitudes toward the pursuit of lifelong health and well-being. Movement routines teach them efficient and effective movement skills, body mechanics, and concepts in all movement categories as well as a functional level of activity-specific motor skills. Personal and social responsibility components in the curriculum develop positive behaviors and intellectual skills through participation in physical activity.

In an effective physical education program, children learn that they need not be elite athletes to establish positive physical activity attitudes, beliefs, and behaviors for lifetime health. In a good program the teachers use various teaching strategies and styles.

## Developmentally Appropriate Movements

Young children need, want, and are innately programmed to move and play. Recognizing this, educators should provide an environment conducive to physical activity for *all* children, not just the youngsters that are genetically talented or who happen to mature early. Teachers are responsible for giving all children developmentally appropriate movement activities that will increase their self-confidence and promote a healthy self-esteem. These activities are all-inclusive: everybody participates and wins. Movements in early-childhood programs should introduce children to different ways of using their bodies. Through movement and play children actually prepare their brains for learning. Research conclusively indicates that when children are engaged in physical activities, the cognitive domains of the brain are naturally stimulated.

Learning experiences are designed to meet the physical, cognitive, and emotional needs of the child. This is what is meant by developing the "whole child." When beginning, select one child to demonstrate the main challenge of the lesson. Proceed slowly to ensure that *every* child understands what will be involved with the activity. Give all students the chance to participate and model for one another.

## *Teaching Strategies*

Various teaching situations have some similarities and definite differences. The differences range from the size, meeting frequency, age and abilities of students, range of equipment, and duration of a class. As a physical educator you must start with well-planned objectives, matched with appropriate activities, and effectively organized to adjust to the similarities and differences among the class's members. This section briefly describes some of the effective strategies you can implement in daily plans.

**Set the Environment.**   Equipment placed around the area sets the stage for easy retrieval. A prearranged activity area allows teachers maximum interaction with the students. Bulletin boards and signs convey that this is an environment created for students to enter and learn. When students are greeted at the door, they know the educator is ready for class and eager to work with them. These simple actions send strong messages to learners, parents, and administrators that a teacher is well prepared and organized.

**Plan and Teach Routines to Use Equipment.**   Each student should have individual equipment to use, rather than having to wait for a turn. An efficient system for handing out and collecting equipment can save valuable time. Equipment should be placed in a safe location around the edge of the activity areas for quick distribution to students. Students hustle as they retrieve equipment in a safe manner, move to an open space, and immediately begin working on the assigned task. It is good practice to have the students place any equipment on the floor, so it is out of their hands, while you give instructions. When an activity uses circuits or stations, equipment should be located next to each station in an orderly manner allowing the children safe movement to subsequent stations.

**Use Music to Enliven Activities.**   Music can motivate most children to move with a smile on their face. If you add some blank intervals between selections when you dub the music onto tape, you'll have more opportunities during playback to model, supervise, and motivate students. Well-timed musical numbers are also useful to help you measure and demonstrate the concept of overload with a gradual extension of exercise time.

**Use Stop and Start Cues.**   The use of cues to start and stop activities will facilitate activity, use class time efficiently, and promote careful listening. The cue to stop must be easily heard and well understood, especially when students are working in groups. Upon the stop cue, students are to cease activity within five seconds. Once students are all quiet and listening, deliver or model directions quickly.

**Use Class Time Effectively.**   Clear, short directions maximize the time you have for instruction and practice. Lengthy explanations and discussions confuse students and lose their attention. Combine a visual demonstration with verbal descriptions whenever possible. Group the students quickly by assigning partners and dividing them into their smaller groups.

**Focus Student Learning.**   Be sure to organize your class so that you give the primary focus of the lesson top priority. Explain exactly what you want the students to learn as a result of the experience or activity. The students' attention should focus on the planned outcome. Students engage in active learning when the purpose of the activity is clear, and it is effective for you to use a phrase or "mental set" to gain their focus. Visual aids encourage and reinforce learning; adding them to verbal directions allows youngsters to utilize more than one sense.

Signs with simple printed directions and pictures provide visual learners with more easily assimilated information.

**Give Positive Reinforcement.**    Positive feedback gives the students reinforcement. You can use it effectively even when they are progressing slowly. Positive experiences and sensing continual progress toward personal and realistic goals are important. Specific feedback directs students in helpful directions.

**Integrate Activities With Other Studies.**    It is important to follow a conceptual format, one that gives students experiences that will help them apply their physical education to the world outside of the classroom. Students benefit from opportunities to solve problems relating to physical activity and program development. Integrating real-world lessons and concepts, such as math or geography, also enhances the overall learning process in physical education.

**Check Often for Understanding.**    If you quickly invite students to pantomime a task, explain directions to a friend, respond as a group to specific questions, or point in the direction of the station rotation, you will be able to assess their understanding of the assigned task before they actually engage in the activity. Particularly if the activity is new, this could save time, which might otherwise be lost due to their confusion.

**Supervise Actively.**    The process of teaching and learning requires active supervision. This includes developing certain patterns: you model the task, occasionally clarify or motivate, move through the activity areas, keep all students in view as much as possible, and provide positive and corrective feedback specific to the assigned task. Through active supervision you reinforce students' on-task behaviors, enhance the quality of practice, and communicate your enthusiasm.

**Use Exercise Time Instead of Repetitions.**    It is always a challenge to individualize learning for all the students in a class. This task becomes particularly difficult with larger classes, broader groupings of ages and abilities, and a complex, dynamic environment. Using *time* as the basis for activities, rather than number of sets or repetitions, directly addresses concerns of individualizing instruction by encouraging students to perform as many quality movements as possible. The key to this system is to get students to hold themselves accountable for quality. Active supervision and frequent interaction with students can significantly help you hold them accountable for the given task.

**Add Closure.**    To close a lesson give a brief overview of what the lesson attempted to do and what students accomplished. Review objectives that might be coming up in future lessons to get the class excited about the next lesson.

To reach every student takes varying your teaching style. Before selecting a particular teaching style, you must decide what the lesson's objective is, clearly identifying what you wish the students to learn. No one teaching method or style is inherently better than any other. The one you choose will depend on the objective of the lesson.

Being innovative or using a variety of techniques and styles adds excitement to learning. Mosston and Ashworth's *Spectrum of Teaching Styles* suggests many practical and easy-to-use teaching methods, including these:

*Command style* is useful when teaching a new activity or lesson. The teacher uses a demonstration and explanation technique. This method is time-efficient, develops listening skills, and streamlines class management.

*Practice style* allows the students to take on more responsibility for learning. Although the learning objectives and class content are still decided by the teacher, the students work at their own pace to perform the task. One easy way to organize several activities at one time is to incorporate the station approach, using task cards to help with instruction. Practice-style teaching affords a teacher the freedom to give individual attention as needed.

*Reciprocal style* allows students to "teach" other class members the objectives and lesson content chosen by the teacher. Students work in pairs in a teaching-learning partnership. Criteria checklists provide a reference for feedback during the activity. Your role as teacher is to stay neutral and act as a facilitator.

*Self-check style* encourages self-responsibility and self-improvement. Decisions are shifted to the learners to promote their greater responsibility. A criteria checklist (used in the reciprocal style) works well for this teaching style, which allows individuals to set their own pace better than they can with a partner.

*Inclusion style* emphasizes everyone's right to participate and be successful. For this style, you establish various levels of performance for each fitness activity. Your role is to encourage learners to evaluate their own performances. This teaching style gives students the right to choose to enjoy mastery of a particular level before moving on. Task cards help implement the learning activities.

## Guided Discovery and Problem Solving

In guided discovery, you (as teacher) establish a predetermined answer to a problem. Then you plan a series of questions and responses to lead youngsters (as learners) to a particular final answer. In the problem-solving style, on the other hand, the answers are unlimited. In either case, you must monitor the class for safety and organization.

Research has shown that traditional fitness-education models and strategies have been unsuccessful in developing lifetime physical activity patterns. Emphasizing how physical education is taught and using the suggested teaching styles and strategies will offer a number of more effective avenues to encourage lifelong fitness patterns among students.

**Holding Students Accountable.**   In an ideal world all students would be self-motivated learners, and the teacher would simply be a resource person to assist the students in pursuing their personal growth. With some students, this model occurs. More often, however, students at all levels need a teacher's encouragement along the way. Your clear communication of the outcomes you expect from learners—through focus statements, prompts, and feedback— will encourage students to stay focused. Your proximity to students during practice further assists youngsters with on-task behavior. This proximity is part of active supervision.

**Actively Monitor Students' Progress.**   As students engage in learning, move throughout the area, observing and fine-tuning their performance by giving specific task-related feedback. By scanning the area and observing students closely, you can determine the need for further group instruction to clarify a task. Or you may discover it is time to move the class on to the next planned task, having assessed that students have already reached the objective.

**Question, and Summarize the Lesson.**   You can intersperse questions throughout the lesson, posing them to individuals or the entire class to direct their learning. As closure for the lesson, quickly assess the students' understanding of the content through oral questioning, pantomiming performance, or a quick written response.

**Don't Forget the Fun.** Children view play as an important ingredient in their lives. When an activity is nonthreatening, success-oriented, and exciting, children naturally become motivated. Children should laugh, sing, play, and interact while engaged in physical activity. They tune into class objectives when they are having fun and enjoying the lesson.

## Evaluating

Evaluation is an important part of the learning experience in physical education. Choosing to be physically active for a lifetime is an ongoing process of developing motor skills, understanding principles of health-related fitness, setting personal goals, and becoming intrinsically motivated to meet self-designed goals. Therefore, the evaluation process for personal fitness must be ongoing, process oriented, and, at some point, personally significant to the individual students.

The evaluation process should be integrated throughout your planning and implementing of instructions. It is also something to consider as you

### Making Objectives Inclusive

Establishing a good objective for a lesson is much more difficult when the class includes a wide range of abilities, particularly cognitive differences. Just as you must vary your teaching style, you must sometimes vary your objective style to reach all students.

When setting objectives, you'll need to adapt the broad national objectives (such as improving cardiovascular endurance) to the particular needs of your class and each student. Instead of a typical activity such as jogging, a student in a wheelchair may do laps around a hardtop track, while another student with a visual impairment may jump rope in place (Craft 1996). An over-detailed objective that requires jogging as the method of improving cardiovascular endurance would fail to include these students, and fail to assist them in meeting the national standard.

One tool for making objectives inclusive is limiting group size. Controlling group size can greatly enhance the learning experience. Smaller groups allow you to tailor the objectives to the members of a particular group, and may also allow you to use unidirectional peer tutoring in appropriate circumstances. Even students as young as third grade are capable of observing and correcting one another's movement errors (Mosston and Ashworth 1986). Smaller groups rotating through different activity stations also helps maximize time on task and may help students with deficit disorders by varying environmental input.

An Individual Education Plan (IEP) offers another tool for making objectives inclusive. The IEP should note a student's significant sensory or processing deficits. You can use this information to determine appropriate objectives for that student.

Remember to avoid cultural and gender barriers to creating appropriate objectives. For example, it is inappropriate to create an objective with a specific time goal for a flexed-arm hang. This performance-based goal emphasizes muscle groups that do not develop equally across genders as adolescence approaches.

choose strategies and styles for teaching. If you have clearly identified the objectives related to fitness skills, knowledge, and behaviors in the planning process and if students have been directed in activities that match those objectives, the evaluation becomes integrated with the doing of the activity and the practice of the skills. By your active supervision, checking for understanding, and class closure, you can accomplish daily evaluations of lesson objectives.

The quality of the teaching determines the effectiveness of a fitness curriculum. In addition to pedagogical skills, teachers must value fitness and enthusiastically implement fitness lessons. You must constantly monitor teaching practices and effectiveness to keep the activities stimulating, motivating, and fun. You accomplish high quality by using developmentally appropriate activities with a lot of activity time, high levels of success, and by reinforcing and rewarding efforts.

Assessment produces information. You then use this information to further the effectiveness of your teaching. Performance categories are easy to measure and are almost always easy to define. The number of push-ups completed or how many laps were run are easy to measure and define. Some social characteristics, such as cooperation and sportsmanship, are more difficult to define and therefore still harder to measure reliably. Assessing the simplest concepts in class, such as "We had fun today," provides an evaluation tool for your teaching practices.

Effective teaching is primarily about what happens to the students. Its main ingredients are keeping students appropriately engaged in the subject matter a high percentage of the available time within a warm, nurturing climate. Learning goals are one way to assess the effectiveness of your teaching.

A *learning goal* is simply a statement of expectations for what students will learn within the school setting, given the constraints of the students' abilities and the teacher's expertise. All physical education teachers can and should have learning goals for their students. As you set and meet realistic goals, you convince yourself and your students that learning is truly part of the program. Review these guidelines as you think about writing learning goals for yourself:

- Write realistic goals.
- Write goals that you want 75 percent of your students to attain.
- Write learning goals for each unit and each grade.
- Limit the number of goals you write.

Teachers can learn a lot about themselves and their expectations for their program as they write realistic learning goals. Often curricular decisions between two important content topics hinge on the teacher's assessment of what the students should learn in order to be involved in an active, healthy lifestyle and become good citizens of the school and community. When physical educators teach from learning goals and students see their own improvement, all are likely to become more interested and motivated.

The ultimate evaluation of whether fitness education is successful comes if and when students choose to be physically active and use the skills and knowledge developed in their school years. Extending the lesson activities to encourage participation in physical activities beyond the physical education class should be integrated into the total fitness-education program.

## Summary

Siedentop (1991, p. 7) defines pedagogy as "the skillful arrangement of an environment in such a way that students acquire specific intended learnings. Pedagogy links the teacher's actions with the student's outcomes." Teaching fitness to children should help them acquire the skills, knowledge, and attitudes that lead to a lifetime of physical activity. Learning should occur in all three domains of human development: psychomotor, cognitive, and affective. Fitness training is a long-term process of educating students about physical fitness and the importance of regular activity. Physical educators choose varied strategies and styles that are developmentally appropriate and effective for the particular student population to reach the goal of pursuing lifetime fitness.

# Chapter 5
# Managing a Health-Related Fitness Program

You must juggle many logistical aspects to teach health-related fitness effectively and efficiently. In this chapter we'll explore many of these aspects, including how to

- strike an appropriate balance between fitness activities and concept education;
- collaborate with volunteers, classroom teachers, and community programs;
- obtain and store equipment;
- manage behavior through prevention and timely troubleshooting; and
- keep students safe.

You can use this concise guide to help you manage your classes more effectively.

## Striking a Balance

Some teachers think fitness education presents only two scenarios:

1. They might spend too much time on health-related fitness concepts in class, and then won't have enough time to engage their students in physical activity itself.

2. They might limit the time they spend covering health-related fitness concepts and concentrate on keeping students physically active during physical education, but then they won't equip students with the necessary knowledge to be physically active and fit for life.

How can you balance the teaching of concepts and the need for actual physical activity? In this section we'll discuss how to expand your students' physical activity time while still teaching them health-related fitness concepts. Keep in mind the cycle illustrated in figure 5.1 as you study this information.

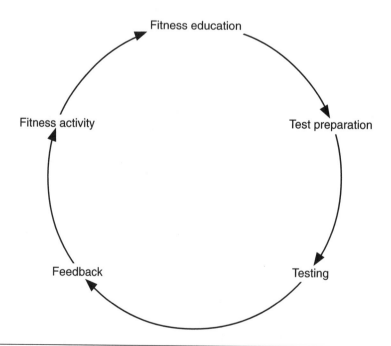

**Figure 5.1**   The fitness education cycle.

### Kill Two Birds . . .

You'll notice that many of the activities in this book involve teaching health-related fitness concepts in a very physically active way. Not only does this "kill two birds with one stone," it also increases the likelihood that students will remember what you're teaching. Indeed, we all remember much better when we actually *do* something as part of learning it. So use the lessons in this book as a model to create your own efficient lessons. Then look beyond physical education class time to further enhance your fitness program.

Keep in mind that teaching health-related fitness does not preclude skill development. Design skill-development activities to be very physically active. Then, as part of the highly active skill-development activities your students are engaged in, discuss health-related fitness concepts. For example, have students (each with his or her own ball) work on dribbling while jogging around the gym. After a few minutes, ask students to stop and feel their heart beating. Discuss why the heart is beating faster during and just after the activity than before. In this way, you actually kill two birds with one stone.

### Creative Scheduling

You can work with administrators and classroom teachers to both schedule additional times for fitness activities and use existing times more fully. The following is a list of ways to increase physical activity time at school so that you can afford to spend more time on fitness concepts during class.

• *Fitness breaks.* The new CDC (1998) guidelines assert that physical activity can be accumulated throughout the day in short bouts, making this an increasingly popular and beneficial option in some districts. As you train classroom teachers to conduct these breaks, offer them concrete reasons for increasing blood flow (e.g., more blood to the brain helps a person think better). Help classroom teachers avoid the boredom of tried-and-true activities by teaching them specific fun activities, suitable for the limited space a classroom can offer (don't assume they can—or will—go outside). Perhaps offer a five-minute summary of several possible activities at each staff meeting and help teachers solve any problems they're having.

• *Recess.* It's shocking, but some schools are actually moving away from providing regular recess time. The theory is that more time can be spent on the "3 Rs" if children aren't wasting time running around. Don't let this happen at your school! Educate administrators, classroom teachers, and parents on how regular physical activity enhances both physical and academic performance. Then ensure that students have ample equipment and input for fun and beneficial physical activities during recess. Don't hesitate to teach fun fitness activities during physical education that students can easily use as well during their free times—then point these out. After all, this can form the beginning of self-responsibility for physical fitness. In addition, you should advocate proper facilities and adequate supervision during recess.

• *Lunchtime.* Free play at lunchtime is simply a longer recess in most schools, but you can make it so much more. Consider making yourself available as a personal fitness consultant to interested students and train student volunteers to conduct fun fitness activities during free-play times or to assist you with younger students in physical education class. You can even start a fitness club and offer fun incentives for participating.

• *Intramurals.* These are physical activity programs conducted between teams of students in the same school. Adapt a program to augment your fitness curriculum in specific, stated ways; work to ensure the program is fun and friendly, welcoming all who wish to participate. When creating teams, be sure to make them as even as possible. Then insist that participants focus primarily on skill, fitness, and social development, not on cutthroat competition. You can run intramural activities before school, during recess, or after school. Find what works for your situation and garner the support you need from people at school and home to run the kind of program that will help children see fitness as a fun, lifetime pursuit.

• *After-school programs.* You can expand any program you normally run during the school day to fill the after-school time slot. Consider creating a new program or working to enhance an existing after-school child-care program. If you cannot commit the time to after-school activities, train others who can, such as parents or senior volunteers or child-care workers. After-school programs can also include evening and weekend activities, such as family fitness nights or developmentally appropriate field days emphasizing fun physical activities instead of competition.

Note that these ideas should all serve as *extensions* of physical education, not as replacements. So make sure that your administration and colleagues understand your intent.

### Fitness Homework

You can introduce a fitness concept in physical education class, assigning homework to reinforce the concept. Use the many projects in this book to involve students in worthwhile physical activity outside of school. Make sure the projects you develop involve the students in applying what they have learned in class to the real world (see figure 5.2).

## Collaboration

You can and should make full use of volunteers, classroom teachers, and community programs to enhance your health-related fitness program. When using other people in your program, take the time to train them so that their approaches and attitudes match those of your program. Likewise, ensure that any community programs you tap into will respect and reinforce your philosophy. Then enjoy the enthusiasm and knowledge all these resources bring to your program.

### Volunteers

Parents, older students, senior citizens, or any other interested, responsible individuals can make good volunteers. If volunteers will be working one-on-one with students, you must train them to be effective, including teaching them how to give general, specific, and corrective feedback and to physically assist a student. Then you must give them chances to practice in simulated class situations. Guest speakers and demonstrators, such as a mother who plays hockey or a father who is a gymnast, are also excellent resources.

# May 1999: FITNESS MONTH

| Monday | Tuesday | Wednesday | Thursday | Friday | Saturday | Sunday |
|---|---|---|---|---|---|---|
| | | | | | | Try a day without television. Do something outside instead.<br><br>**1** |
| To be totally fit, nutrition is important also. Eat from all levels in the food pyramid each day.<br><br>**2** | Go for a 30-minute walk with a friend. Yes, the dog can count as your friend.<br><br>**3** | When you choose a snack today make it a healthy snack. *Suggestion:* **Ants on a Log** Celery with peanut butter in the groove and raisins on that.<br><br>**4** | Ride your bike for 30 minutes. Tell a parent where you are going. Make sure you use hand signals and follow the laws of the road. **Be safe!**<br><br>**5** | The heart pumps about 7 quarts of blood per minute. Plug the sink and dump in 7 × 4 cups of water to see how much volume is 7 quarts. **6** | Make up an exercise routine & put it to music. Pump up your muscles, not the volume.<br><br>**7** | **8** |
| Jump rope during recess. Try a new trick today or make up a routine with several tricks.<br><br>**9** | Always warm up when exercising. Start slowly then stretch. Warm muscles work better. Cool down also. Do not stop suddenly.<br><br>**10** | When going to the grocery store have your parent park in the parking space far away from the store. **Walk!**<br><br>**11** | The best time to drink liquids is *before* you get thirsty. Sip some water before you exercise.<br><br>**12** | Fitness is being the best **you.** Competing against others has nothing to do with fitness. Do it for yourself.<br><br>**13** | Try a carryover (lifetime) sport this weekend. Go to the driving range & hit some golf balls. Go to the tennis court & hit some tennis balls. Fitness comes in all shapes & sizes just like us.<br><br>**14** | **15** |
| Exercise helps you to fall asleep more easily at night. Sleep tight.<br><br>**16** | Organize a neighborhood running & tagging game. Play for 20 minutes. Include everyone.<br><br>**17** | How many bones make up your skeleton? If you said 207 you were right. It takes a lot of muscles to move around 207 bones.<br><br>**18** | Go to the nearest basketball hoop & play **Around the World, "21",** or try 25 free throws.<br><br>**19** | All exercises are not created equal. Some build strength. Some build stamina. Some build flexibility.<br><br>**20** | Rake the yard for 30 minutes. Wear gloves & watch out for blisters. Jump in & over the leaf piles. Bag the leaves.<br><br>**21** | **22** |
| Play catch with a (1) football, (2) softball, (3) frisbee, (4) dog. Don't throw the dog, throw something to the dog.<br>**23** | Exercise helps you do better in school. Yes, you still have to study but you are less stressed & more relaxed & ready to learn.<br>**24** | Set up a game of 4 square during lunch recess. While you are waiting for a turn, do trunk twisters, jumping jacks, or any exercise of your choice.<br>**25** | When you are physically fit you have more energy for work and play. **Exercise = Energy.**<br><br>**26** | Create a fitness rap or poem. Give it to your physical education teacher. **Look out Will Smith!**<br><br>**27** | Try walking up & down the stairs for 10 minutes without stopping. **Use the handrail & keep a slow steady pace.**<br>**28** | Children need 10 to 12 hours of sleep to remain healthy. **This is per day not per week.** Try it you might like it.<br>**29** |
| **Memorial Day** Celebrate the holiday with the fitness activity of your choice.<br><br>**30** | You should drink lots of water (8 glasses) especially when the weather is warm. Pop or soda does not count as water.<br>**31** | | | Take care of your body, it is the only one you will get. | | |

The banner across the top of the calendar reads:

**May 1–7 PHYSICAL EDUCATION WEEK**

**GET PHYSICAL . . . . . . . EDUCATION**

**Figure 5.2**  A fitness month calendar.

### Classroom Teachers

Sometimes your greatest ally in the quest to improve the fitness levels and understanding of your students is a classroom teacher. Beyond including fitness breaks during class (discussed earlier in the chapter), classroom teachers can set up learning centers that reinforce the science and math of health-related physical fitness. Offer classroom teachers specific ideas that they can tailor to their students' abilities and other studies. Some examples are calculating heart rate, learning about the cardiorespiratory system, learning about geography by actively "traveling" from one place to another, and so on. In addition, consider offering specific lesson plans for classroom teachers to follow on the days you cannot teach physical education to their students.

Some specialists find it relatively easy to persuade classroom teachers and school administrators to extend meaningful physical activity into the rest of the school day. Others, however, struggle to overcome the perception that physical activity is just a way to allow students to blow off steam (or even a complete waste of time). How can you overcome such attitudes? Start slowly, asking for what you feel should be relatively easy for the classroom teacher to do. Provide support materials, such as activity and task worksheets. Your enthusiasm will be contagious if you are sensitive toward nonspecialists' fears and misperceptions regarding physical activity. To this end, provide adequate in-service training to give classroom teachers the information, support, and motivation they need to help you enhance students' fitness and knowledge about fitness. When classroom teachers see the physical and academic benefits of regular physical activity and of students' understanding how important fitness is as a lifetime pursuit, you should have the support you need.

### Community Programs

Exposing students to physical activity programs in the community can be the ideal way to demonstrate that fitness is a lifetime pursuit that goes beyond the confines of school. To use these valuable resources, you can bring in visitors for demonstrations, talks, and lessons. Or you can take students on field trips to see and experience local facilities, such as a fitness center or the YMCA, and to learn about opportunities to be physically active outside of school.

# Equipment

Obtaining and storing an adequate supply of equipment can be daunting tasks, but they're essential to running an effective fitness program. In this section we'll briefly describe how you can tackle this important aspect of your job.

### Obtaining Enough Equipment

Effective class management and maximal time on task, both of which lead to maximal learning and fitness gains, depend largely on students having the equipment they need to be active during most of the class time. A little creativity, persistence, and planning can help you obtain enough equipment to effectively teach health-related physical fitness (Davison 1998). Here are several ways to garner additional equipment:

- *Finding free equipment*—obtain sound hand-me-downs from middle and high schools, athletic teams, and fitness centers and donated equipment from fitness equipment stores in exchange for mentioning their generosity to parents.
- *Raising funds*—organize creative fitness activities for which students obtain sponsors, family fitness nights with a small admission fee, PTA or PTSO support, and so on.
- *Making equipment*—make sit-and-reach boxes, jump ropes, markers for running courses, throwing targets, and streamers, to name a few.
- *Having students bring their own equipment*—bringing balls, jump ropes, and so on—can help augment your supply. Make sure students put their names on their equipment to prevent misunderstandings and losses. It is prudent to use this equipment only within the owner's class to better protect it.

Wherever you obtain equipment, you must ensure it is the appropriate size to foster success and that it is otherwise safe to use. If possible, accept all donations graciously so as not to discourage a donor's generosity—you never know when someone will come through with a valuable item. However, discard any items that are too worn or damaged to repair for safe use.

Finally, organize lessons into learning stations to stretch an inadequate supply of equipment. That way, if you have only one sit-and-reach box, for example, you can rotate an entire class through a sit-and-reach station, keeping everyone active at other stations as they wait to use this equipment. Learning stations have other advantages, such as enhancing social interactions and allowing you to focus on one small group at a time while still engaging the rest of your students in appropriate activity.

## Creating a Complete Collection

The following is a basic list of items you need to run a viable fitness program. Ensure that you have enough of each to maximize students' time on task.

- Sit-and-reach boxes
- Skinfold calipers
- Tape or CD player and music brought in by students (preview for appropriateness)
- Heart rate monitors
- Cones for marking boundaries
- Tubing or light dumbbells for strength training
- Mats
- Manipulatives for physical activities, such as balls and jump ropes

In addition, insist that students wear proper shoes and recommend that for fitness testing they wear loose-fitting clothing.

## Storing Equipment

Appropriate storage can increase the longevity of equipment, facilitate class management, and save you precious time. You can make this process more efficient by

- using see-through bins, baskets, and bags whenever possible, particularly for small items;

## Inclusion

Inclusion is a philosophy that supports placing all students with disabilities within their home school and in regular education classes. This can be a complex issue, and it has been variously interpreted by different people.

The Individuals with Disabilities Education Act (IDEA) states that individuals with disabilities should be educated in the least restrictive environment, that is, an environment that will promote the most success and the best opportunities for improving their present level of performance. In this sidebar we'll look at some ways in which you can meet the needs of individuals with disabilities during the initial inclusion phase and ongoing instructional phase.

### Tips for Initial Inclusion

Your attitude, approach, and organizational skills will greatly impact the chances for successful inclusion of each student with disabilities into your program. Use this checklist to help a student with disabilities make a smooth transition into your program.

- Be positive. Make the student feel a part of the class, model appropriate interactions for students without disabilities, and make efforts to accommodate the student's unique needs.

- Prepare the individual with disabilities for the integration process. Give the student time to adjust; remain fully available to resolve concerns or problems the student or her parents may have.

- Prepare students without disabilities for the process of inclusion by explaining who will be integrated and any unique needs these individuals may have. So that changes are more widely accepted, involve students in making any necessary new rules and in changing the activities for the individuals with disabilities.

- Learn as much as possible about the student with disabilities: his medications, health problems, emergency procedures, and present level of gross motor, cognitive, and affective functioning. Review the goals and objectives, unique behavior problems, and activity interests and skills listed in the Individual Education Plan (IEP) and Individualized Family Service Plan (IFSP).

- Use peers to assist you with the students who have special disabilities. Peers can help with pushing a student from station to station, making sure a student with mental retardation knows which station to go to, and giving feedback to a student with sight impairment.

- Visit other places where inclusive physical education is being implemented successfully.

- hanging bags from a wall or ceiling;

- organizing baskets and bins on shelves by type, unit, or other logical order;

- labeling each storage container and its place in the storage room neatly and clearly; and

- regularly inspecting equipment and repairing or replacing items as needed.

In addition, if classroom or other teachers also use the physical education equipment, develop a sign-out procedure and carefully oversee timely and accurate returns.

## Managing Behavior

A natural outcome of creating and running a well-planned, well-organized, and fun fitness program is an enhanced ability to manage students' behavior. In this section we'll outline how to prevent and deal with problems that may arise—without harming kids' attitudes toward physical activity.

### Preventing Problems

Thorough lesson planning can prevent many problems. In tandem with thorough planning, you can prevent most behavior problems by attending to several other important areas: establishing helpful protocols, avoiding negative practices, and motivating students. Let's look closely, now, at each of these.

**Establishing Helpful Protocols.** Protocols are set procedures that help you maximize students' time on task by minimizing the time wasted on noninstructional procedures, such as distributing and returning equipment and portfolios. In addition, protocols can prevent injury and misbehavior, as they establish orderly routines. The following list outlines several areas in which you should establish protocols, along with giving you helpful hints to use in forming your own specific procedures:

• *Entering and leaving the activity area.* Establish a set routine that encourages calm, cooperation, and efficiency, such as entering without talking, reading posted warm-up instructions, and quickly following those instructions.

• *Signaling for attention and giving directions.* Choose a signal, such as blowing a whistle or beating a drum, to signal that students are to freeze, holding equipment, bodies, and mouths still so you can give them instructions. It is wise to make a rule that students gently place all equipment at their feet—to make it easier for them to leave it alone while you are speaking.

• *Distributing and collecting equipment.* Use multiple containers or have group leaders guide activities to avoid the entire class simultaneously struggling to get the equipment from one small area.

• *Assigning groups.* Use one of the many sensitive and quick ways to assign groups, such as organizing students by birth month, favorite color or ice cream flavor, or playing card they picked (all hearts or 4s together, for example).

• *Handling emergencies.* Train students as to what you need them to do and not do should injury, illness, or emergency occur.

## Tips for Instruction

Use this list to help make general changes in your teaching approach:

• Make simple adjustments in your teaching style choices. For example, use more demonstrations and provide more physical assistance for students with mental retardation. Avoid elimination games and modify rules so the student with disabilities can be successful. Modify equipment so students with limited strength or coordination can succeed. Use small groups and station activities with a range of challenges.

• Provide clear, concise, and brief verbal cues and demonstrations.

• Provide extra opportunities for practice.

• Observe individual behavior and provide adequate feedback, pairing positive feedback with corrective feedback.

• Maximize on-task behavior and minimize off-task behavior. For groups that include individuals with a variety of ability levels, design activities that allow them to work at their own levels.

The following are more specific guidelines for teaching individuals with disabilities:

• Use success-oriented activities.

• Incorporate an appropriate awards program.

• Post only the names of youngsters who meet their goals, rather than their actual scores.

• Increase intensity more gradually than usual.

• Modify distance goals and areas of play for individuals with limited movement abilities.

• Lower or enlarge the size of goals.

• Reduce the number of points needed to win a game.

• Use equipment that varies in shapes, sizes, and textures to stimulate interest.

• Preselect teams.

• Give individuals adequate time to process information.

• Limit distractions whenever possible.

Once you have designed and taught the protocols you feel you need to run the class smoothly, spend some time having students practice them. The class time spent in practicing protocols will be made up many times over by the time saved in efficiently run lessons.

**Avoiding Negative Practices.**    As you probably well know, your approach to health-related physical fitness will either turn your students on to physical activity or turn them off. Indeed, students who hate physical activity will not learn to enjoy it if you choose to engage in certain practices. Avoid these practices (Safrit 1995):

*Remember, fitness is a process. It's more important to continue to be active than to score high on a fitness test and then become inactive.*

- Using fitness activities as punishment
- Denying (or allowing others to deny) fitness or skill education because of poor performance elsewhere in school
- Overemphasizing fitness testing
- Underemphasizing the importance of self-esteem by making negative comments about poor performance

By creating a positive learning atmosphere instead, seek to motivate students to enjoy and do their best in physical activity.

**Motivating Students.**    Creating a fun and relevant learning atmosphere not only will reduce discipline problems, it will also increase the likelihood that students will see fitness as a worthwhile and satisfying lifetime pursuit—our central objective in bringing this program to you. What motivates children? Play and fun, social interaction, feelings of physical competence, and chances for self-expression (Virgilio 1997). So plan these into your health-related fitness program.

Here are some specific motivational strategies you might consider (Virgilio 1997; Safrit 1995):

- *Teach basic skills.*    Give students the tools they need to succeed.
- *Choose success-oriented activities.*    Pay close attention to developmental appropriateness to ensure all students can succeed.
- *Have fun, fun, fun.*    Children naturally love to move, so take advantage of it. Virgilio (1997) insists, "Children should laugh, sing, play, and interact while engaged in physical activity." To add spark to your lessons, play music and choose activities that use a child's imagination.
- *Add creative equipment.*    Rotate the equipment you use to teach various concepts to renew interest in physical activity.
- *Create a colorful environment.*    Dec-orate the gym attractively according to your current theme.
- *Provide incentives.*    Extrinsic motivators, such as healthy treats and awards that reward effort rather than prowess, have their place in fitness education (see chapter 2).
- *Be a role model for your students, fellow teachers, and principal.*    Dress professionally in sharp-looking warm-ups or other appropriate clothes. Let children see you enjoying physical activity and eating appropriate nutrients.
- *Accentuate the positive.*    Use gestures and words of encouragement to reinforce positive behavior and increase the likelihood of progress.
- *Keep students moving and otherwise engaged.*    Minimize lecturing.
- *Encourage self-direction.*    Show students how to apply the knowledge they're learning in the real world. Teach intermediate level students to manage their own fitness education portfolios, giving them the necessary tools to direct their own fitness training after they leave your program.

Most of these motivators are intrinsic. In other words, they make physical activity a reward in and of itself, thereby increasing the likelihood that students will pursue physical activity on their own. Not surprisingly, motivated students are more cooperative, making your job that much easier.

Finally, cooperative learning approaches enhance motivation by providing the social interaction students enjoy and thrive on. Moreover, students learn from each other in cooperative groups, empowering them to apply their knowledge in other situations as they practice helping each other succeed. So plan cooperative learning experiences as often as possible.

## Dealing With Problems

Prevention is your watchword: You've established protocols. You've planned in appropriate motivators. You're still, however, dealing with a few problems. Don't despair—we all face similar situations. Here are some trouble-shooting hints:

- Don't allow problems to fester; deal with them quickly and decisively to prevent them from spreading.

- Modify protocols that don't seem to be working.

### Fitness Is for Everyone

Health-related fitness is equally important to boys and girls. Don't lower expectations for girls! It is critical to developing a gender-equitable learning environment that you understand, monitor, and develop student-to-student interactions. These dynamics establish a student "pecking order." Without intervention, some of these interactions could be damaging to girls and boys alike. To encourage gender-equitable interactions, encourage appropriate verbal and physical interactions between students, praise positive interactions, turn both positive and negative interactions into "teachable moments," and set the stage for cooperative activities between boys and girls. When you present examples, make them of both men and women. For example, Michael Jordan has to be in great shape to be successful—and so does Mia Hamm!

You should also consider the factors that contribute to making a message and its dissemination special for a given population. Such factors might include demographic parameters, individual families' values and beliefs, the students' perceptions of engaging in a specific health activity, the channels available for communication, and the influence of community leaders and groups. In addition, be aware that clothing may present problems. Some religious tenets, for example, preclude wearing the very type of apparel that many people consider appropriate for participating in physical activity.

- Add appropriate protocols as you note the need arising.

- Engage the help of parents, classroom teachers, a special education teacher, or administrative staff when a child persistently disrupts class. Ask for insights and hints that will help this particular child experience success.

- Work out a specific plan with the child and other advisors to overcome the disruptive behavior.

- Include special incentives tailored to the particular child's interests. For example, allow the child to choose a favorite activity when he or she has cooperated to a set degree or amount.

# Safety

Thorough planning, effective class management, developmentally appropriate equipment and activities, and equipment and facilities in good condition are the keys to safe physical education. Here are reminders specific to fitness education that Safrit (1995) cites:

- Have children warm up the large muscles of the body before they engage in vigorous and extensive exercise.

- Help children learn to identify the difference between fatigue and pain that may lead to injury.

- Always ensure that environmental conditions are safe for the fitness lesson.

- Educate yourself and your students as to harmful exercises. Stay up to date in safety issues.
- Make sure students are wearing appropriate clothes and shoes and that they are not wearing jewelry, such as long necklaces or earrings, that could become tangled by equipment or ensnare classmates.

Stay alert to potential dangers to *prevent* problems.

## Summary

With foresight, persistence, and timely troubleshooting, you can run classes that are effective, enjoyable, and safe. Use the suggestions in this chapter to help you maximize time on-task and minimize disruptions. Teach in safe and developmentally appropriate ways. Above all, keep fun as the focus of your health-related fitness program to ensure that students will want to make fitness a lifetime focus.

# Chapter 6
# Assessing
# Health-Related Fitness

You are responsible for assessing what your students have learned in physical education, based on the goals and objectives you have set. You cannot, however, achieve truly authentic assessment by basing it solely on any one indicator. Rather, you must use a variety of assessment tools, including fitness tests, to create a true picture of each individual's achievements. Moreover, you must assess in all domains—physical, cognitive, and affective—by monitoring actual student performance in authentic, real-world settings. Ultimately, you must look more at the process than at the product, gathering evidence of progress over time. In other words, you must teach the processes you're assessing, including proper techniques and fitness knowledge. Your lessons must emphasize the *how* and *why* of education, rather than stressing current physical ability, if you want to empower students to assume personal responsibility for fitness.

Yet the realities of assessment—a teacher's time commitment, organizational challenges, and limited class time, to name a few—may tempt you to avoid developing and implementing a formal approach. In this chapter we'll explore the importance of assessment, define and discuss authentic assessment, show you how to apply authentic assessment tools to fitness education (including management tips), and, finally, discuss the issues of grading.

## Importance of Assessment

The most important benefits of authentic assessment are enhancing student motivation and learning. When you emphasize self-assessment, self-responsibility, and goal setting, you motivate students to improve their performances. When you teach students the "hows" and "whys" of health-related physical fitness, you give them the knowledge they need to become responsible for their own fitness. Most importantly, however, you teach students *how* to learn—the processes of self-analysis and self-direction—something they can take with them when they leave your program. So a carefully constructed assessment approach empowers students to reach our ultimate goal—that of self-directed, active lifestyles.

Beyond this, assessment serves several other purposes (Graham 1992). It

1. forces us to look carefully at each individual, if only for a few moments;
2. gives us an overall assessment of the program when we see the gains fifth or sixth graders have made since kindergarten;
3. increases our credibility as professionals when we provide recorded evidence of individual and program progress; and, finally,
4. becomes a self-imposed accountability measure, forcing us to look at the results of our teaching.

Rink and Hensley assert in summary, "Assessment is the cornerstone of education reform, enabling educators to create high-level goals, set standards, develop instructional pathways, motivate students, provide diagnostic feedback, monitor progress, communicate progress to others, and make appropriate decisions about students and programs" (1996, p. 39).

## Authentic Assessment

As you probably well know, fitness testing has been widely abused by some educators in the past. Even today, some insist that fitness testing has no place in the authentic assessment movement. We couldn't disagree more! In this section we'll show you how to make fitness testing a valuable part of authentic assessment.

First, however, what is authentic assessment? Assessment may be called authentic "if the student demonstrates the desired behavior in real-life situations rather than in artificial or contrived settings" (Melograno 1998, p.10). Applied specifically in physical education, developmentally appropriate authentic assessment means that "Teacher decisions are based primarily on ongoing individual assessment of children as they participate in physical education class activities (formative evaluation) and not on the basis of a single test score (summative evaluation)" (Graham et al. 1992, p. 7). Thus, for fitness testing to be a viable component of authentic assessment, it must

1. demonstrate the desired behavior,
2. link directly to the curriculum,
3. occur on an ongoing basis, and
4. make students both capable of and likely to apply the tests and the physical gains outside the classroom.

Gains evidenced by authentic assessment should be made in the physical, affective, and cognitive domains, meaning an individual develops health-related fitness, a positive attitude, and fitness knowledge.

## Putting Fitness Testing in Context

Some may argue that fitness testing is "artificial or contrived," but there is a significant correlation between performance on health-related fitness tests and actual health-related fitness (CDC 1998). Furthermore, health-related fitness testing that is part of a sound, ongoing educational program gives students the basic knowledge they need to be fit for life. Moreover, fitness testing provides a kind of "snapshot" of each individual's current fitness level, and an opportunity to plan for future improvement (in the same manner as does a math or reading test).

## Measuring Progress Over Time

Of course, a single test score cannot tell you anything about an individual's progress. This is why you must plan for ongoing assessment for it to be truly authentic. But given the workload associated with testing hundreds of students, how can you accomplish this overwhelming task? One answer is to train older students to assess themselves informally and to train volunteers to help you assess younger students.

These are some major benefits of training students to assess themselves:

- Teaches students specific tests they can apply throughout their lives
- Gives students guided practice in applying their knowledge of fitness testing
- Simulates a self-directed approach to fitness
- Shows students exactly what you expect them to learn—and then teaches and assesses it, thereby linking fitness testing directly to the curriculum in students' minds
- Makes assessment time double as learning time

- Gives students ongoing feedback in the form of test results and teacher guidance
- Provides built-in respect for individual abilities and progress
- Adds ongoing input for realistic goal setting

If you have too little class time for assessments, you can send self-assessment task sheets as homework for trained students to complete outside of physical education class time. You know you're on to a valuable teaching practice when it saves your valuable time and energy while helping students achieve your ultimate goals!

Peer assessment leads to the same benefits as self-assessment. In addition, peer assessment enhances social development.

Periodically, however, you should conduct formal fitness tests, rotating the classes you're focusing on and thus spreading out the paperwork. Within each class, use the learning station approach so that you can oversee a testing station, ensuring correct technique and accurate data. While assessing students, be sure to reinforce the reasons for fitness testing and fitness itself, thereby connecting this activity to real life. Figure 6.1 offers a handy checklist to ensure you're ready to formally assess students.

## Applying Authentic Assessment Tools to Fitness Education

Your assessment of an individual must be based on a variety of assessment tools—not just formal and informal fitness testing—to teach and assess student progress in fitness education. This creates a balanced approach to assessment, allowing students to show you the "big picture" of their learning. Table 6.1 lists several authentic assessment tools that are appropriate, along with examples of their application in fitness education. Note, too, that these tools give students the opportunity to display different types of intelligence; a child who is weak in one form of intelligence can shine in another while still developing the weak area. Strive to use a variety of assessment tools in your program.

## Preparing for Fitness Testing

❑  1.  Sequence the tests.

❑  2.  Schedule and organize testing.

❑  3.  Consider safety factors.

❑  4.  Obtain necessary equipment.

❑  5.  Find or design efficient scoring sheets.

❑  6.  Locate and train assistants.

❑  7.  Send a letter home to parents, letting them know the date of the tests and asking that children come to class in appropriate clothes and shoes.

*(continued)*

**Figure 6.1**  Planning for fitness testing will make your job easier (adapted from Safrit 1995, p. 78).

Name _____   Classroom _____

# Start Off on the Right Foot—Be Safe!

*Directions:* (Circle) the shoes below that are safe for you to wear in physical education.
Put an X on the shoes that are not safe to wear in physical education.

(Circle) the days you have physical education class:

**MONDAY   TUESDAY   WEDNESDAY   THURSDAY   FRIDAY**

**Figure 6.1**   *(continued)*

## Table 6.1    Appropriate Authentic Assessment Tools

| Tool | Description | Example |
|---|---|---|
| Self-assessment | Student assesses herself based on goals or teacher-set criteria. | Student uses a sit-and-reach box to monitor flexibility between doing more formal tests. |
| Peer assessment | Peers observe each other's performances & offer feedback based on teacher-set criteria. | Students observe each other stretching, completing a criteria task sheet to help each other learn to stretch safely and effectively. |
| Journal | Student assesses himself by recording his activities or feelings in writing. | Student records each bout of physical activity he engages in outside of physical education class and notes how he feels afterwards. |
| Reflection | Student thinks about the learning process to improve her performance & attitude. | Student lists three specific ways she can improve her one-mile run time. |
| Observation | Teacher observes and records physical and affective information. | Teacher monitors student testing at a learning station, rating her observations on a criteria task sheet. |
| Individual project | Student investigates an area of interest under teacher's guidance, setting goals, planning how to achieve those goals, & striving for those goals. | Student explores how to apply health-related fitness concepts to his favorite sport & tests his theories as to what will help improve his sport performance. |
| Group project | A group of students learns in a situation in which interdependence, cooperation, & accountability are required. | A group works together to design a game that builds cardio-respiratory endurance. They then teach it to another group. |
| Role-playing | Students assume roles & explore social & psychological issues in simulated affective activities. | Partners take turns counseling a "friend" who is reluctant to participate in physical activity. |
| Event task | Students problem-solve, using a type of role-playing that simulates real-world experiences & offers open-ended tasks. | The teacher challenges groups of students to design & demonstrate several ways they can use to help include a student with a disability in physical activity. |

| Tool | Description | Example |
|---|---|---|
| Fitness testing | Give standardized tests of each area of health-related fitness to help teachers & students plan how to maintain or improve each one. | Student practices muscular strength & endurance tests, takes the tests, & records the results. She then plans how she will improve over time. |
| Portfolio | Student collects samples of her work to show her effort, progress, & achievement over time. | Student puts her plans for improving muscular strength & endurance in writing, along with her test scores, adding this information to her portfolio. |

Melograno, 1998.

Let's now examine more specifically how these tools can help you assess students in the physical, cognitive, and affective domains, discussing appropriate methods and effective uses of results.

## Physical Domain

During periods of fitness testing and education you will assess students in the physical domain, of course, but you should also monitor their applications of the health-related fitness components when they are in skill and sport settings. In this section we'll discuss various authentic assessment tools that can help you assess student progress in the physical domain.

**Useful Assessment Tools.**  Fitness tests (e.g., *FITNESSGRAM*) are the most obvious and structured way to assess fitness in the physical domain. Another forum for observing students' fitness is their performing both general and sport-specific skills, allowing you to note those that are weak in one or more health-related fitness components. For example, after such observations you can work more closely with a student who lacks the flexibility or strength to master gymnastics stunts or one who doesn't have the stamina to keep running in basketball or soccer. As you look for each health-related fitness component in a real-world context, you can better tailor your program to meet individual needs. Other means of assessing students in the physical domain include

- self-assessment,
- peer assessment,
- individual projects, and
- event tasks.

*Remember, fitness is individual. Encourage children who show low levels of fitness by explaining to them that any improvement will be significant. Challenge children with high levels of fitness to do even better. Support children with significant disabilities in the activities they can engage in. In short, challenge children at their appropriate levels.*

In these examples you can see how fitness testing serves to confirm a teacher's concerns and helps her monitor individual progress. Thus, fitness testing can serve your program, rather than your program serving fitness testing.

Finally, always attend carefully to safety when you and your students engage in fitness testing. Figure 6.2 offers a safety checklist.

# Safety Checklist for Fitness Testing

❏   1.   Give students plenty of chances to practice before the test.

❏   2.   Check for proper form, correcting when necessary.

❏   3.   Ensure that the test has enough space, its surface is suitable, and the area is free of hazards, such as glass.

❏   4.   Provide mats for curl-ups and flexibility testing.

❏   5.   Check equipment to ensure its proper functioning.

❏   6.   Remind students of emergency procedures.

❏   7.   If you're testing outdoors, monitor environmental conditions for cardiovascular testing.

❏   8.   Have students warm up with a general cardiovascular activity and stretching.

**Figure 6.2**   Always test under safe conditions (adapted from Safrit 1995, p. 80).

**Using Results Appropriately.**   We cannot emphasize too much that fitness testing must be part of your quest to individualize and otherwise improve instruction, not a contest to see who is the fittest among students. Thus, strive to use fitness testing results in the following ways (Safrit 1995; Graham 1992):

• Be sensitive to students' feelings and keep results and records confidential, even if it means locking up files. Insist that students not share results among themselves. Finally, reward persistence, improvement, and effort—instead of elite performance.

• Relate fitness testing results to fitness education. Talk specifically about how students can improve or maintain their results. Help them plan realistic goals and steps toward those goals.

• Inform and involve parents—both before and after testing. Send information about what tests you're giving and why, emphasizing your philosophy regarding fitness testing. Explain fitness basics and the meanings of results at a parent-teacher conference, if at all possible, or at least in writing.

## Cognitive Domain

The cognitive domain automatically comes into play as you empower students to take increasing responsibility for their fitness testing, goal setting, and individual fitness planning. In other words, as you teach students how to apply the fitness test results, including goal setting and planning how to improve their performances, you are asking them to think. In this section, we'll explore ways to assess individuals' progress in understanding the learning processes they are going through.

**Useful Assessment Tools.**   When choosing cognitive assessment tools, you must select instruments that reflect what you have taught students regarding fitness knowledge and that are manageable to administer. One quick way to assess understanding is to simply observe how students perform the fitness tests and discuss this performance with them. Do they use correct technique consistently? Do quick reminders help them perform correctly or do you need to spend more time with them? When you debrief the class at the end of a testing day, do you find they have a good sense of why they are taking the tests and how they might improve performance? Make a statement or series of statements regarding health-related fitness and have students signal thumbs-up for true and thumbs-down for false. These methods, which don't take much administrative time and energy, can give you valuable (albeit informal) information to help guide your planning for future lessons.

Written tests are a tried-and-true way to test the cognitive domain. Include one at a station on a circuit or consider asking the classroom teacher to administer a short test. In any case, keep such tests short and to the point—no more than three to five multiple choice questions to give you the feedback you need without taking too much instructional or teacher time. Figure 6.3 presents a sample written test appropriate for fitness education assessment in the cognitive domain.

One clever way to assess cognitive understanding of fitness concepts is to present a fictitious character and his fitness troubles (Graham 1992). Ask students to write or dictate a short letter or simulated e-mail message offering the character advice about how to improve his health-related fitness. Ask students to draw pictures of what they think the fictitious character might look like before and after taking their advice. Here again, the classroom teacher may be willing to provide time and help for this activity, as it ties into language arts. Post students' advice on a bulletin board.

Ask students to analyze their own performances; you can add a "Thinking About Learning" box at the bottom of task sheets to encourage thoughtful reflection (Schiemer 1996). Make sure, however, that they feel it's safe to tell the truth about their performance assessments: emphasize the importance of process (self-analysis) rather than product (actual performance). Of course, this activity also touches on the affective domain.

Other assessment tools you can structure to reveal knowledge of fitness concepts include the following:

- Reflection in journals
- Individual projects
- Role-playing, including event tasks

Most importantly, you can use all these tools to help students learn *how to learn* as they apply the facts you've taught them in different ways.

**Using Results Appropriately.**   Like any authentic assessment tool, oral checks for understanding or written tests to assess cognitive development should only be a part of your whole assessment approach. Use the information you gather to help you tailor your teaching plans to both the class's abilities in general and to specific individual needs. If you wish to use written tests as part of your grading system, ensure they are just that—*part* of a system that takes many types of assessment into account (see also "Grading" later in this chapter). Finally, as you work to develop the cognitive aspects of fitness education, emphasize that students need to learn this information because health-related fitness is temporary; therefore, each one of us must become equipped to plan how to maintain or improve our own fitness level on a continuing basis.

Name _____ Classroom # _____

# *Lesson:*
# Cardiovascular endurance

*Directions:* Circle the activities that help improve cardiovascular endurance.

**Watching TV**

**Sleeping**

**Riding a bike**       **Jogging**       **Swimming**

**Bowling**

**Jumping rope**

**Walking**

**Playing horseshoes**

Choose one of the activities you circled and do it for 15 minutes at least once before your next physical education class. If you have several days between now and your class, repeat the activity or choose another one you have circled. Draw a line under any circled activity you did. Ask your mom, dad, and other family members to participate with you.

After you have completed this sheet have your mom or dad sign at the bottom. Return the signed sheet during your next physical education class.

Remember . . . try your best! Good luck!

❑ Check here if mom or dad did the activity with you.

Parent signature: _____ Date: _____

**Figure 6.3** Sample quiz.

## Affective Domain

Perhaps you view the affective domain as being secondary to what your program is doing in the physical and cognitive domains—something, that is, to attend to and monitor if there's time. Don't fall into this trap! The affective domain is actually the heart of a successful program, a program that inspires enthusiasm for physical activity and a desire for fitness in each student, no matter his or her abilities or interests. Think about it this way: no matter how well-versed students are in health-related fitness concepts, no matter how many hours per week they engage in appropriate physical activity now, if they hate what they're doing, they'll surely stop it as soon as they are out of your program. So carefully assess affective development on an ongoing basis to alert you to potential problems.

**Useful Assessment Tools.**   You can slant various assessment tools toward assessing the affective domain. For example, ask students to reflect in their journals on what they are feeling about your program or a particular activity. Take a written or oral survey, such as the one shown in figure 6.5. Present role-playing challenges to partners and have one partner pretend to love fitness activities and the other, to hate it. You'll be amazed as you eavesdrop by how articulate students are about their positive and negative feelings. And simply being allowed to air negative feelings in a safe context can do much to dissipate them. You have no time? Use these suggestions as two-minute closure activities. Assign written assessments as homework.

**Using Information Appropriately.**   Obviously, you should not condemn a child for a poor attitude toward health-related physical fitness. Rather, you should seek

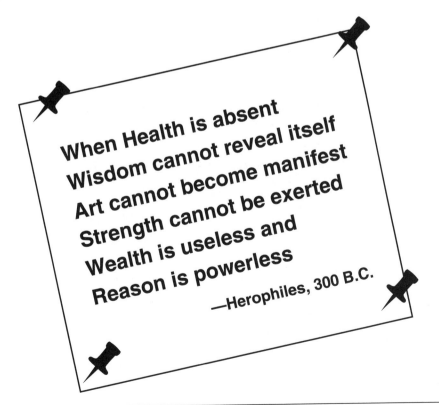

When Health is absent
Wisdom cannot reveal itself
Art cannot become manifest
Strength cannot be exerted
Wealth is useless and
Reason is powerless

—Herophiles, 300 B.C.

**Figure 6.4**   Bulletin board.

# Sample Survey

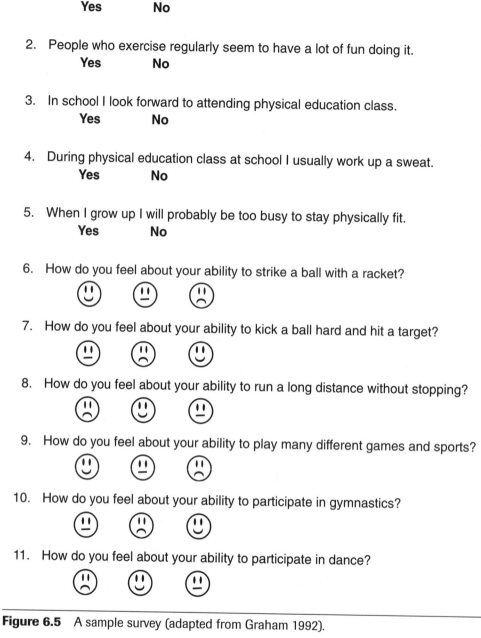

1. I would rather exercise or play sports than watch TV.
   **Yes**        **No**

2. People who exercise regularly seem to have a lot of fun doing it.
   **Yes**        **No**

3. In school I look forward to attending physical education class.
   **Yes**        **No**

4. During physical education class at school I usually work up a sweat.
   **Yes**        **No**

5. When I grow up I will probably be too busy to stay physically fit.
   **Yes**        **No**

6. How do you feel about your ability to strike a ball with a racket?

7. How do you feel about your ability to kick a ball hard and hit a target?

8. How do you feel about your ability to run a long distance without stopping?

9. How do you feel about your ability to play many different games and sports?

10. How do you feel about your ability to participate in gymnastics?

11. How do you feel about your ability to participate in dance?

**Figure 6.5**    A sample survey (adapted from Graham 1992).

to help that child overcome negative feelings through providing a fun program, helping the child set realistic goals, and empathizing with the child's hidden fears. This process may include helping parents overcome their negative feelings toward physical activity as well. If you notice widespread negativity, brainstorm with students and colleagues about how to make your program more fun. Keep in mind, however, that sometimes even the best programs take time to overcome bad feelings created by negative past experiences. Regularly evaluate your teaching and program, then move ahead confidently and enthusiastically. Your persistence will pay off.

## *Portfolios—Putting It All Together*

We believe portfolios can be a vital part of authentic assessment because, when well conceived and organized, they provide a handy reference for overall assessment, grading, and parent-teacher conferences. Moreover, portfolios can travel with students from grade to grade and school to school, so that both the students and future physical educators can monitor long-term progress and persistent problems. In this section, we'll focus on how you can streamline the administrative tasks associated with portfolios.

As you probably well know, the gap can be quite wide between theory and practice with authentic assessment in general and portfolio keeping in particular. Use these tips to help turn portfolios into the teaching, learning, and assessing tools they are meant to be—without your having to spend 16 hours a day at school:

• Obtain or have students or volunteers make sturdy portfolios. For each use a traditional three-hole folder, a folded piece of 12- by 18-inch construction paper with pockets added, a flat box, a hanging file, or other appropriate container.

• Store portfolios by class in milk crates, portable hanging file boxes, or larger bins. Try to get the classroom teacher to store the container.

• Train students to file their papers for themselves or for younger students.

• Establish protocols for passing out and collecting portfolios.

• Periodically, select (or have students select) representative pieces from their assessment activities to retain in their portfolios. This leaves fewer bits and pieces for you to sort through. Designate how many pieces to select, taking the time to discuss what creates a good cross-section of items. Send the rest home after stamping them with a message such as "COMPLETED ON TIME" to indicate you do care but that you're not using it as part of your assessment of a student. This will eliminate paperwork in a professional manner. *Note*: If you designate pieces to select after the work is completed, students will be motivated to try their best on each assignment.

• Staple or glue certain ongoing assessments, such as a fitness testing record sheet, into the front or back cover of each portfolio.

• Decide whether you wish to staple in several sheets of paper to form journals inside each portfolio, use a separate notebook for journals, or add individual sheets to portfolios with journal-type entries as they are written.

Ask other teachers in your building and district for additional ideas regarding the logistics of sane portfolio management.

### Ensuring Gender Equity

Evaluations free of gender bias place equivalent expectations on females and males. In addition, evaluators can spend equal time interacting with girls and boys in praising, disciplining, instructing, and providing other types of feedback. Educators must take care that evaluative instruments are free of gender bias and that student performance is not evaluated on the basis of male experience alone.

## Grading

Assessing and grading are not one and the same. Indeed, they have very different purposes. Assessment tells you and your students how they are improving or what they need to work on. Grading attempts to communicate in a single letter or number, addressed primarily to parents, all that the individual child has done in your physical education program (Graham 1992). Alongside of assessment, grading can help you recognize the strengths and weaknesses of your physical education program.

In order to grade students fairly, you must develop criteria for testing and grading, including the weight you will assign each component of the grade. Then you must communicate these parameters to students and parents—*before* collecting data. Safrit (1995) makes these suggestions:

• Don't use improvement in fitness-test scores as the basis for grading unless you have provided sufficient class time for improving fitness.

• Use evidence of cognitive development as long as you have taught the concepts you're measuring.

Finally, you must collect explicit documentation to maintain accountability. A portfolio system can do much of the record keeping for you.

But a grade in physical education doesn't tell students and parents much about how an individual is doing. For example, a student who has very poor flexibility may receive a "Satisfactory" simply for behaving in physical education class and trying hard (Graham 1992). You can overcome this problem by providing separate grades for affective, physical, and cognitive performance. Develop and use your own form to send home with the rest of the report card. On this form, note areas of improvement and offer tips as appropriate about how the student can overcome problem areas. You can also use such a form at the end of each unit, whether it's grading time or not. Even if you must still enter a total grade on the regular report card, by offering students and parents specific information, you will help students learn through grading, thereby making it a more worthwhile use of your time.

Indeed, objective and thorough grading should do the following:

• Help the student understand where he can improve
• Help the teacher recognize if program objectives are being met
• Show the teacher where changes in the program should occur
• Promote the physical education program to the school and community
• Justify the ongoing need for physical education in the curriculum

## Summary

Assessment is an indispensable component of all effective teaching; fitness education is no exception. You can and should use a variety of assessment strategies across the fitness education curriculum to gather data on each student's achievement. Portfolios can provide the foundation of an authentic assessment approach. You can have students complete several different types of assessment tools. Managing assessment takes thought and planning but is well worth the effort.

Finally, when you give a physical education grade, you should offer specific data, well documented across the physical, affective, and cognitive domains. In this way, you will demonstrate that you do, in fact, provide a balanced, worthwhile curriculum.

# Chapter 7

# Nutrition and Health-Related Fitness

The science of nutrition defines and explains the human body's dietary need for specific chemical substances to maintain life. We all have the same general nutritional needs, but the amounts of specific nutrients that we each require vary according to age, gender, heredity, and lifestyle. Each of us has several diet options that can afford pleasurable eating while meeting individual nutritional requirements. Thus the amount of energy and the quantity of nutrients we require are best tailored individually. The challenge we each face is to obtain all the essential nutrients from our particular diets.

## What Is Diet?

Diet is the total intake of food (and supplements, if taken) consumed in a five-to-seven day period. No single food or single meal defines the diet. Over a 70-year life span, a person will eat some seventy thousand meals—about a thousand each year—plus snacks. Is it any wonder that eating is automatic?

Although all foods have nutritional value—there are no "junk" foods with absolutely *no* nutritional value—clearly some foods are more valuable than others. In assuring a person good nutrition the fundamental goals are to

- provide a variety of different foods,
- supply all the nutrients in adequate amounts, and
- supply sufficient energy (calories) to maintain an ideal body mass.

There are infinite ways, which are often decided by taste, culture, and economics, for an individual to meet these dietary needs. Nevertheless, experts have developed broad, useful guidelines to encourage individuals to obtain the essential amounts of the nutrients they need to promote growth and development and to maintain an ideal body mass. These are some well-known developers of such guidelines:

- The Committee on Dietary Allowances, which establishes guidelines called the Recommended Dietary Allowances (RDA). The RDA cite the amount of each nutrient required on an average day to meet the needs of most healthy people under usual environmental conditions in the United States.

- The Food and Drug Administration, which developed a standard format for food labeling.

- The U.S. Department of Agriculture (USDA), which designed the Food Guide Pyramid to graphically show the most necessary nutrients within each food group, the number of recom-

**Figure 7.1** Illustration of a typical food label.

mended servings, the size of such servings, and foods within each group categorized by nutrient and density.

## Behavioral Foundations of Diet

For countless generations food choices were largely determined by what people could grow (farm) or catch. During these historic times, knowing and choosing what to eat was fairly easy—people simply ate what was available. Having a much greater variety of choices today, we often find it less easy to decide what food to eat. We must *learn* how to make appropriate choices.

All people require the same nutrients, but in amounts that vary from individual to individual and from stage to stage in a person's life. Neonatal and infant nutrition set the stage for the later interaction of home and school in influencing a child's nutritional habits. After undergoing explosive growth during the first year of life, a child continues to develop and change, but somewhat less quickly. The cumulative

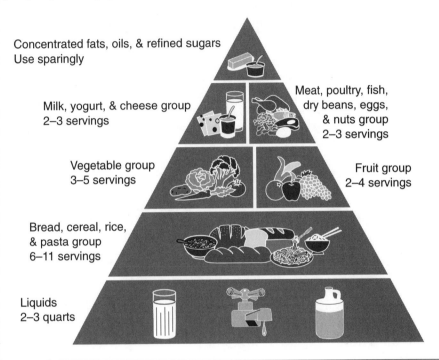

Concentrated fats, oils, & refined sugars
Use sparingly

Milk, yogurt, & cheese group
2–3 servings

Meat, poultry, fish, dry beans, eggs, & nuts group
2–3 servings

Vegetable group
3–5 servings

Fruit group
2–4 servings

Bread, cereal, rice, & pasta group
6–11 servings

Liquids
2–3 quarts

**Figure 7.2** A modified Food Guide Pyramid focusing on daily intake.

effects over the next decade are remarkable. A child enters the school system at a critical stage of growth and development, which will continue through the elementary, middle, and high school years. To have a healthy diet, a child must eat food that provides all of the nutrients—(particularly iron, trace elements, calcium, protein, and vitamins) in adequate quantities over a five- to seven-day period—all the time.

The childhood years offer the best chance for parents and teachers to influence not only current but also future food choices, and thus to help develop good eating behaviors. Parents are the gatekeepers; they control and influence the availability and choices of food in their children's environment. Teachers must actively help educate parents about nutrition. It is critical that parents and teachers help establish appropriate eating habits at the elementary-school level and make students aware of the relationship between nutrition and health, both now and for the future. The concept of balance and moderation to obtain and maintain an ideal body weight is crucial in preventing such eating disorders as anorexia.

A person's total nutrient needs are greater during adolescence than at any other time of life except pregnancy and lactation. According to the USDA guidelines, during adolescence girls need 2,200 calories a day, whereas boys require 3,000 calories a day (Saltman 1993). Nutrient needs rise throughout adolescence and then level off (or even diminish slightly) as an adolescent becomes an adult.

Adolescents make many more choices for themselves than do young children, both about their activity level and what they eat. Social or peer pressures may push them to make both good and bad choices. Children and adolescents acquire information—and misinformation—on nutrition from personal, immediate experiences. They are concerned with how diet can improve their lives and looks *now*, so they may engage in crash dieting or the latest fad in weight gain or loss. It is common also to see increased calorie consumption, especially of fats and carbohydrates, among adolescents.

Poor childhood habits in both physical activity and nutrition often lead to health problems in adulthood. For example, obese children seldom develop heart disease, cancer, or gall bladder diseases as children. However, childhood obesity may set the stage for adult obesity, when the threat of these and other diseases associated with obesity does increase.

The interactions of physical activity and nutrition are important in every person's life. We need physical activity as much as we need all 45 nutrients in our diets.

## Counting Calories

A calorie is the amount of energy it takes to raise the temperature of one gram of water one degree Celsius. The body's needs are much greater than water's, of course, so we measure energy in kilocalories (1,000 calories, or one kcal). Popular sources often shorten the term *kilocalories* to simply *calories,* which can be confusing. We will refer to calorie counts in this book, rather than using the less-familiar term kilocalorie. Different types of food have different energy values for equal weights (see table). *Nutrient density* refers to the amount of a given nutrient per calorie. A variety of foods with high nutrient densities should predominate in a diet. Basing a diet on foods with low nutrient densities, for example, risks either overeating to obtain adequate amounts of necessary nutrients or doing without those necessary nutrients.

| Food | Amount | Calories |
| --- | --- | --- |
| American cheese | 50 gm (about two slices) | 185 |
| Fast-food fried chicken drumstick | 54 gm (one) | 135 |
| Hard-boiled egg | 50 gm (one large) | 80 |
| Breaded fish sticks | 55 gm (two) | 100 |
| Pork (breakfast) sausage links | 50 gm (three) | 185 |
| Flour tortilla | 53 gm (one 8 inch) | 155 |

When you read the labeling on a food package, you'll notice that calories are based on a defined serving size, which may or may not accurately reflect normal consumption. For example, the labels on some 12-ounce cans of soft drinks list values based on two servings per can, although many people consume a whole can as a single serving.

Of course, we don't always eat equal weights of different foods. "Virtuously" eating reduced-fat and reduced-sugar foods will not necessarily lead to consuming fewer calories if you eat them in a greater volume! A boy who eats one tablespoon of peanut butter (about 45 calories) consumes fewer calories than a girl who eats a plain baked potato (about 140 calories). Even though peanut butter has more calories per gram than the baked potato, the potato weighs a lot more, and thus has more total calories than the peanut butter.

## Six Fundamental Needs

There are six important nutritional concepts that you as a teacher should emphasize to students at all levels. This chapter focuses on them, relating the concepts to youths and integrating their present diet with their future development by promoting the development of good health habits now. Your task is to help students integrate the science of nutrition with their own social, economic, and cultural backgrounds so that they can develop and enjoy lifelong, healthy habits of nutrition and physical activity.

By applying knowledge from nutrition, medicine, and physiology and committing to physical activity, a student can achieve the ancient Greek ideal of a sound mind *and* a sound body. A balanced diet supports a healthy lifestyle by meeting the six fundamental nutritional needs to

1. ensure and maintain proper hydration and electrolyte balance,
2. develop and maintain an ideal body mass,
3. develop and preserve a lean body mass,
4. provide adequate carbohydrates to optimize metabolism,
5. maximize oxygen delivery, and
6. develop a high-density skeleton.

## Ensure and Maintain Proper Hydration and Electrolyte Balance

It is important to maintain proper hydration and electrolyte balance, particularly during physical activity. Water constitutes 55 to 60 percent of an adult's body weight, and an even higher proportion of a child's weight. Sweating, vomiting, or urinating can cause dehydration. Conversely, excessive water intake can cause water intoxication.

The body attempts to maintain *homeostasis* (the proper level of hydration) by regulating both water intake and loss. When the concentration of *solutes* (which are dissolved chemicals, usually fairly simple compounds such as salt) in the blood is too high, receptors in the brain trigger the thirst sensation to make you want to drink. The brain regulates water loss through sweating, urination, and other mechanisms using similar signals.

While thirst signals the body's need for water, time-wise it lags behind that need. Dehydration leads to poor thermal regulation, loss of circulating water in the blood, and increased concentrations of sodium and potassium. Changes in electrolyte concentrations alter the performance of the heart and other neuromuscular systems. In addition, loss of circulating water in the blood reduces blood pressure. Students must know that they need to replenish lost water by drinking fluids (of any type) before, during, and after activity, rather than only when they become thirsty.

*Although sweating causes a loss of salt along with water, people don't usually lose enough salt to require salt supplements. Americans take in plenty of salt through their diets. In fact, excessive salt consumption in some individuals can result in hypertension (high blood pressure) and other ailments, and is a serious public health problem.*

## Develop and Maintain an Ideal Body Mass

As children mature through the stages of life, they gain greater independence in creating a lifestyle. The choices that children make determine their ability to maintain an ideal *body mass*, which is defined as the sum of lean body tissue (primarily muscle and organs) and stored (depot) fat.

Physiological parameters that define an ideal body mass include growth, development, circulation, respiration capacity, and physical activity. For many years we have defined the ideal body mass by drawing on growth and activity tables from a large population, which figure them as a function of age, gender, and height. However, the Body Mass Index (BMI) is a more accurate measure of an individual's relative health. Population studies suggest that a BMI between 20 and 25 is ideal. A BMI lower than 20 indicates insufficient stores of body fat, which may reduce growth and activity. A BMI between 25 and 30, on the other hand, indicates overweight, and a BMI greater than 30 indicates obesity with a possibility of serious health impairment.

*Females tend to have a greater percentage of body fat, with the ideal ranging from 18 to 23 percent body fat (compared with 16 to 19 percent for males). The body uses sexual hormones to regulate its body fat.*

### Determining Body Mass

Body Mass Index is the weight in kilograms (kg) divided by height in meters (m) squared (that is, $kg/m^2$). For example, a 145-pound (66-kilogram) adult who is 67-inches (1.7 meters) tall has a BMI of $66 / (1.7 \times 1.7) = 23$, which is in the "ideal" range.

Other ways to measure body fat include using convenient skinfold calipers (*FITNESSGRAM*); weighing the body underwater; and performing an isotope assay (the most accurate and expensive method). The BMI and calipers methods determine body composition quite accurately, and they are both convenient and inexpensive.

Obesity is now the biggest nutritional problem among youths. In our complex society, however, we cannot focus only on obesity. In fact, psychological and social pressures to look thin have driven many youngsters to the extremes of anorexia and bulimia, which pose serious health risks. Helping your students achieve and maintain an ideal body mass requires teaching them the right combination of caloric intake, caloric expenditure, and behavior modification. Behavior modification includes the frequency of eating, the portion sizes of food, and commitment to physical activity.

## Develop and Preserve a Lean Body Mass

Exercise both builds and breaks down muscle protein. Maintaining and increasing muscle mass requires optimal protein synthesis. Efficient production of new muscles results only when the diet provides all the amino acids, particularly the essential amino acids. A healthful diet includes enough high-quality protein to support muscle growth and sufficient energy sources to preserve amino acids for building muscle. This is particularly important during the growth years.

## Provide Adequate Carbohydrates to Optimize Metabolism

All dietary sugars, complex and simple, are metabolically equal. The body breaks down starches and sucrose into simple sugars for absorption. Sugar is both a fuel and an essential intermediate for burning fats and amino acids. For most individuals, young and old, the diet should supply enough carbohydrates to store glycogen in the muscles and liver as fuel for activity. However, excessive carbohydrate consumption can lead to weight gain, just as can excessive fat or protein consumption.

## Maximize Oxygen Delivery

The diet must provide certain trace elements, particularly iron and copper, necessary to synthesize hemoglobin. In the red blood cells hemoglobin binds oxygen and carries it to the tissues. The rate of metabolism, and thus the generation of energy, is a direct function of oxygen utilization. Maximizing the delivery of oxygen to the red blood cells requires developing an optimal lung capacity for gas exchange. Physical activity greatly enhances the capacity of the lungs and the circulatory system's functioning.

Iron-deficiency anemia prevents the body from synthesizing hemoglobin. Anemia, therefore, is a special concern in children during their fast growth spurts. It also is important to avoid in early adolescence as girls approach menarche.

## Develop a High-Density Skeleton

Throughout a life the body continuously builds and breaks down bone. Humans turn over their skeleton every 7 to 10 years. The bone is built from minerals (primarily calcium) and an organic matrix, much like reinforced concrete (see figure 7.3). Bone development depends on physical activity, nutrition, and heredity. Nutritional factors affecting bone density include calcium, vitamin D, and fluoride to build the mineral matrix and trace elements to build the collagen of the organic matrix. Dairy foods are the primary source of calcium for children and adolescents. The synthesis of bone is stimulated by weight-bearing exercises and hormone production.

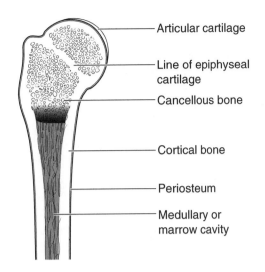

**Figure 7.3**    Cross-section of the femur.

# Biochemistry of Meeting the Six Fundamental Needs

The body is a complex chemical factory that takes raw material from the diet and the air and creates an astounding array of products—including the human body itself. The body needs different nutrients to meet each of its six fundamental needs. In this section, we'll look at how the body processes these nutrients.

## Water and Electrolytes

Water is essential to life. No other substance is as widely involved in so many diverse functions. Water

- makes up slightly more than half of the normal body weight,
- transports nutrients throughout the circulatory system for delivery to cells and tissues,
- removes waste products by transporting them from cells and tissues through the circulatory system to the kidneys and then out of the body in the urine,
- plays an important role in the buffering system, which maintains the acid-alkaline balance in the body,
- is an important coolant as a temperature-regulation mechanism, and
- is involved as a reactant or solvent in almost every chemical reaction that occurs in the body.

Water may be bottled or delivered by tap. It comes also by way of milk and juices, which contain additional nutrients. Fruits, vegetables, and other foods as well contain water and nutrients. Water, however, is the most important nutrient. The body loses two to three quarts of water per day through normal activity—and even more with greater physical activity. Therefore, one must consume at least two to three quarts of various beverages and water daily to maintain adequate levels in the body. Humans can only survive four to five days without water.

*In females very low body fat can limit the body's ability to produce female hormones, thus leading to brittle bones and osteoporosis—even in children. Maintaining an ideal body mass (ensuring that the body has enough fat) and performing weight-bearing activity to stimulate bone production will help prevent osteoporosis and brittle bones.*

*Some beverages can actually lead to greater water loss. Caffeine (found in many soft drinks, tea, and coffee) and alcohol are both diuretics—that is, they cause the body to lose more water, usually through increased kidney function. Active people need to replenish their water, not lose even more.*

## Energy Sources and Building Blocks

Food provides the fuel for maintaining the energy-requiring processes that sustain life. We must constantly replenish energy reserves through nutrients that provide "burnable fuel": carbohydrates, fats, and proteins. Energy is measured in calories. Every calorie, no matter what the source, is equal.

The First and Second Laws of Thermodynamics show us the relationship between energy and nutrition. The First Law tells us that energy can neither be created nor destroyed. It can, however, be converted from one form to another. In nutritional terms, if energy is taken in as food and not used, it is stored as fat. The Second Law states that all systems in the universe have a tendency to become disorganized and chaotic. Preventing this chaos requires continuous energy expenditure. In nutritional terms, there are millions of cells in our body breaking down every second. Nutritional fuels provide the energy to repair, replace, and operate these cells.

Metabolism is a series of chemical reactions in which the body converts food to useful energy and heat, which it then uses to operate, build, and repair body tissues. Two processes work at the same time. One process, called *anabolism,* joins smaller molecules together to form larger molecules; it occurs, for example, in the growth and repair of cells and tissues. The other process, called *catabolism,* splits larger molecules into smaller molecules; it occurs, for example, when the body splits complex carbohydrates into simple sugars.

### Metabolic Rates

Each individual has his or her own rate at which to convert the potential energy available in foodstuffs into stores of body energy. Through physical activity and proper nutrition a person can improve this rate of conversion: the *resting metabolic rate* (RMR)—or the amount of energy the body requires at rest to carry out such basic physiological functions as breathing, blood flow, and basal nerve and muscle activity. These functions alone consume 60 to 75 percent of the body's daily energy budget.

RMR varies with genetics, age, sex, physical activity level, and body type. Body type is determined by bone and muscle structure. A muscular person will have a higher RMR than a less muscular person of the same weight because muscle tissue requires more energy to maintain itself than does fat tissue.

Another consequence of the First Law of Thermodynamics is the need to take in building materials. Just as we can only change the form of energy, not create or destroy it, we can only change the form of matter, not create or destroy it. The matter forming the body must come from somewhere; that somewhere is the diet. The body uses nutrients in different ways as raw material for life's energy and structures, just as we might use wood to heat houses or build them.

**Carbohydrates.** Carbohydrates, both sugars and starches, are the body's principle source of energy. One gram of carbohydrate yields four calories (kilocalories). The body converts all sugars to glucose, the form of sugar that the cells use for energy. Glucose is the building block for other sugars (lactose, maltose, and galactose), amino acids, and nucleic acids.

The body stores any glucose it does not immediately use, since (under the First Law) it can't simply destroy the energy. It converts some of the glucose to glycogen and stores it in the liver and muscle; it converts the rest of the glucose to fat.

Dietary fibers are complex, indigestible carbohydrates that come from plants. *Insoluble* fiber absorbs water and helps provide the diet with needed bulk for the proper elimination of waste. *Soluble* fiber combines with waste substances to assist in their removal from the body.

Almost all foods, both natural and processed, contain carbohydrates. Grains, fruits, vegetables, and sweets, such as candies and baked goods, all contain both simple and complex carbohydrates to fuel the body. Whole grains and fruit or vegetable seeds and skins contain insoluble dietary fiber, whereas oat bran, apples, barley, beans, carrots, and other vegetables contain soluble fiber.

**Proteins.** The body uses protein both for fuel and as raw material for synthesizing tissues and hormones. Proteins are giant molecules consisting of chains of various of the 20 amino acids, strung together like beads. Protein synthesis requires the simultaneous presence of all 20 amino acids. The body can synthesize 10 of these amino acids, so they are termed *nonessential*. The other ten amino acids, called the *essential amino acids*, must come from the diet because the body is unable to make them. The breakdown and synthesis of protein is a normal function of the human body. As already mentioned, sugars are the primary fuel for the body. Proteins can be used for fuel if necessary. Proteins have the same caloric density as carbohydrates–that is, one gram of protein equals four calories.

## The Sweet Things in Life

Although all cells require some glucose, the brain and nervous system rely almost completely on glucose for energy. The brain and nervous system use two-thirds of the glucose the body requires—about 500 calories a day. Although one can survive longer without carbohydrates than without water, feelings of hunger, sluggishness, and irritability set in when the glucose levels in the blood drop.

When carbohydrate intake is too low, the glucose and glycogen stores in the liver will be depleted within 24 hours. Although the body can use fat for two-thirds of its energy requirements, it cannot use fat directly for energy in the brain and nervous system. Furthermore, in the absence of sugar, the body breaks down fat into toxic ketone bodies, leading to *ketosis*. The body must look for other stores of glucose to help fuel the brain and nervous system; it breaks down protein sources in the body to make amino acids, which are converted in turn to sugars to prevent ketosis.

Based on a 2000-calorie daily diet, an adult needs between 250 and 300 grams of simple and complex carbohydrates each day to provide sufficient glucose. There are two types of carbohydrates. The simple sugars—glucose, fructose, sucrose, galactose, and lactose—are found primarily in fruits, vegetables, soft drinks, cakes, candies, and milk. The bloodstream rapidly transports these simple carbohydrates to body tissues. Starches are complex carbohydrates containing linked glucose molecules, and they occur in grains, grain products, and potatoes.

Dietary protein is broken down into amino acids, which are then absorbed into the blood stream. Each cell synthesizes the proteins it needs, including enzymes to facilitate and direct chemical reactions and key structural elements of the cell. The body also uses proteins as building blocks for antibodies (which protect the body from invading organisms), blood clots, hormones (such as insulin), and neurotransmitters. Finally, amino acids are precursors in the construction of the nucleic acids DNA and RNA.

The nutritional value of proteins depends on their complement of essential amino acids and their ease of digestion and absorption. Not all sources of proteins in the food supply are equal. A complete protein meal contains all the essential amino acids in the correct amounts required by the human body. Animal sources, such as poultry, meat, fish, eggs, and milk, provide complete proteins. Vegetable sources of protein, such as legumes and grains, are incomplete because (with the exception of soy protein) they don't provide all the essential amino acids. Vegetarians can obtain complete proteins (and still not eat animal products) by consuming legumes and grains together to create a complete protein.

**Fats.** Fats play important roles not only as fuel sources for the body, but also by adding pleasure, satiety (feeling of satisfaction), and taste to foods. The term

## Kinds of Fats

Triglycerides, the most common form of fat, are composed of three long-chain, fatty acid hydrocarbon molecules joined to a glycerol. Like carbohydrates, fatty acids are composed of carbon, hydrogen, and oxygen. However, fatty acids have many more atoms of carbon and hydrogen in proportion to their oxygen, and so they supply more energy per gram. Few fatty acids that occur in foods or the body are free. Instead, they are usually found incorporated into triglycerides. In the body, 99 percent of the stored body lipids are triglycerides.

There are two major types of fatty acids: saturated and unsaturated. Saturated fatty acids, found in shortening and animal fats, are usually solid at room temperature and contain the maximum number of hydrogen atoms per carbon atom; thus they have no double bonds. Unsaturated fatty acids contain one or more double bonds; they tend to remain liquid at room temperature and to come from plants. Oils such as olive and canola are rich in monounsaturated fatty acids, which have only one double bond. Polyunsaturated fatty acids, which are found in vegetable and some fish oils, contain more than one double bond. Margarine is a chemically saturated vegetable oil.

Stored body fat (triglycerides) provides a source of energy, thermal insulation, and protection from mechanical shock. Fatty acids serve as starting materials for important hormonal regulators. The phospholipids and sterols contribute to the cells' structures. Cholesterol serves as the raw material for steroid hormones, vitamin D, and bile. The lack of fat in the diet may lead to hair loss, abnormal skin conditions, failure to resist infection, and poor absorption of fat-soluble vitamins.

*fat* refers to all lipids: triglycerides (fats and oils), phospholipids (lecithin), and sterols (cholesterol). Fats are the most dense caloric energy source—one gram of fat equals nine calories.

Fats can be found in a wide variety of foods, in varying forms and amounts. Triglycerides in the diet deliver fat-soluble vitamins, bring flavor, aroma, and tenderness to foods, slow digestion, and contribute to a sense of satiety. Fats are found in foods of both plant and animal origin. They also are in processed sources, including breads, cakes, candy, dairy products, and cooking fats such as oils, shortening, and butter. In food, 95 percent of the lipids (triglycerides) are fats and oils, and the remaining 5 percent are such other lipids as phospholipids and sterols.

Only when fats are consumed in high quantities do they become a threat to an individual's health and well-being. Fats eaten with awareness and appreciation can bring pleasure to a meal. If eaten unconsciously and unnecessarily, however, they offer no such benefits. While eating special low-fat foods can, in theory, be beneficial for weight management, most people tend to eat *more* of these reduced fat foods, and may therefore fail to reduce their caloric intake.

### Other Nutrients

Carbohydrates, proteins, and fats are the body's sources for energy for most of its structure. But these nutrients by themselves aren't enough. The body also needs vitamins and minerals to build chemical structures and to make and use energy.

**Vitamins.**    Vitamins are small organic molecules. After it was discovered that a deficiency of vitamins causes disease, they were determined to be essential substances. Only very small amounts of each vitamin are typically required in the diet. Vitamins differ from carbohydrates, fats, and proteins in many ways: They cannot be synthesized by our bodies, and must be obtained instead from the diet. Furthermore, some can be oxidized, or broken down, and rendered unable to perform their duties. Consequently, vitamins must be treated with respect in cooking and storing food.

We know enough about the structure and function of each vitamin to be able to synthesize all of them. Synthetic vitamins are identical in their activity to those

## Table 7.1   Water-Soluble Vitamins

| Vitamin | Functions | Sources |
|---|---|---|
| **Thiamine (B$_1$)** | Assists in energy metabolism; has a site on nerve-cell membrane to aid in muscle and tissue response. | Whole-grain foods |
| **Niacin** | Energy-transfer reactions and the metabolism of glucose, fat, and alcohol; oxidation-reduction reactions. | Milk, eggs, meat, poultry, fish, whole-grain and enriched breads and cereals |
| **Riboflavin (B$_2$)** | Coenzymes in energy metabolism; supports vision and skin health. | Milk, yogurt, cottage cheese, meat, green leafy vegetables, whole-grain bread and cereals. |
| **Biotin** | Part of coenzyme used in energy metabolism, fat synthesis, amino-acid metabolism, and glycogen synthesis. | Widespread in foods |
| **Pantothenic acid** | Energy metabolism. | Widespread in foods |
| **Pyridoxal (B$_6$)** | Helps make red blood cells; energy metabolism, amino-acid metabolism. | Green leafy vegetables, meats, fish, poultry, legumes, fruits, whole grains |
| **Folate** | New cell formation; nucleic-acid metabolism. | Green leafy vegetables, legumes, seeds, liver |
| **B$_{12}$** | New cell synthesis; maintains nerve cells; helps break down some fatty acids and amino acids. | Animal products (meat, fish, poultry, dairy, eggs) |
| **Vitamin C** | Collagen synthesis; antioxidant; amino-acid metabolism; absorption of iron. | Citrus fruits, cabbage-type vegetables, dark green vegetables, cantaloupe, strawberries, peppers, tomatoes, potatoes |

of natural origin. The body converts all vitamins to either coenzymes, which assist enzymes with cell metabolism and energy production, or regulatory hormone-like molecules.

The nine water-soluble vitamins (see table 7.1) dissolve in water and cannot be stored in the body. Therefore, water-soluble vitamins need to be consumed more often than fat-soluble ones.

The four fat-soluble vitamins (see table 7.2) dissolve in fat and can be stored in the body. They are found in oils, greens, milk, and eggs. Given the proper precursors, the body can manufacture vitamins A and D. For example, the body

## Table 7.2 Fat-Soluble Vitamins

| Vitamin | Functions | Sources |
|---|---|---|
| Vitamin A | Vision, maintenance of the cornea, epithelial cells, mucous membranes; growth of skin, bone, and teeth. | Fortified milk, cheese, eggs, spinach, broccoli, orange fruits and vegetables |
| Vitamin D | Bone metabolism. | Sunlight, fortified milk, egg yolk, liver, fatty fish |
| Vitamin E | Antioxidant, stabilization of cell membranes. | Plant oils, green leafy vegetables, wheat germ, egg yolks |
| Vitamin K | Blood clotting; bone metabolism. | Liver, green leafy vegetables, milk |

## Table 7.3 Major Macrominerals

| Macromineral | Functions | Sources |
|---|---|---|
| Calcium | Bone building; regulation of muscle activity; vision. | Milk products |
| Magnesium | Bone building; glucose utilization. | Nuts, avocados |
| Phosphorus | Bone building; cellular structure; cellular energy transfer. | Meat, fish, milk products |
| Sodium | Electrolyte balance; nerve and muscle function. | Salt |
| Potassium | Electrolyte balance; nerve and muscle function. | Bananas |
| Chloride | Electrolyte balance; nerve and muscle function. | Salt |
| Sulfur | Joint lubrication (in body-synthesized amino acids); allergic inflammation. | Meat, fish, milk products |

can convert beta carotene, which is found in melons, squash, and carrots, to vitamin A. Sunlight on the skin helps transform cholesterol to vitamin D.

**Minerals.** Minerals are inorganic elements that dissolve in water to become charged particles. Minerals cannot be changed and they keep their chemical identity. Nevertheless, they may be incorporated into proteins and other body structures. Minerals are involved in many aspects of the body's functioning. They are important in both electrolyte balance and acid-base balance. Nerve and muscle functioning depends critically on minerals, and many enzymes require minerals as a cofactor in order to function. So, too, the structure of many cells and tissues, particularly bone, relies on minerals.

The body requires the major minerals (*macrominerals*) in the largest amounts (see table 7.3). Minerals, except for calcium, are readily absorbed into the blood, freely transported, and rapidly excreted by the kidneys. As a result, the only mineral that the body stores is calcium; the others are quickly used or lost in waste products. Mineral-rich foods must be eaten regularly to replenish the body's supply.

Minerals are plentiful in the food supply, except for calcium and magnesium. Not enough people eat dairy products, which can supply 80 percent of the available calcium in a typical diet. Inadequate dietary calcium is the most common serious deficiency of minerals. While we must realize sodium's importance, too much sodium can lead to high blood pressure in some individuals.

## Table 7.4   Trace Elements

| Trace element | Functions | Sources |
|---|---|---|
| Iron | Hemoglobin protein; oxygen transport; respiration. | Red meats, fish, poultry, shellfish, eggs, legumes, dried fruits. |
| Zinc | Insulin; genetic material and proteins; immune reactions; transport of vitamin A; taste perception; wound healing; bone metabolism. | Protein-containing foods; meats, fish, grains, vegetables |
| Iodine | Thyroid hormone. | Seafood, bread, dairy products |
| Copper | Respiration; heme synthesis; collagen synthesis; bone metabolism. | Meats, shellfish, nuts |
| Manganese | Enzyme cofactors; bone and collagen. | Meats, nuts |
| Selenium | Oxidation-reduction, antioxidants. collagen. | Grains, seafood |
| Fluorine | Tooth and bone development. | Grains |
| Chromium | Maintains glucose homeostasis. | Meats, unrefined foods, fats, vegetable oils |
| Molybdenum | Facilitates (with enzymes) many cell processes. | Legumes, cereals, organ meats |
| Cobalt | Part of vitamin $B_{12}$; nerve formation and blood formation. | Meat, milk, dairy |

*Trace elements* are also vital to one's health. They are the minerals (see table 7.4) that must be consumed in small amounts, hence they are called *microminerals*. There are 10 essential trace elements, the best known of which are iron, copper, zinc, iodine, and selenium. Trace elements, used as enzyme cofactors, are a crucial part of systems for oxygen transport, respiration, and the regulation of metabolism.

# Consequences of Unhealthy Diets

We all want to believe in magic when it comes to nutrition and physical activity. Students must be taught, however, to separate magic and myth from reality. The belief that one can get something for nothing and achieve success without effort does not stand up to the First and Second Laws of Thermodynamics. No single diet or supplement is magical for losing or gaining weight, maintaining beautiful skin or hair, or imparting strength or agility.

Remembering the First Law of Thermodynamics, we can extend the principle to calories: all of them are equal, no matter what food source they come from. Consider some of the fashionable diets. Low-fat diets can provide pleasure in eating along with fewer fat calories. Consumed in large amounts, however, the reduced-fat items actually provide excessive calories. High-protein, moderate-fat, and low-carbohydrate diets suppress the appetite and lower calorie consumption, but such regimens may have toxic side effects. High-carbohydrate diets, which are low in fat and protein intake, restore carbohydrate depots for athletes, but this style of eating may compromise overall energy intake and provide too little protein.

If the diet provides inadequate levels of specific vitamins and minerals, nutritional supplements such as vitamin pills can make up the difference. There is little proof that supplementing the diet with vitamins and minerals *beyond* the RDA significantly benefits performance or enhances nutrition.

There are plenty of strategies you can use to help youngsters learn good eating habits. Here are some underlying principles. Remember as you plan your activities with students that strategies for good eating should include these:

1. Individual eating habits should respect family lifestyles.
2. Begin the day with breakfast to provide energy and nutrients.
3. Control calorie consumption by spacing meals and snacks throughout the course of the day.

---

### Dietary Disorders

Obesity (overweight) is an all-too-common consequence of poor lifestyle habits. While some individuals may be genetically predisposed to becoming overweight, everyone can avoid obesity through a healthful diet and by increasing physical activity. Obesity results from one dietary factor alone: excessive caloric intake. Remember that all calories are equal. Those excess calories commonly come from eating too much fat, but they could come just as easily from simply eating too much. Obesity can have serious consequences, such as heart disease, diabetes, joint and bone injuries, and kidney disease. Limiting or eliminating excess weight is a matter of reducing the excessive caloric intake. The best way to reduce the excess is through a combination of healthier eating—consuming fewer calories—and greater physical activity, which burns off calories through both the activity itself and raising the RMR.

An obsession with overweight—or the perception of being overweight—can also result in serious harm, however. An individual who is seriously underweight is also unlikely to be fit. The most common eating disorders associated with underweight are anorexia and bulimia. Advertising showing all body and dietary fat as "bad" only complicates the issue. Once again, a healthful diet, appropriate physical activity, and fitness knowledge are the best defenses against the eating disorders.

4. Find pleasure in food while being aware of its nutrient and caloric content.

5. Practice balance, variety, and moderation. Understand that there are no health foods and no junk foods.

6. Enjoy good food. Enjoy good health. Enjoy life.

## Summary

The most serious consequence of an inadequate diet is an ongoing failure to achieve one's physical best. Diet provides both energy and building blocks for everyone, regardless of activity level. A fit individual eats a healthful diet. It's impossible to build aerobic endurance without having the energy to keep the heart rate elevated. Muscular strength and endurance require building new muscle tissue with nutrients. Good flexibility requires a healthy skeleton, also built from sufficient nutrient intake. And an ideal body composition clearly depends heavily on an appropriate diet. Good diet alone cannot create fitness; neither can activity alone.

In most school-based programs, the concepts of nutrition are taught in health or biology-related courses, while the concepts of physical activity are assigned to physical education classes. Both of these very important concepts must fit into our lives and the lives of our students as one integrated concept, especially since we are constantly bombarded with sound bites about nutrition and exercise information from marginally informed media sources and word-of-mouth.

# PART II Activities

# Chapter 8
# Aerobic Fitness

# 1 Red Light, Green Light

## Primary Level

**Aerobic** means "with oxygen." **Aerobic endurance** is when your heart and lungs are doing a good job of sending oxygen to your muscles so you can exercise for a long period of time. To do the best job, your heart and lungs need food as fuel and plenty of good exercise.

## Purpose

Students will understand that (1) the heart, lungs, and muscles work together when performing aerobic activities; (2) food is the fuel that keeps the body running; (3) oxygen is needed to burn the fuel for energy to do physical activity; (4) the longer and harder one does physical activity, the more fuel and oxygen the body needs; and (5) drinking liquid before, during, and after activity is important.

## Equipment Needed

- Red, green, and yellow cards
- Music, preferably a car song

## Relationship to National Standards

**Physical Education Standard 4:** Student achieves and maintains a health-enhancing level of physical fitness—Student will engage in sustained physical activity that causes an increase in heart rate and breathing rate.

**Health Education Standard 3:** Student will demonstrate the ability to practice health-enhancing behaviors and reduce health risks—Student will demonstrate strategies to improve or maintain personal health.

## Set Induction

Ask students to share what green, yellow, and red traffic lights mean. Explain that today they are going to imagine they are cars and follow the traffic lights to help them exercise their hearts. Review or teach how to take a pulse rate. Explain that raising the heart rate through physical activity is good for their hearts. Mention that eating and drinking enough fluid are healthy for the body and are also good for the heart. In today's lesson the green card means "Go" and to go perform the locomotor skill. "Yellow" means slow down and walk; you're running out of fuel (oxygen, food, and liquid). "Red" means that the car is out of fuel (oxygen, food, and water) and to check your pulse by putting your hand over your heart. Have students check their pulses before beginning the activity.

## Procedure

1. Have students find a spot in the activity area.
2. Flash the green light card. Choose a locomotor skill with which to move. Have the students perform the locomotor skill for 30 seconds.
3. Flash the yellow light card to signal students to slow down and walk.
4. Finally, flash the red light card to signal students to stop. Have each student place one hand over the heart and use the other hand to demonstrate the heartbeat (by opening and closing the hand).
5. When students have felt their pulses, flash the green light and increase the activity time (from 30 seconds to a minute).
6. Repeat the yellow and red lights, and then have students check for increased heart rates. Ask, "Is it faster?" Repeat the activity until they see that their body is using up oxygen, food, and fuel when it performs activity.

## Teaching Hints

Make sure students have a general understanding of how to feel the heart rate by placing a hand on the chest. You can play this game at the beginning of the year to teach stop and start commands.

## Closure and Assessment

### Written and Oral

- Tell what part of the body helps you be active over a long period of time.

### Project

- Discuss with a friend or the class their favorite aerobic activity.

## Extending the Lesson

- Have students draw a picture explaining what their bodies need to move. What are the key ingredients to having a healthy heart, lungs, and muscles?
- Ask the art teacher to have students draw their own cars and demonstrate how aerobic endurance is like a car.

# 2 Benefit Pickup

### Primary Level

**Benefits of aerobic endurance** are gained from increased physical activity and appropriate nutrition. Having aerobic endurance helps you learn better, enjoy life, and feel good. Physical activity encourages your heart to beat stronger, your lungs to breathe better, and your muscles to get stronger. Appropriate nutrition, which includes eating balanced meals, drinking plenty of water, and not eating too much or too little food, gives you the energy to be physically active.

## Purpose

Students will understand (1) the benefits of having aerobic endurance; (2) physical activity will increase the lungs' ability to take in more oxygen and the heart's ability to beat stronger; (3) the importance of balance, variety, and moderation of foods; (4) the role of nutritional variety, including protein to help build muscles, and carbohydrates and fats for energy; and (5) the importance of drinking fluids before, during, and after activity.

## Equipment Needed

- Large containers (hoops, buckets, and the like)
- Aerobic Endurance Health Benefit Cards
- Any medium-paced music

---

**Aerobic Endurance Health Benefit Card Suggestions**
Design several cards decorated with pictures and then laminated, or popsicle sticks with the health benefits from aerobic endurance written on them. Examples of health benefits: healthy heart, breathing healthy, stronger muscles, feel better, learn better, play harder, more energy, healthy body composition.

---

## Relationship to National Standards

**Physical Education Standard 4:** Student achieves and maintains a health-enhancing level of physical fitness—Student will engage in sustained activity that causes an increased heart rate and increased breathing rate.

**Health Education Standard 3:** Student will demonstrate the ability to practice health-enhancing behaviors and reduce health risks—Student will identify personal health needs and demonstrate strategies to improve or maintain personal health.

## Set Induction

Brainstorm with students about the benefits of aerobic exercise. For very young students who cannot yet read, ask them about the benefits of aerobic exercise and read several of the health benefit cards to them to introduce the activity.

## Procedure

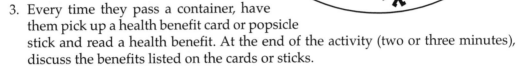

1. Place the health benefit cards in a central location at each end of the activity area (in containers, hoops, or the like).

2. Have the students begin moving clockwise or counterclockwise around the activity area using various locomotor patterns. Play music.

3. Every time they pass a container, have them pick up a health benefit card or popsicle stick and read a health benefit. At the end of the activity (two or three minutes), discuss the benefits listed on the cards or sticks.

## Teaching Hints

Encourage students to move at a pace that is best for them. The younger the students, the more time you should spend introducing the concepts of health benefits due to aerobic endurance before beginning the activity.

## Closure and Assessment

### Written and Oral

• Share the health benefits that were learned in today's activity.

### Project

• Share with another class member what health benefits were picked up and what type of activity you performed to increase aerobic endurance.

## Extending the Lesson

• Develop a bulletin board with the caption "(School Name) Kids Are Active Kids." Have students bring in pictures to display of themselves in their favorite aerobic activities at home, in school, and in the community.

• Bring in a model or a poster of the heart and discuss what happens to the heart and cardiovascular system when these organs are healthy.

# 3 Grab Bag

## Primary Level

**Frequency** is how many days per week you perform aerobic activity. Being active three or four days a week is good, but doing some form of activity *most* days of the week is *best*. You should be aware of the foods you eat every day, so you can balance the amounts and types of foods you need to make activity and food fun and enjoyable.

## Purpose

Students will understand and demonstrate how many days a week they should perform aerobic activity and will record activity and food consumed during the week.

## Equipment Needed

- Several activity cards that depict physical activities that improve aerobic endurance (see sidebar)
- 5 labeled bags (see sidebar)

---

**Grab Bag Ideas**

Prepare cards listing physical activity ideas such as the following:

Grab Bag 1:   Activities I Do by Myself
                    Bicycle ride (solo)—role-play for 30 seconds
                    Walk/jog (solo)—role-play for two minutes
                    Jump rope (solo)—role-play for two minutes

Grab Bag 2:   Activities I Do With Friends
                    Bicycle with a friend—role-play for 30 seconds
                    Jump rope with a friend—role-play for two minutes
                    Walk/jog with a friend—role-play for two minutes

Grab Bag 3:   Activities I Do With My Family
                    Shovel snow, rake leaves—role-play for 15 seconds
                    Mow the lawn—role-play for 15 seconds
                    Walk the dog—role-play for 15 seconds

Grab Bag 4:   Activities I Do in School
                    Chase and flee (tag) for three minutes
                    Jump rope in threes for three minutes
                    Play two-square for three minutes

Grab Bag 5:   Activities I Do in the Community
                    Swim—role-play for 15 seconds
                    Skate—role-play for 15 seconds
                    Soccer—role-play for 15 seconds

---

## Relationship to National Standards

**Physical Education Standard 3:** Student exhibits a physically active lifestyle—Student will engage in moderate to vigorous physical activity outside of physical education class.

**Health Education Standard 3:** Student will demonstrate the ability to practice health-enhancing behaviors and reduce health risks—Student will demonstrate strategies to improve or maintain personal health.

**Dance Education Standard 6:** Student makes connections between dance and healthful living—Student will explain how healthy practices (such as nutrition, safety) enhance his or her ability to dance.

## Set Induction

Explain that to have healthy heart we need to do aerobic activity most days of the week (at least three). Then brainstorm a list of heart-healthy foods. State that, today, students will be trying to raise their heart rates through doing a variety of physical activities, and you will be checking to see if they remember several heart-healthy foods.

## Procedure

1. Choose a student to name several heart-healthy foods (designate the food group, if desired).

2. Draw or have a student draw a physical activity card from one of the grab bags.

3. Direct the whole class to role-play the activity chosen.

4. Have another student name another heart-healthy food, then draw a second activity.

5. To reinforce the concept that people should eat heart-healthy foods and engage in physical activity most days of the week, continue to draw out and perform activities, suggesting that each draw represents a new day.

## Teaching Hints

Encourage students to work at their own paces. If time limits the number of activities the class can complete in one session, summarize and remind by saying "In class, we drew (number) cards representing (number) days of the week. How many more days do we need to be healthy this week?" Or draw the remaining cards and simply read them to the class.

## Closure and Assessment

### Written and Oral

- Tell by raising your fingers how many days per week you should give your heart, lungs, and muscles a workout and name a physical activity you could do on each day.

### Project

- Give each student a one-week calendar to complete at home or during recess. During the week, have each student draw or cut out a picture of the activity he or she did to give his or her heart a workout on each day of the week.

## Extending the Lesson

- Construct a FITT bulletin board as described in Activities 12 through 15, applying the concepts to aerobic fitness, beginning with the "F" and continuing as appropriate through the activities in this chapter.

- Go for a walk with a grandparent or another older adult. Describe how you felt and what you talked about. Answer the question "Is activity important for older people?"

# 4 Locomotion

## Primary Level

**Intensity** is how hard you do your physical activity. As you work harder, your lungs breathe harder to bring in more oxygen, and your heart beats faster to move the blood through your body to deliver oxygen and nutrients to the muscles. As the blood flow increases, you get hotter and begin to sweat. To replace the sweat you lose, you should drink plenty of water before, during, and after activity.

## Purpose

Students will (1) recognize and differentiate between which locomotor skills are aerobic activities that make their heart rates and breathing rates increase and which are not; (2) understand they need to drink fluids before, during, and after activity; (3) understand that dehydration can lead to severe illness so they should not wait until they are thirsty to drink water; and (4) understand the harder they work, the harder their hearts beat, the faster they breathe, and the hotter their bodies get.

## Equipment Needed

- Performed in an activity area or gym
- Segmented music tape or a tambourine

## Relationship to National Standards

**Physical Education Standard 4:** Student achieves and maintains a health-enhancing level of physical fitness—Student will engage in sustained aerobic activity that causes an increased heart rate and breathing rate.

**Health Education Standard 3:** Student will demonstrate the ability to practice health-enhancing behaviors and reduce health risks—Student will demonstrate strategies to improve or maintain personal health.

## Set Induction

Ask students to share the benefits of aerobic activity. Explain the concept of *intensity*. State that today students will be working harder and harder, checking their heart rates to see what their hearts do as they work harder. Ask students to predict what will happen (accept all answers and discuss correct answer after activity). Have students practice feeling their heart rates by placing one hand over the left side of the chest; this will give a baseline heart rate to which they may compare during the activity. Ask, "What else might your body do when it's working hard?"

## Procedure

Direct students to do the following:

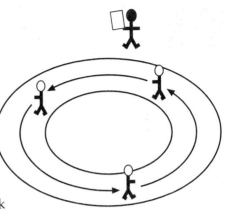

1. Work in their own space, all moving clockwise or counterclockwise around an activity area.

2. Check their heart rate by placing one hand over their hearts. Simulate the heart pumping with the free hand whenever checking heart rate during this activity.

3. Walk for 30 seconds, then check heart rate.

4. Gallop (or skip) for 30 seconds, then check heart rate.

5. Jog for 30 seconds, then check heart rate.

6. Sprint for 30 seconds and check heart rate one last time.

## Teaching Hints

Before beginning the activity, ensure that all students know how to feel their heart rates by placing their hand over the left side of the chest.

## Closure and Assessment

### Written and Oral

• Tell me how you know when you are working harder at a physical activity.

### Project

• During other classes, have students record which locomotor patterns increased their heart rate more, due to the various intensities of activities performed.

## Extending the Lesson

Have the classroom teacher read a book about different kinds of animals, and have the students act out the movements to each animal in the story. Make Animal Locomotor Cards to visually represent the movements to be performed.

## 5 | Off the Wall

### Primary Level

**Time** is how long you should perform an activity to improve your heart rate, breathing rate, and muscle capability. You should do physical activity at least 10 minutes at a time without stopping. You should accumulate up to 30 minutes of aerobic activity most days of the week. Time depends on the kind of activity chosen—some activities don't use up as much oxygen, food, and water as others.

## Purpose

Students will (1) identify time as it relates to aerobic endurance; (2) understand that their fuel supply (oxygen, food, and water) depends on the time they spend doing the activity; (3) understand that the longer they do an activity, the more fluids are necessary to hydrate the body; and (4) learn how to stay at an even pace so their fuel supply lasts as long as possible in order to do the activity for 30 minutes or more.

## Equipment Needed

- Off the Wall Cards (see sidebar)
- Music (optional)

---

**Off the Wall Card Ideas**

Cards with locomotor patterns written on them, or other cards that incorporate a sport skill such as dribbling a basketball or soccer ball.

Place the cards on the walls opposite each other. Wall Cards (↔ = Your choice with change of direction or pathway [e.g., forward, backward, sideways, straight, curved, zigzag]):

Walk ↔ Jog

Hop ↔ Jump

Slide ↔ Gallop

Skip ↔ Leap

Make five sets of five cards.

---

## Relationship to National Standards

**Physical Education Standard 3:** Student exhibits a physically active lifestyle—Student will engage in moderate to vigorous physical activity.

## Set Induction

Explain that in order to get the most benefit from physical activity, people need to keep moving for at least 10 minutes at a time.

## Procedure

1. Select a method of locomotion and direct students to travel back and forth from sideline to sideline (i.e., off the walls). If you use a pair of cards (e.g., walk and jog) at a time, place the walk card at wall A and the jog card at wall B. Have students travel back and forth according to the wall card directions for two minutes.

2. After two minutes, change the cards to the next set.

3. Continue until students have used all sets for a total of about 10 minutes of aerobic activity.

## Teaching Hints

There are two ways to perform "Off the Wall." The first way is that the entire class can perform the locomotor skill or activity and go across the gym once for one minute, and then the teacher calls out another locomotor skill or activity. The second way is for the class to be divided into station groups, and at each station is a new locomotor pattern or physical activity—after one minute, the teacher rotates the stations.

## Closure and Assessment

### Written and Oral

• List or tell how much time you should spend giving your heart, lungs, and muscles a workout.

### Project

• Draw a picture showing how you felt during the different time intervals.

## Extending the Lesson

Start a "Lub Dub Club" for which members supplement class time with 15 to 20 minutes of at-home aerobic activity time. Have students take home an information sheet explaining the program to their parents. Have parents sign the sheet to verify the student's home performance. To reward each student's additional effort, display a small heart with the student's name. Reward consecutive efforts by placing a small sticker on the student's display heart.

# 6  Aerobic Exploration

## Primary Level

**Specificity**, or **type**, means what kind of activity you participate in to improve or maintain your aerobic endurance. You must perform the aerobic activities with nonstop, continuous movement. The activities you select should be fun and enjoyable to you.

## Purpose

Students will identify and choose several different activities that maintain or improve their aerobic endurance and aerobic activities they enjoy doing.

## Equipment Needed

- Soccer balls
- Basketballs or playground balls
- Scrap paper
- Cones
- Signs with station instructions on them
- Any other equipment that is included in their choices or in the stations

## Relationship to National Standards

**Physical Education Standard 3:** Student exhibits a physically active lifestyle—Student will identify at least one activity associated with each component of health-related physical activity.

**Health Education Standard 3:** Student will demonstrate the ability to practice health-enhancing behaviors and reduce health risks—Student will demonstrate strategies to improve or maintain personal health.

## Set Induction

Explain that, today, students will have several opportunities to explore a variety of aerobic experiences through actual physical activity as well as through role-play. Introduce how to take the pulse at the neck (see Teaching Hints) and ensure students can do so by having each make a baseline check. Briefly introduce the stations you have set up. Encourage students to think about which activities they like best as they move from station to station. These are the ones they should do outside of physical education class.

## Procedure

1. Signal students to rotate through the following stations:

   - Skating—can use two pieces of scratch paper for skates.
   - Cross-country skiing—role-play, using hockey or pillow polo sticks for poles.
   - Soccer dribble—dribble soccer ball around cones.
   - Power walking—do laps around gym.
   - Basketball dribble or defensive slide as in guarding (or both)—dribble playground ball around cones.
   - Swimming—role-play crawl or backstroke.
   - Additional stations—choose a variety of stations that are aerobic and included in your physical education sport skill theme, dance, or gymnastic program.

2. To increase students' awareness that they are doing activities that can improve aerobic endurance, have them check their pulses before each rotation.

## Teaching Hints

Primary students can find the pulse with index finger at neck and show "how fast" by opening and closing the other hand (like a heart pumping) or putting their hand on the left side of the chest and counting the beats.

## Closure and Assessment

### Written and Oral

- Thumbs up or thumbs down: Activities that give your heart, lungs, and muscles a workout are called aerobic activities.

### Project

- Create a list of different activities you could use for the Aerobic Exploration Stations and have the students circle those that increase aerobic endurance.

## Extending the Lesson

Have the students create "sayings" or a commercial about aerobic activity.

# 7 Getting Started

## Primary Level

To ensure healthy heart, lungs, and muscles, you need to be active most days of the week. The goal of improving aerobic endurance (demonstrating **progression**) requires doing more than usual, meaning you must participate in aerobic activity more often, harder, or longer. This also means that it takes a longer time to use up oxygen, food, and water during increased physical activity. This is **progression**.

## Purpose

Students will demonstrate progression from baseline fitness performance toward a realistic goal selected by the student with help from the teacher.

## Equipment Needed

- PACER tape and/or CD (get from Cooper Institute – *FITNESSGRAM*)
- Measured area 20 meters (21 yards, 32 inches) or running area equal to 1 mile

## Relationship to National Standards

**Physical Education Standard 4:** Student achieves and maintains a health-enhancing level of physical fitness—Student will sustain moderate to vigorous physical activity for short periods of time.

## Set Induction

Explain that, over time and with aerobic practice, the heart, lungs, and muscles will get stronger, making the task seem less difficult. The way to know if you're improving is to measure your ability today and then later repeat the test to see if you're making progress (that is, feeling better afterward or lasting longer). Emphasize that this is not a competition; instead, everyone should try their best, then work on improving during the rest of the school year. State that you will help each student set a reasonable goal in this area.

## Procedure

1. Choose which assessment you are going to practice.

2. Have students practice the assessment tasks you have selected.

3. Explain that over time and with practice, aerobic endurance will increase. State that later each student will repeat the assessment tasks to see if he or she is improving.

4. Help each student set a personal goal.

5. Students can write their goals down on record sheets.

| Days | Assessment |
| --- | --- |
| Monday | |
| Tuesday | |
| Wednesday | |
| Thursday | |
| Friday | |

## Teaching Hints

Remember to emphasize finishing and—over time—improving, not scores (see chapter 2). See the Appendix for sample forms. After collecting baseline data, provide opportunities for students to practice aerobic activities. Keep in mind that the PACER is an excellent activity for aerobic practice as well as an assessment tool. Over the course of the school year, periodically reassess and identify progress as individuals or as a whole class.

## Closure and Assessment

### Written and Oral

- Have students report that upon reassessment that "It felt easier" or "I lasted longer."

### Project

- Have students log their scores and write realistic goals with your help.

## Extending the Lesson

- Create a "Century Club" for which students (with assistance from parents) log 100 minutes of aerobic activity in one week (or longer).
- Have the students interview their family members to find out what types of activities or exercise they perform to remain aerobically fit.

# 8 Full Speed Ahead

## Primary Level

Students report that upon reassessment the activities felt easier or they could perform the activities longer. This also means that it takes a longer time to use up oxygen, food, and water during increased physical activity. This is **progression**.

## Purpose

Students will participate in aerobic activity that demonstrates progression and understand that good nutrition with adequate proteins, carbohydrates, and fats support an increase in frequency, intensity, time, and type of activity.

## Equipment Needed

- Segmented medium-beat music that students can use to pace themselves
- Any equipment necessary to do locomotor activities

---

### Making a Segmented Audio Tape for Full Speed Ahead

Increase the activity time and decrease the rest time as the tape progresses. A sample tape may look like this:

15 seconds music (for activity), 15 seconds quiet (for resting)

15 seconds music, 15 seconds quiet

20 seconds music, 10 seconds quiet

20 seconds music, 10 seconds quiet

25 seconds music, 5 seconds quiet

25 seconds music, 5 seconds quiet

30 seconds music—Full Speed Ahead!

---

## Relationship to National Standards

**Physical Education Standard 4:** Student achieves and maintains a health-enhancing level of fitness—Student will recognize the physiological indicators that accompany moderate to vigorous physical activity.

**Health Education Standard 3:** Student will demonstrate the ability to practice health-enhancing behaviors and reduce health risks—Student will demonstrate strategies to improve or maintain personal health.

## Set Induction

Explain to students that to become more fit, you need to do a little more activity and work a little harder each time you are active. It can be helpful to alternate bursts of activity with periods of rest as well. Explain that today students will be starting out moving slowly and gradually increase speed until they are going Full Speed Ahead! This is *progression*.

## Procedure

1. Have students find a self-space in the activity area.
2. Select a locomotor movement to demonstrate this concept. Have younger students begin by walking and second and third graders by skipping or jogging.
3. Practice using the tape.

## Teaching Hints

Monitor the intensity level of the activity with your students. When ready, have students progress to starting with more intense forms of locomotion.

## Closure and Assessment

### Written and Oral

- Tell or write three things that demonstrate progression in an aerobic endurance workout.

### Project

- Talk to a classmate and share the difference between performance when they first started performing the exercise or activity and the way they feel now.
- Draw a picture of an activity you can do with a friend or family member to improve your aerobic endurance.

## Extending the Lesson

- Make a chart that shows how an athlete increases their workload and decreases their rest during training, which is similar to how the heart, lungs, and muscles work harder each time the music plays.
- Have students draw pictures of activities they enjoy that show aerobic endurance.

# 9 Move and Shape Up!

## Primary Level

A **warm-up** prepares your body for activity. It increases your heart rate and breathing rate gradually. A **cool-down** lets your body return to a normal heart rate and breathing rate gradually.

## Purpose

Students will experience and explain the importance of warming up and cooling down.

## Equipment Needed

- Shape signs (optional)

## Relationship to National Standards

**Physical Education Standard 4:** Student achieves and maintains a health-enhancing level of physical fitness—Student will identify the physiological signs of moderate physical activity.

**Health Education Standard 3:** Student will demonstrate the ability to practice health-enhancing behaviors and reduce health risks—Student will demonstrate strategies to improve or maintain personal health.

## Set Induction

Discuss the changes that occur when the body begins to be active. (Your heart beats faster and you breathe harder. Blood vessels that carry oxygen get bigger. Your body gets warmer because it is burning energy.) Explain that a warm-up lets the body make these changes slowly, which is healthier and safer than making the body work hard without preparation. Explain to students that walking before jogging is an example of a gradual warm-up. Ask if they can name others. A cool-down gradually returns the breathing and heart rate to normal after vigorous physical activity.

## Procedure

1. Have students stretch muscles they will use during the main activity.

2. Direct students to move using various locomotor movements, starting slowly.

3. Add changes in direction, size of movement, levels, pathways, and so on.

4. Signal students to gradually increase the intensity of the warm-up.

5. Ask students what is happening to their breathing and heart rates as the warm-up progresses.

6. Have students stop to rest and perform a shape, learning or practicing a variety of shapes they can make with the body, such as a circle, line, or square. You can either name the shape or hold up one of the optional shape signs to designate a shape for practice.

7. At the end of the lesson, repeat the activity as a cool-down. Finish with an easy walk to completely reverse the process.

## Teaching Hints

Be sure to start slow and easy.

## Closure and Assessment

### Written and Oral

- Ask "When should you warm up—before or after exercising? What should you do after exercising—warm up or cool down? What important things happen to your body when you warm up? What important things happen to your body when you cool down? Tell me one important rule about warming up. Tell me one important rule about cooling down."

### Project

- Ask the students to come up with several suggestions for the class warming up and cooling down, allowing them to assist in leading these warm-up and cool-down activities.

## Extending the Lesson

- Design a place mat for the students' daily snacks that explains the importance of aerobic endurance and being healthy.

# 10 Taking Your Heart Rate

### Intermediate Level

Aerobic means with oxygen. **Aerobic endurance** is the ability of the heart, lungs, and muscles to perform activity over a sustained period of time. Your body needs fuel from food, including carbohydrates, fats, and proteins, to perform well. The muscles also need oxygen transported by blood to burn these fuels for energy. The body also needs plenty of liquid in order to avoid becoming dehydrated. Your heart rate represents how fast your heart pumps blood to your body. As the body requires more oxygen to be transported to the muscles, your heart beats faster and you breathe harder.

## Purpose

The students will understand (1) physical activity increases the heart rate, lung capacity, oxygen delivery, efficiency to burn fuels for energy, and circulation of fuels through the body; (2) the heart pumps, the lungs bring oxygen into the blood, and muscles provide mechanical energy; (3) nutrients, such as carbohydrates, fats, and proteins, provide fuel during endurance activity; (4) the body needs liquid to keep it from becoming dehydrated; and (5) the definition of heart rate and the significance it has in physical activity.

## Equipment Needed

- Heart rate monitors (if available) or a clock with a second hand
- Task cards (with pictures if you have students with reading difficulties)
- Equipment for a circuit of station activities that show differences in aerobic endurance (e.g., sports skills such as dribbling a basketball or soccer ball; recreational activities such as jumping rope, or role-playing climbing a mountain; outdoor activities such as cross-country skiing, swinging on a swing, or walking; work such as using a computer or reading a play; pretending at a beach by tossing and catching a Frisbee)
- Pencils and task sheets (see the Appendix)

## Relationship to National Standards

**Physical Education Standard 4:** Student achieves and maintains a health-enhancing level of physical fitness—Student will engage in sustained physical activity that causes increased heart rate and breathing rate.

**Health Education Standard 3:** Student will demonstrate the ability to practice health-enhancing behaviors and reduce health risks—Student will demonstrate strategies to improve or maintain personal health.

## Set Induction

Define *aerobic endurance.* Brainstorm a list of activities that are more and less aerobic in nature. Explain that today, students will be collecting information on how strenuous various activities are by checking and recording heart rate after each activity. Tell them that if they are role-playing they should try to be as active as they would be either in real life or in sports and athletics. Review how to take a heart rate accurately.

## Procedure

1. Divide students into the same number of small groups as you have stations.

2. Have students perform each task card activity for one minute at each station and record their heart rates on a task sheet (see the Appendix).

3. Every 60 seconds, signal students to rotate to the next activity.

4. Discuss differences in heart rates compared to the types of activities performed.

## Teaching Hints

- Remind students that a healthy diet with all essential nutrients will give their bodies the fuel they need to be active.

## Closure and Assessment

### Written and Oral

- Write a definition of aerobic endurance.

- List activities from today's lesson that were aerobic.

### Project

- Have students work in small groups to design new stations for aerobic and nonaerobic activities.

- Have a group of students modify a game or sport skill drill to increase aerobic activity and therefore raise heart rates.

## Extending the Lesson

- Construct a "Mind Map" bulletin board picturing the heart, lungs, and muscles working over a clock.

- Have the students prepare a graph depicting heart rates for a variety of activities and the value of each in the development of the aerobic system.

# 11 Heart Obstacle Course

## Intermediate Level

**Aerobic endurance** improves the ability of the heart, lungs, and muscles to do work over a long period of time. Together good nutrition and physical activity will promote lifelong **health** benefits and disease prevention. But to feel good and enjoy life, physical activity and nutrition should be fun, individual, and pleasurable.

## Purpose

Students will learn (1) the importance of aerobic endurance to personal needs and interests; (2) health risks of lack of activity and poor nutrition; (3) the fact that physical activity increases the lung capacity for oxygen exchange to burn fuels; and (4) that each person is unique in nutritional and physical activity needs.

## Equipment Needed

- Blue and red beanbags
- Blue and red chalk
- Scooter boards and cones
- Small (8-ft.) parachute
- Mats
- Red and blue balls
- Jump ropes
- Blue and red signs signifying oxygenated and deoxygenated blood
- Warning signs with risk factors
- Tunnel
- Weights or other load to carry

## Relationship to National Standards

**Physical Education Standard 4:** Student exhibits a physically active lifestyle—Student will identify the benefits derived from regular physical activity.

**Health Education Standard 3:** Student will demonstrate the ability to practice health-enhancing behaviors and reduce health risks—Student will demonstrate strategies to improve or maintain personal health.

## Set Induction

Discuss each of the Purpose aspects (see worksheet in the Appendix). Discuss each of these controllable risk factors with the students. Explain that today students will be "traveling" through a "heart" just as the blood does through our bodies. State that red means the blood has enough oxygen and blue means it does not have enough oxygen. Display a diagram or model of the heart and point out the corresponding stations while describing the path the blood flows along. Organize the students according to your preference (see Procedure). Have students check their heart rate before and after the obstacle course.

## Procedure

At each heart station, post signs that list what the heart part is and what it means and one benefit of aerobic activity.

There are two ways to do the course:

1. Station approach—Students spend 2-3 minutes at a station and travel to the next station through the valve to the next chamber.

2. Continuous movement—Students pick up a blue beanbag and hold onto it as they travel through the right side of the heart. They drop the blue beanbag in the lungs and pick up a red beanbag and travel through the left side of the heart. At the vena cava, students drop the red beanbag and pick up a blue beanbag, and so on.

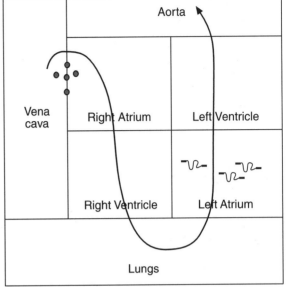

## Teaching Hints

If using the station approach, use a segmented music tape (30 seconds and 10 seconds, 40 seconds and 10 seconds, or the like) to signal work and rest intervals.

If using the continuous movement approach, start two to four students at each station so they do not have to wait in line. Continue long enough for students to gain aerobic benefits from participating. Make sure that you have enough red and blue beanbags.

## Closure and Assessment

### Written and Oral

- Tell or write four benefits of participating in aerobic activities and two risks of heart disease.

### Project

- Have the students fill in a task sheet as they work their way through the parts of the heart, listing the benefits of aerobic exercise and the risk factors for heart disease.

- Draw a cartoon strip using the following characters: Harry the Heart and Ruby the Red Blood Cell. Show how aerobic endurance is beneficial to your health and reduces the risks of disease.

## Extending the Lesson

- Review the flow of the blood throughout the body with your students, using a model or chart of the heart. Have students outline their bodies on large sheets of paper and label the heart, lungs, head, shoulders, knees, and toes. Trace the flow of the blood as it moves throughout the heart and body. Use red and blue crayons to distinguish between blood leaving the heart and moving through the arteries and blood returning to the heart through the veins.

- Develop a bulletin board entitled "Heart Disease Risk Factors."

- Walk with an older person. How do you feel? How does he or she feel?

- Work with the classroom teacher in studying the cardiorespiratory system.

- Teach students the relationship among aerobic endurance, physical activity, and nutrition.

# 12 Aerobic Flip Card File

### Intermediate Level

**Frequency** is how many days per week you should perform aerobic activity to improve your heart rate, breathing rate, and muscle function. You should perform activity that is pleasurable and fun a minimum of three days a week. For best results, you should do some activity most days of the week. You should be aware of the foods you eat and the amount of activity you do to ensure your diet is the best it can be for growth and development.

## Purpose

Students will participate in a variety of activities to allow them choices to stay active most days of the week and record the type and amounts of foods and physical activity during a designated time period.

## Equipment Needed

- Equipment needed for activity stations
- Four or five 3 x 5 index cards for each student
- Yarn, string, or a metal ring to connect cards for each student
- Class chart to record student's frequency of practice (optional)
- Pencils or markers

## Relationship to National Standards

**Physical Education Standard 3:** Student exhibits a physically active lifestyle—Student will identify several moderate to vigorous physical activities that provide personal pleasure.

**Health Education Standard 3:** Student will demonstrate the ability to practice health-enhancing behaviors and reduce health risks—Student will demonstrate strategies to improve or maintain personal health.

## Set Induction

Review the importance of aerobic activity and healthful eating to heart health. Explain that today students will be making a personalized flip card file of their choices of aerobic activities (or that they will be adding to their flexibility flip card file; see chapter 9, Activity 12 on page 144 and chapter 10, Activity 13 on page 184).

## Procedure

Set up four stations with choices of aerobic activities, for example:

Station 1—step-ups, basketball dribbling around cones, and soccer dribbling around cones

Station 2—aerobic dance routine, step aerobics routine, and jump rope routine

Station 3—jump rope (solo), jump rope (with partner), and jumping medley (scissors, jacks, skier)

Station 4—lap run, shuttle run (PACER)

Direct students to do the following:

1. Go to each station and select one aerobic activity to copy onto a 3 x 5 card.

2. Practice the activity.

3. Rotate to the next station upon the signal.

4. When finished with the stations, you should have four cards for your personalized flip card file.

5. Connect cards with yarn (or string or a metal ring).

6. Use your file to do the activities you chose most days of the week during any free time at school, such as, in class (with teacher's permission) or during breaks or at home.

7. Record how often you do aerobic activity.

## Teaching Hints

Have students put their names on their flip cards and help them think of ways to be responsible for keeping track of them. You could establish a lost and found spot. Keep in mind not every student will be self-motivated to use the cards. Therefore, use prompts and a system of accountability. To have students record frequency, have them check it off on a class chart or list it on a fifth 3 x 5 card attached to the file.

## Closure and Assessment

### Written and Oral

• Tell or write a definition of frequency.

### Project

• Compare your choice of activities with two other students in the class and ask them why they chose those activities to stay aerobically fit. Report to the class the reasons that activities are chosen.

## Extending the Lesson

• Write a one page paper on "How You Feel When You Are Active." One paragraph should discuss what happens to your body when you exercise; the second paragraph should discuss how you feel and how exercise and activity increases your ability to learn; finally, discuss how exercise and activities influence how you feel about yourself when you work out and stay fit.

• Construct a "Choices of Our Students" bulletin board from the choices made during the project assessment.

• Construct a bulletin board to represent the FITT formula. Use the caption "To Be Fit, You Must Think FITT." List the FITT acronym down the left side of the bulletin board. Explain to students that the "F" stands for frequency.

# 13 | Jump to It

## Intermediate Level

**Intensity** is defined as how hard you have to work in your chosen aerobic activity to make your heart pump the blood faster and your lungs breathe faster to supply more oxygen to your muscles. As a result, your body temperature rises and you sweat to cool off. To replace the sweat you lose during activity, you must drink fluids before, during, and after aerobic activity.

## Purpose

Students will (1) demonstrate the principle of intensity by participating in a series of activities that require them to increase repetitions or workload or both; (2) learn to take their pulses to monitor the intensity of each activity; and (3) learn to recognize the signs of dehydration and reasons to continually take fluids into the body.

## Equipment Needed

- Jump to It signs—jump back and forth over a line, side to side, over a line, zigzag down a line, jumping jacks and jills, scissors jump over a line, jump rope
- Equipment needed to follow sign instructions (e.g., jump ropes)
- Recordkeeping worksheet (see the Appendix)
- "Jump" by Van Halen or other energetic music (optional)

## Relationship to National Standards

**Physical Education Standard 4:** Student achieves and maintains a health-enhancing level of physical fitness—Student will identify several activities related to each component of physical fitness and begin to develop a strategy for the improvement of selected fitness components.

## Set Induction

Review or introduce the definition of *intensity*. Play Van Halen's "Jump" to the students, and tell them they are going to work on the concept of intensity during aerobic activity.

## Procedure

This activity is performed over a few days.

1. Divide students into even groups.
2. Start with a group of students at each jump station.
3. Have the students work at each station for 15 seconds and then rotate to the next station.
4. Have the students record their heart rate in the middle and at the end of the activity.
5. The next day, have the students increase the intensity of the exercises by increasing the time at each jump station from 15 seconds to 20 seconds. Alternatively, have the students perform each station for 10-15 seconds and then when they either finish or complete half of them, increase the length of time to 15-20 seconds.

## Teaching Hints

When revisiting this lesson, increase the active time allotment. Encourage students to work harder and try to perform more repetitions at each activity. Was the heart beating faster? Compare to previous worksheets.

## Closure and Assessment

### Written and Oral

- Tell or write a definition of intensity. Then tell how you varied the intensity of the workout in this activity.

### Project

- In small groups, have students design a different set of stations using other locomotor activities. Have them name each station game and tell how you can vary the intensity in the activity.

## Extending the Lesson

- Instruct the students about the various heart rates in different work environments. Then have them take their heart rates at home performing various types of tasks.
- Design a bumper sticker showing intensity.
- Talk about fatigue symptoms, such as dehydration, stress, and muscle cramps.
- Explain to students that the "I" in FITT stands for intensity. Turn the "I" on the FITT bulletin board (see Activity 12) into "Intensity = How Far!"

# 14 Time Card Contract

## Intermediate Level

**Time** is how long you need to be physically active to improve or maintain your aerobic endurance. You should accumulate 30 minutes of aerobic activity most days of the week. Time will vary according to the **intensity** and the **type** of activity chosen.

## Purpose

Students will (1) define the time concept for aerobic endurance; (2) learn that as you increase time you need to replenish fluids; and (3) learn that as you increase time you need more oxygen, food (complex carbohydrates vs. the simple sugars), and water.

## Equipment Needed

- Time cards
- Hole punches, one per station

Equipment for aerobic station activities might include the following:

- Volleyballs
- Soccer balls
- Basketballs
- Jump ropes
- Instructions for step dance or other forms of dance

## Relationship to National Standards

**Physical Education Standard 3:** Student exhibits a physically active lifestyle—Student will select and participate regularly in physical activities for the purpose of improving skill and health.

**Dance Education Standard 6:** Student makes connections between dance and healthful living—Student will explain how healthy practices (such as nutrition, safety) enhance his or her ability to dance.

## Set Induction

Remind students that the Surgeon General's Report states that it is important to perform at least 30 minutes of aerobic activity most days of the week. Explain that to help them remember to get enough aerobic activity, they will be using time cards and setting individual contracts. The contracts will include the type of activity and the length of time performing that activity. They will meet portions of the time card contract in school and the rest outside of school. You will record the portions they do in school. The students should record how long and what types of activity or exercise they performed at home. These records can be kept in a pocket folder and considered part of their physical education portfolio. Discuss the importance of drinking fluids before, during, and after physical activity, and eating the right foods for maximum performance. Finally, remind students that a healthy heart can deliver oxygen to the body more efficiently.

## Procedure

1. Set up five continuous action stations that involve three minutes of aerobic activity each.
2. Every time a student completes a station, the time card is punched.
3. Continue rotating students through the stations until they have accumulated 15 minutes of activity.

## Teaching Hints

Remind students that they should perform the station activities nonstop. Relate the three minutes of activity at each station to the accumulation of 30 minutes of aerobic activity. Make sure to emphasize that students need to complete the other 15 minutes of aerobic activity outside the physical education setting.

| Activity |
| --- |
| Jump Rope |
| Step Dance |
| Basketball |
| Soccer Dribble |
| Volleyball Juggle |

## Closure and Assessment

### Written and Oral

- Tell or write a definition of time (duration).

### Project

- Give each student an activity sheet to complete for one month at school and home. During the month, have the student draw or cut out a picture of the activity he or she did to give his or her heart a workout and how much time he or she spent on the activity. Relate this to the accumulation of 30 minutes of aerobic activity for that day.

## Extending the Lesson

- Have the student prepare a chart of heart rates for various activities. Following each activity, list duration for each, based on working heart rates.
- Explain to the students that the first "T" in FITT stands for time. Remind them to perform at least 30 minutes of aerobic activity most days of the week. Turn the first "T" on the FITT bulletin board into "Time = How Long!" Place a clock on the bulletin board next to the "T" for time.

# 15 Healthy Heart Tag

## Intermediate Level

**Type** means certain activities use more oxygen and require you to breathe faster and your heart to beat faster. You must learn to choose the activities that strengthen your heart.

## Purpose

Students will (1) identify five heart-healthy activities they enjoy participating in to develop their aerobic endurance; (2) begin to understand how frequency, intensity, and time influence the type of activity done to improve aerobic endurance; (3) understand their bodies need food sources including carbohydrates to store reserves in the muscles and liver for long duration activity; (4) understand that their bodies call upon these stores depending on the type, time, and intensity of the activity; and (5) learn the difference between aerobic and anaerobic activities by taking their pulses and noting their breathing rates.

## Equipment Needed

- Healthy Heart Tag signs
- Segmented music tape with rest intervals
- Equipment necessary for activity stations

## Relationship to National Standards

**Physical Education Standard 3:** Student exhibits a physically active lifestyle—Student will select and participate regularly in physical activities for the purpose of improving skill and health.

## Set Induction

Review the importance and components of being heart-healthy (see Purpose). Then describe how to play Healthy Heart Tag: when students are tagged once, they must hold their hearts and keep moving. When students are tagged the second time they must go to their favorite aerobic activity and participate in the activity listed on the sign. They return to the game when they have completed the activity on the sign.

## Procedure

Because this game is vigorous, use a segmented music tape with rest intervals already programmed into the music. During the resting segments, have students feel their pulses to check for increased heart rates. In addition, have them monitor their breathing rates.

1. Place the Healthy Heart Tag signs around the perimeter of the activity area.
2. Choose three to five students to be taggers.
3. Select a locomotor movement to use for the activity.
4. Change taggers often.

## Teaching Hints

Make sure the rest segments on the music tape are long enough for students to check their pulses.

## Closure and Assessment

### Written and Oral

- Tell or write a definition of type.

### Project

- Using the criteria of "vigorously," "continuously," "using large muscle groups," and "over a long period of time," have each student develop a list of activities and player positions that will provide exercise for the heart, lungs, and muscles.
- Have the students discuss with one another how they feel when they participate in community activities.

## Extending the Lesson

Explain to the students that the second "T" in FITT stands for type. Turn the second "T" on the FITT bulletin board into "Type = Which Exercise!" Have students bring in pictures of people involved in a variety of aerobic activities to add to the bulletin board.

# 16 On Your Way

## Intermediate Level

To make sure you have a healthy heart and healthy lungs and muscles, you need to be active most days of the week. The goal of improving aerobic endurance (demonstrating **progression**) requires doing more than usual, participating in aerobic activity more often, harder, or longer.

## Purpose

Students will demonstrate progression from a baseline fitness performance toward a realistic goal selected by the student with help from the teacher.

## Equipment Needed

- PACER tape
- Measured area of 20 meters (21 yards, 32 inches) or one-mile running area

## Relationship to National Standards

**Physical Education Standard 4:** Student achieves and maintains a health-enhancing level of physical fitness—Student will meet the health-related standards as defined by *FITNESSGRAM*.

## Set Induction

See Activity 7, Getting Started, earlier in this chapter.

## Procedure

1. Choose which assessment you are going to practice.
2. Have students practice the assessment tasks you have selected.
3. Explain that over time and with practice, aerobic endurance will increase. State that later each student will repeat the assessment tasks to see if he or she is improving.
4. Help each student set a personal goal.
5. Students can write their goals down on record sheets.

| Days | Assessment |
|------|------------|
| Monday | |
| Tuesday | |
| Wednesday | |
| Thursday | |
| Friday | |

## Teaching Hints

At this age introduce idea of keeping personal scores confidential. It is, however, appropriate to publicly reinforce the whole class for demonstrations of progression. You can introduce the formal goal-setting process at this age; see chapter 2 and the sample forms in the Appendix. Keep in mind that fourth graders are often still only nine, in which case, *FITNESSGRAM* does not recommend focusing on lap or time standards. Teacher discretion in goal setting is necessary. Each segment of the tape decreases by one half of a second.

## Closure and Assessment

### Written and Oral

- Ask the students to share examples of activities they have participated in that demonstrate the FITT principle to become more aerobically fit.

### Project

- With another classmate or alone create a two-week workout schedule of aerobic activities that demonstrates improvement in the FITT principles.

## Extending the Lesson

- Create a "Century Club" (see Activity 7).
- Have students prepare a fitness goal, then work to show progression, explaining how to achieve this goal.
- Have students describe how it feels to walk, jog, or run. Discuss "How would you progress in each?"
- Ask the math teacher to work with the students to graph the differences in the amount of activity and the time taken to perform the activity than when the activity was first introduced (e.g., laps in the PACER test, or length of time in dribbling between two cones) in activities they perform.

# 17  High Five

## Intermediate Level

Students demonstrate improvement on baseline measurement at time of reassessment (**progression**).

## Purpose

Students will explain one example of progression in an aerobic activity.

## Equipment Needed

- Fun, fast-paced music

## Relationship to National Standards

**Physical Education Standard 4:** Student achieves and maintains a health-enhancing level of physical fitness—Student will participate in moderate to vigorous physical activity in a variety of settings.

## Set Induction

Introduce or review the concept of *progression*. Offer a few examples of progressively longer or more intense physical activity.

## Procedure

1. Have students spread out in general space.

2. On signal (music beginning), direct students to move aerobically and try to "high five" as many students as possible while the music plays.

3. Stop the music to signal students to feel their heart rates and rest.

4. Repeat the activity three or four times.

## Teaching Hints

Use skipping to start the activity. Progress to running once the students are demonstrating safe dodging and fleeing skills. Moving from a skip to a run also demonstrates progression because of the change in intensity. Progression also occurs because of the time factor on the tape, which should increase activity time and decrease rest time (in seconds: 15-15, 15-15, 20-10, 20-10, and so on).

## Closure and Assessment

### Written and Oral

- Tell or write a definition of progression as it relates to aerobic endurance.

### Project

- Show the concept of progression in a FITT workout plan to meet the personal goal you set on your aerobic endurance fitness assessment.

## Extending the Lesson

- Have students bring pictures of people involved in various physical activities. Construct a bulletin board that illustrates how progression can be applied in the activities to improve conditioning.
- Brainstorm a list of activities that may increase in intensity or time, showing progression. Include activities in the home and the gym.

# 18 You Should Be Dancing

## Intermediate Level

A **warm-up** prepares your heart, lungs, and muscles for activity by slowly increasing blood flow and body temperature. It is important to warm up so you do not injure your muscles. A **cool-down** slowly brings your body back to normal temperatures and the blood flow back to normal.

## Purpose

Students will understand why a warm-up and cool-down is important in aerobic activity and how to do both properly.

## Equipment Needed

- 20-30 laminated dance step cards (square dancing, folk dancing, line dancing, or any other dance movements; see samples in sidebar)
- Music

### Suggested Dance Steps

The following are examples of dance steps:

- Polkas
- Skipping in place
- Grapevine R-L
- Charleston
- Mexican hat dance
- Jitterbug (Lindy)
- Do-si-do R-L
- Hustle
- Elbow swing R-L
- Hopscotch step
- Two hands around R-L
- Leg kicks front and back
- Slide step
- Twist
- R hand star, L hand star
- Ski jumps, 1-8

## Relationship to National Standards

**Physical Education Standard 3:** Student exhibits a physically active lifestyle—Student will analyze personal interests and capabilities in regard to one's exercise behavior.

**Dance Education Standard 6:** Student makes connections between dance and healthful living—Student will explain how healthy practices (such as nutrition, safety) enhance his or her ability to dance.

## Set Induction

Review the importance of and rules for warming up and cooling down, relating these to heart rate. If desired, discuss what the target heart rate is for the class's age group. Brainstorm types of movements that are considered warm-up activities such as aerobic exercise versus muscular strength or stretching. Explain that dancing is an excellent way to increase the heart rate, thereby benefiting the heart.

## Procedure

1. Scatter the dance step cards around the room.
2. Begin the activity by having the students first listen and then clap to the music, in order to get the beat.
3. Have students skip, jog, or use another traveling action to travel to a card. The traveling actions should be done to the beat of the music.
4. Direct them to perform the steps on the card, sustaining the movement until they have increased the heart rate for a period of time or reached and held the target heart rate for the time you indicate.

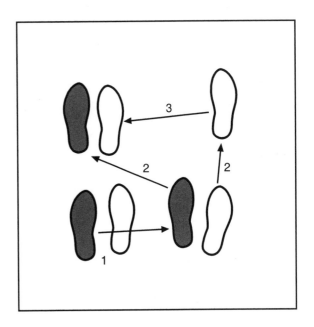

## Teaching Hints

Make sure students know the dance steps from previous lessons or introduce a few before beginning activity. Encourage students to start dancing slowly and warm up gradually.

## Closure and Assessment

### Written and Oral

- Explain the reasons why warming up and cooling down benefit the body.

### Project

- Select and record appropriate activities that will warm up and cool down the body for participation in the *FITNESSGRAM* PACER, or the one-mile run or walk, or for your favorite aerobic activity.

## Extending the Lesson

- Interview people of various ages about their warm-up and cool-down procedures. What were (or are) they? Do they differ from ours? Why?
- Create a bulletin board called "Aerobic Workout Warm-Up and Cool-Down," demonstrating various ways to perform each activity.

# Chapter 9 ⎯⎯⎯⎯⎯⎯⎯⎯⎯⎯⎯

# Muscular Strength and Endurance

# 1   Mix It Up

## Primary Level

**Muscular strength** is the ability to move your body or an object as hard as you can once. It is the greatest force that can be produced by a group of muscles. **Muscular endurance** is the ability to move your body or an object over and over again without getting tired. For most physical activities, both muscular strength and endurance are needed. To build muscle mass for activity requires good nutrition, especially getting enough protein.

## Purpose

Students will learn that (1) strength is needed to do a task once; (2) endurance is needed to do a task many times; (3) muscular strength and endurance are individual, indeed, everyone is different; and that (4) good nutrition helps a person achieve muscular strength and endurance.

## Equipment Needed

- Scooters
- Jump ropes
- Bathroom scale
- Pull-up bar for flexed-arm hang
- Station signs (see list of stations in sidebar)

## Relationship to National Standards

> **Physical Education Standard 3:** Student exhibits a physically active lifestyle—Student will identify at least one activity associated with each component of health-related physical fitness.

## Set Induction

Define *muscular strength* and *endurance*. Explain that each person is unique in how much muscular strength and endurance they have. State that today's lesson is designed to show the difference between muscular strength and muscular endurance with several stations. Describe the stations and their purposes. Identify and discuss safety concerns at Scooter Push-Away (Station 1).

## Procedure

1. Divide students into eight groups and send one group to each station.
2. Signal students to perform the station activity and remain there until the signal to rotate.
3. Continue to rotate students until every group has visited all eight stations.

---

**Stations for Mix It Up**

*Note*: The stations alternate between muscular strength and muscular endurance activities.

**Station 1: Scooter Push-Away** Seated on scooter facing the wall, the student uses one big push with the feet to see "how strong" his or her legs are from that one effort (muscular strength).

**Station 2: Scooter Travel** Seated on the scooter, the student travels from point A to point B to experience pushing with legs over and over again (muscular endurance).

**Station 3: Maximum Vertical Jump** Student stands with side to the wall and performs a maximum vertical jump (muscular strength).

**Station 4: Repeating Jump** Student stands side to wall and continues to jump vertically over and over again for 20 seconds (muscular endurance).

**Station 5: Maximal Horizontal Jump (Long Jump)** Student jumps forward (from standing) one time with maximum strength (muscular strength).

**Station 6: Jump Rope** Student jumps rope continuously for 20 seconds (muscular endurance).

**Station 7: Press Down** In a push-up position, student presses a bathroom scale to see how high the scale goes (muscular strength).

**Station 8: Flexed-Arm Hang** Maintain a flexed-arm hang for as long as possible (muscular endurance).

---

## Teaching Hints

Use the sample station ideas all in one lesson or as individual examples over a period of several lessons.

## Closure and Assessment

### Written and Oral

- Tell me an activity from one of the stations that uses muscular strength.
- Tell me an activity from one of the stations that uses muscular endurance.

### Project

- Cut out or draw a picture of an activity that uses muscular strength.
- Share with a classmate the activities that produce strength and those that produce muscular endurance.

## Extending the Lesson

- Ask "What daily activities use muscular strength and endurance?" Have students make a collage of pictures of people doing activities that require both muscular strength and endurance.
- Muscle-a-Day poster: Draw or demonstrate daily activities using the specific muscle.
- Teach students that a well-developed skeleton requires muscular strength and endurance activities as well as a diet sufficient in proteins and calcium. Using a skeleton, show where muscles attach and what bones they move.
- Construct a bulletin board titled "Strong Bones, Strong Body!" that portrays calcium building strong bones and protein as the building blocks for muscles.

# 2 | Talk to the Animals

## Primary Level

Strong muscles allow us to participate in a variety of activities, including chores, work, and play. The muscles that have good endurance allow us to play and work safely for long periods of time. There are many **benefits to having good muscular strength and endurance** such as good posture, strong bones, strong muscles, and so on.

## Purpose

Students will identify several benefits related to muscular strength and endurance and learn how muscular strength and endurance play a role in developing strong, healthy bones.

## Equipment Needed

- Animal Walk Cards (one side of the card has a picture of an animal and the other side lists a benefit; see sidebar)
- Music tape

---

### Examples of Animal Walk Cards

Giraffe—good posture

Rabbit—strong leg muscles

Seal walk—strong upper body muscles

Injured animal (picture of animal on crutches)—prevents injuries

Turtle (or elephant) walk—play and work longer

Puppy dog—strong upper body muscles

---

## Relationship to National Standards

**Physical Education Standard 4:** Student achieves and maintains a health-enhancing level of physical fitness—Student will support body weight momentarily by taking weight on hands.

## Set Induction

Define *muscular strength* and *endurance* and discuss their benefits. Explain that today students will be performing animal walks to develop muscular strength and endurance. Review the Animal Walk Cards, ensuring students know what to do for each animal. Remind students to stay in self-space while traveling about the activity area.

## Procedure

For students who don't read:

1. The teacher should discuss the health benefits of muscular strength and muscular endurance before the activity.

2. The teacher then holds up an animal card and has the students walk like the animal while the music is on. When the music is stopped, the teacher asks them a question about the health benefits of muscular strength and endurance.

3. The teacher then holds up another animal card and students move like this animal.

For students old enough to read:

1. The cards are scattered all over the activity area. Small groups of students begin at each Animal Walk Card, turning it over to learn the health benefit. When the music begins, they return the card to the floor and perform the animal walk around the area.

2. When the music stops, the students perform a locomotor pattern to another card and read it. When the music starts again they perform this animal walk.

3. Keep repeating the activity until you have discussed several health benefits and students have each performed several animal walks, using both muscular strength and endurance.

4. After the activity is over, discuss the health benefits that the students picked up.

## Teaching Hints

Spend more or less time previewing the Animal Walk Cards before beginning the activity, depending on the age and reading abilities of the students. Be sure to reinforce that the animal walks and other traveling develop muscular strength and endurance as they learn about the benefits of these two parts of health-related fitness.

## Closure and Assessment

### Written and Oral

- Tell two benefits of muscular strength and endurance you learned in this activity.
- Tell the benefit that is written on the back of the Animal Walk Card I'm holding up.

### Project

- Select one benefit that is important to you and develop a poster showing why that benefit is important.

## Extending the Lesson

- Create a "Muscular Strength and Endurance Benefits" bulletin board. Display student drawings, depicting benefits important to their personal needs and interests.
- Make a large body outline. Attach pictures of activities of a muscle at work at the location of the working muscle. For example, a construction worker using a hammer exercises the biceps and triceps. Discuss the muscles being used to support the body so it can be healthy.

# 3   Classercise

## Primary Level

**Frequency** is how many days per week you should perform muscular strength and endurance activities. You should participate in strength and endurance activities one to three times a week. Daily chores and tasks require muscular strength and endurance.

## Purpose

Students will understand (1) the number of days a week they should perform muscular strength and endurance activities; (2) that muscular strength and endurance will define and increase the intensity of physical activity of sport and recreation; and (3) that a balanced diet, complete with all the building blocks and energy needs, helps build muscular strength and endurance.

## Equipment Needed

- Calendar worksheet (list days of the week across long edge)

## Relationship to National Standards

**Physical Education Standard 3:** Student exhibits a physically active lifestyle—Student will engage in moderate to vigorous physical activity outside of physical education class.

## Set Induction

Review the difference between muscular strength and muscular endurance. Discuss the importance of performing activities that require muscular strength and muscular endurance at least three days each week. Review activities that can be performed in the classroom or at home.

## Procedure

This activity begins in physical education, but extends to the classroom as a fitness break. After learning about the concept of frequency in physical education class, the physical educator and students will each design an activity calendar (illustrating the concept of frequency) that can be performed for a week improving muscular strength and endurance. Several of the activities can be done in class but the rest of the activities should be done outside the gym. Ask the classroom teacher to allow the students to take a fitness break using a few of the designed muscular strength and endurance activities; for

| Days | Activity |
|------|----------|
| Monday | |
| Tuesday | |
| Wednesday | |
| Thursday | |
| Friday | |

example, push-ups, curl-ups, Crazy Jumps, and so on. Other times the activities on the calendar will be performed at recess, or as a homework assignment.

## Teaching Hints

Suggested activities for the calendar: perform animal walks across the classroom; climb across the playground equipment; push someone on a swing; jump rope; play hopscotch; play wall ball variations; accompany an adult on a hike; carry groceries; carry laundry.

## Closure and Assessment

### Written and Oral

- List the number of days per week you should perform muscular strength and endurance activities. List an activity you could do for each day.

### Project

- Have students complete Classercise Calendar on their own for one week. Collect at the end of the week and check for appropriateness of frequency and activities.

## Extending the Lesson

- Design a FITT bulletin board to illustrate the concepts of muscular strength and endurance. Add information to the board as students learn about each component (see chapter 8, Activity 12).
- Take or draw pictures of people in the community using their muscles.

# 4 | Seek Your Peak

## Primary Level

**Intensity** is the amount of weight or resistance your muscles must work against to become stronger. By increasing the intensity and developing your muscles, you become stronger.

## Purpose

Students will recognize activities that make the muscles work harder and start to learn that proper nutrition must provide not only the fuel but also the building blocks needed to build strength and endurance for growth and development.

## Equipment Needed

- Mats (for the curl-up activities; optional)

## Relationship to National Standards

**Physical Education Standard 4:** Student achieves and maintains a health-enhancing level of physical fitness—Student will sustain moderate to vigorous physical activity for a short period of time.

## Set Induction

Define *intensity*. Discuss how today's activities will become more and more intense to help students improve their muscular strength and endurance levels. Emphasize that everyone's level will be a bit different and that everyone can improve if they increase intensity gradually and safely. You are looking for those who are trying to improve—not who's best.

## Procedure

Have each student find a self-space. Direct students to perform sequences that allow them to experience muscular strength and muscular endurance activities at varying intensity levels, such as the following examples. Ask students if they feel their muscles working harder with each new activity.

A push-up sequence might look like this:

1. Start on knees, raise one hand, the other, a foot, the other.
2. Lift knees, raise one hand, the other, a foot, the other.
3. Start in push-up position, make hands go over, over, back, back over a line.
4. Start in push-up position, sink to the ground (stomach touches ground).
5. Start in push-up position, bend elbows but do not let stomach touch ground.
6. Elevate one foot on top of the other and try a push-up.
7. Place both feet on an elevated surface (step, box, or the like).

A curl-up sequence might look like this, starting in a sitting position:

1. While sitting, pick up one leg and shake it.
2. While sitting, bend knees and slowly lower back to the floor.
3. Lie down, lift head, and look at your toes.
4. Lie down, lift head and one leg, and then the other leg.
5. Lie down, wave a leg at a friend. Repeat with other leg, but *never* lift both legs at the same time.
6. Lie down with knees bent and sit up and touch toes.
7. Lie down and lift and hold shoulders off floor a few seconds.
8. Lie down with knees bent and hands on thighs and sit up, sliding fingers to knees.
9. Lie down with knees bent, hands on floor, and slide hands along finger pads until even with knees.

## Teaching Hints

This is a great beginning-of-the-year activity to help you discuss individual differences in muscular strength and endurance. Be a role model and show how intensity affects your physical fitness performance as well. Encourage all children to work at the intensity level that is best for them! For safety, demonstrate proper form and have students model you.

## Closure and Assessment

### Written and Oral

- Ask the students which push-up or curl-up is the intensity they need to use to improve their muscular strength or muscular endurance. (Approximately number three or four in the push-up or curl-up sequence.)

### Project

- Have students participate in an intensity sequence for a teacher-selected activity for two weeks. Following each exercise sequence, have students rate from 1 to 5 if they think their muscles feel stronger.

## Extending the Lesson

- List in order of intensity (from easiest to heaviest) the following jobs:
  - Baseball player
  - Construction worker
  - Postal carrier
  - Secretary
- Collect pictures of people working out at different intensities.
- Have the classroom teacher cover nutrition, including protein sources for building strong muscles and calcium sources for building strong bones.

# 5 Reps and Sets

## Primary Level

In relation to muscular strength and muscular endurance, **time** (duration) refers to the number of repetitions and sets. A **repetition** (rep) is one complete movement of an exercise. A **set** is a fixed number of repetitions. **Rest** occurs between each set. To start with, experts recommend performing one set of 8 to 12 repetitions. Increasing the time spent exercising (number of repetitions and sets) with increased muscular strength and endurance depends on both the goal and the type of activity.

## Purpose

Students will (1) identify time (rep and set) and rest (between sets) as it relates to muscular strength and endurance; (2) learn that energy (carbohydrates and fats), proteins, and oxygen are just as important in muscular strength and endurance activities as in aerobic endurance; and (3) understand that the time necessary to achieve benefits is based on an individual's personal interests, goals, and genetics.

## Equipment Needed

- Equipment for other repetition challenges may be needed, but none for Push-Up Fun

## Relationship to National Standards

**Physical Education Standard 4:** Student achieves and maintains a health-enhancing level of physical fitness—Student will support body weight by momentarily taking weight on hands.

## Set Induction

Define *time* (repetitions and sets) in relation to muscular strength and endurance. Demonstrate these concepts with one activity, such as curl-ups. Teach that rest is important between sets. Explain that a healthy diet as well as efficient oxygen intake enhance muscular strength and endurance. Outline the specific activities you have chosen for today's lesson.

## Procedure

This activity teaches repetitions and sets using any muscular strength and endurance activity.

For example, using Push-Up Fun (see sidebar), the student performs as many reps as possible in 15 seconds for the first set. Then, the student rests for 10 seconds. The student repeats the task for a second set (and for a third set, depending on the grade level). Other activities include curl-ups, animal walks, push-up variations, dyna bands, and so on.

---

**Push-Up Fun**

Assume the push-up starting position. On signal, begin "walking" first one hand and then the other over a line, and then back again.

---

## Teaching Hints

Ensure students understand what repetitions and sets are before proceeding with the activity. Showing an illustration of these can help explain them. For example, count eight curl-up repetitions, resting after that set of eight reps, and then performing the set again. Encourage children to rest between sets.

## Closure and Assessment

### Written and Oral

- Stand up if you agree with this statement: For muscular strength and endurance, time is made up of repetitions and sets.

- Answer all together: Is one complete movement of an exercise a set or a repetition?

### Project

- From a list, have each student select one muscular strength activity to perform 8 to 12 repetitions for homework each night of a week, and then rate on a homework sheet how they feel about increasing their muscular strength and muscular endurance. Have each student record the activity and number of repetitions on a calendar to be turned in to you.

## Extending the Lesson

- Give students a challenge to perform at recess (e.g., climb the ladder rungs, flexed-arm hang, reverse pull-ups, and pull-ups). Have the students continue practicing the challenge throughout the week. Stress that the goal should be to increase the length of time each student can perform the challenge.

- Continue to use the FITT bulletin board (see chapter 8, Activity 12). Stress that time in muscular strength and endurance is different than with the other fitness components. Place the repetition and set definitions under the time concept on the bulletin board.

# 6 FUN-damentals of Fitness

## Primary Level

**Type** means what kind of activities are good for developing muscular strength and endurance. You develop muscular strength and endurance by performing specific exercises for each muscle group in your arms, legs, and trunk.

## Purpose

Students will identify what kind of activities develop muscular strength and endurance in specific muscles and understand that each person performs muscular strength and endurance activities at his or her own level.

## Equipment Needed

- Muscle chart
- Poster-size picture of a child

## Relationship to National Standards

**Physical Education Standard 4:** Student achieves and maintains a health-enhancing level of physical fitness—Student will identify several activities that relate to a component of physical fitness.

## Set Induction

Define *type* (specificity). Demonstrate a few exercises and discuss which specific muscles the exercises develop. Explain that in today's activity, students will learn to identify what kinds of activities develop muscular strength and endurance in specific muscles. Then remind students that each person performs muscular strength and endurance activities at his or her own level.

## Procedure

1. Select a muscle on which to focus (see table).
2. Have students practice saying the muscle name.
3. Help students locate the muscle on a muscle chart or poster-size picture of a child.
4. Demonstrate the exercise, then direct students to perform it.
5. Help students identify the action of the targeted muscle as they perform the exercise.

| Muscles | Location | Fundamental sport skill | Exercise |
| --- | --- | --- | --- |
| Triceps | In back of upper arm | Throwing | Push-ups |
| Biceps | In front of upper arm | Bowling, underhand throw | Popeye flex |
| Gastrocnemius | In back of lower leg | Jump rope, hopping | Toe raises |
| Quadriceps | In front of upper leg | Punting, kicking | Wall sit |
| Hamstring | In back of upper leg | Flutter kick | Lunges |
| Deltoid | On top of shoulder | Swimming (crawl) | Arm circles |

## Teaching Hints

You can teach this lesson with either a guided discovery or command style approach. Be sure to have students touch the muscles they are learning about as they're performing each exercise. Can they feel the muscle working? You could use all the muscles listed in this activity all in one day or each as a quick introduction to muscular strength and endurance activities on consecutive days.

## Closure and Assessment

### Written and Oral

- Ask students to name a motor or sport skill which uses each muscle they are learning about. Can they name an exercise to strengthen each muscle?

- Choose the activity that improves muscular strength and endurance in the upper body (e.g., throwing a ball, hopping on one foot, striking an object, push-ups, crab walk).

- Choose the activity that improves muscular strength and endurance in the lower body (e.g., kicking, climbing on the monkey bars, and the like).

### Project

- Have students select one to six activities (sport skills or exercises; number depends on age and ability) and identify the area of the body that the activity would be useful for developing muscular strength and endurance.

## Extending the Lesson

- Have students choose a "Muscle of the Week" and draw three or four activities they like to do that use that muscle.

- Have students choose 2-3 exercises and create an exercise routine that would increase the muscular strength and endurance in an activity they choose (e.g., playing baseball).

## 7 Getting Started

### Primary Level

**Progression**: The goal of improving muscular strength and muscular endurance (demonstrating progress) requires your muscles to do more than usual (more often, increased intensity, more time). Doing more than usual is another way of saying **overload**.

## Purpose

Students will demonstrate progression from baseline toward a realistic goal selected by the student with help from the teacher.

## Equipment Needed

- Record sheets
- Goal-setting worksheet (see the Appendix)

Other equipment depends on the assessment items you choose:

- Curl-up—curl-strips and cadence tape
- Push-up—cadence tape
- Modified pull-up—modified pull-up bar
- Pull-up—pull-up bar
- Flexed-arm hang—pull-up bar

## Relationship to National Standards

**Physical Education Standard 4:** Student achieves and maintains a health-enhancing level of fitness—Student will meet the health-related fitness standard as defined by *FITNESSGRAM*.

## Set Induction

Explain that today students will participate in assessments that will measure their baseline (current) muscular strength and endurance. (Choices from *FITNESSGRAM* include curl-ups, push-ups, modified push-ups, pull-ups, flexed-arm hang, and trunk lift). Demonstrate the procedures for each assessment you wish to use in this lesson. Explain the principle of progression means that working on each FITT component should over time lead to progress, that is, increased muscular strength and endurance. State that today they'll be measuring their current muscular strength and endurance so they can measure their progress later in the school year.

## Procedure

1. Choose which assessment you are going to practice.
2. Have students practice the assessment tasks you have selected.
3. Explain that over time and with practice, muscular strength and endurance will increase. State that later each student will repeat the assessment tasks to see if he or she is improving.
4. Help each student set a personal goal.
5. Students can write their goals down on record sheets.

| Days | Assessment |
|------|------------|
| Monday | |
| Tuesday | |
| Wednesday | |
| Thursday | |
| Friday | |

## Teaching Hints

Ensure students practice and warm up before doing the assessments. Monitor the assessments to ensure students do them correctly. Have students practice muscular strength and endurance activities over time. Reassess and identify progress as individuals or as a whole class.

## Closure and Assessment

### Written and Oral

- Explain to students how the principle of overload will help them improve or maintain their muscular strength and endurance.

### Project

- Have students report on their progress throughout the school year.

## Extending the Lesson

- Have students ask their family what kinds of exercises they perform to increase muscular strength and muscular endurance.
- Bring in a book about muscles, and show how the muscles look and how they are attached to tendons and ligaments.

# 8 Fitness Fun and Games

**Primary Level**

The goal of increasing muscular strength and muscular endurance requires your muscles to do more than usual (more often, increased intensity, more time) to achieve **progression**.

## Purpose

Students will participate in muscular strength and endurance activities that demonstrate progression.

## Equipment Needed

- Scooters (optional)

## Relationship to National Standards

**Physical Education Standard 3:** Student exhibits a healthy lifestyle—Student will identify at least one activity associated with each component of health-related physical activity.

## Set Induction

Discuss the concept of *progression*. Explain that today students will play a fun fitness tag game that shows progression by increasing the amount of time you play each round of the game.

## Procedure

1. Have students begin spread throughout an activity area.

2. Select three or four taggers.

3. Assign all taggers and other students to move either in crab position or on scooters, directing taggers to try to touch as many students as they can using their hands only.

4. There are two rounds to the game. The first round lasts for 30 seconds.

5. When a player is tagged they perform a muscular strength exercise, such as five curl-ups or push-ups, and then return to the game.

6. After 30 seconds, allow the students to rest. Then replay the game for 60 seconds to see if the taggers can increase their score. This is round two.

7. Choose new taggers after each game.

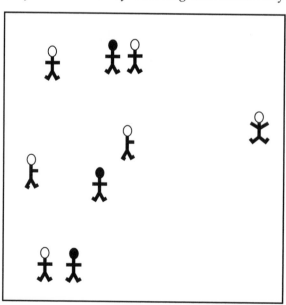

## Teaching Hints

The activity area must be the correct size for the ratio of taggers to players. It should not be too large or no one will get tagged.

## Closure and Assessment

### Written and Oral

- Raise your hand when you hear the correct answer: To show muscular strength and endurance progression you need to do the same amount, do less than usual, or do more than usual.

### Project

- Students select an activity and list ways to do more than usual.

## Extending the Lesson

Research the Greek mythology story entitled "Milo of Croton" and either read or tell the story to the class. In brief, Milo of Croton carried a calf around his neck. As the calf grew, he continued to become stronger, which enabled him to continue to carry the calf until it grew into a bull. The story relates to progression in that he became stronger as the calf grew larger, in order to protect and carry the calf. Milo is a figure that participated in the ancient Olympics and can be called the "father" of progression.

## 9 Warm-Up–Cool-Down

### Primary Level

The purpose of **warm-ups** is to get the muscles ready for activity and avoid injury. To warm up your muscles before muscular strength and endurance activities, you should do some form of light aerobic activity or do the muscular strength or endurance activity without resistance slowly for about five minutes. **Cool-downs** after muscular strength and endurance activities should involve stretching the muscles used. Drinking fluids is also very important during warm-ups and cool-downs.

### Purpose

Students will understand (1) why a warm-up is important for muscular strength and endurance activities; (2) how to do both properly; (3) that to warm up muscles you may slowly do the activity you are going to perform without resistance; and (4) that a proper cool-down for the muscular strength and endurance activities involves stretching.

### Equipment Needed

- Equipment necessary for warm-up and cool-down activities chosen
- Fun walking and stretching music (optional)

### Relationship to National Standards

**Physical Education Standard 4:** Student achieves and maintains a health-enhancing level of physical fitness—Student will begin to develop a strategy for the improvement of selected fitness components.

### Set Induction

Introduce or review the importance of warming up and cooling down. Discuss specific, appropriate activities for each. Mention that drinking fluids during warm-ups and cool-downs is important. Explain that today students will practice a warm-up and cool-down that is appropriate for the main activity.

## Procedure

1. Begin the lesson with a total body warm-up by having students walk around the room at a normal pace.

2. Gradually increase the speed. Explain that the walking warms up the large leg muscles first. While walking, have students vary the directions, step sizes, levels, and pathways.

3. Stop the walking and have students warm up the arms by performing easy arm circles.

4. Do warm-up activities specific to today's main activity.

5. Conduct the main activity.

6. Have students cool down by performing easy stretches of those muscles used during the day's activities.

## Teaching Hints

Play fun walking and stretching music; it's more motivating for students during warm-ups and cool-downs. Use various dance elements in creating the warm-up.

## Closure and Assessment

### Written and Oral

- Why is it important to warm up before muscular strength and endurance exercises?
- Why is it important to cool down after muscular strength and endurance exercises?

### Project

- Have students create a list of activities they can use in a warm-up or cool-down for muscular strength and endurance exercises.

## Extending the Lesson

- Use gum to provide an analogy for importance of warming up. Have the students think of chewing the gum until it is soft. Have them imagine wrapping it in plastic and saving it overnight. Compare the gum to a muscle that gets stiff when it cools down. Imagine how if you were to chew the gum again (yuck!), it would lose its stiffness. Just as chewing serves as a "warm-up" for the gum, your muscles need a warm-up to prepare them again for activity.

- Demonstrate more warm-up routines.

# 10 Muscle Hustle

## Intermediate Level

**Muscular strength** involves the strongest force possible to perform a task that can be produced by a group of muscles. **Muscular endurance** is the ability to move your body or an object over and over again without getting tired. For most activities you use both muscular strength and endurance. If you don't use your muscles regularly, they can lose strength and endurance. Muscles require appropriate nutrition, especially getting enough protein.

## Purpose

Students will understand the definition of muscular strength and endurance by participating in several circuit activities that involve these components.

## Equipment Needed

- Muscle Hustle station signs (listing a sport, skill, or activity that requires muscular strength or endurance; see sidebar)
- Equipment needed for stations: volleyball, soccer ball, basketball, and the like
- Cones
- Segmented music tape (optional)

## Relationship to National Standards

**Physical Education Standard 4:** Student achieves and maintains a health-enhancing level of physical fitness—Student will identify several activities related to each component of physical fitness and at least one activity associated with each component of health-related physical fitness.

## Set Induction

Define *muscular strength* and *endurance*. Share or have students share a few examples of each. Explain that today students will participate in a circuit designed to build muscular strength and endurance, which, in turn, will enhance physical activity and sport performance. Describe the station activities to students.

## Procedure

1. Divide students into small groups and have each group go to a station.
2. Signal students to perform the activity on their station's Muscle Hustle sign for 30 seconds.
3. Have students rotate from station to station.
4. Continue as long as desired.

---

**Muscle Hustle Sample Stations**

Basketball rebound (shoot a basketball at a wall, jump up and grab the rebound)

Volleyball serve (at a wall)

Basketball guard position—slide

Kicking a Nerf soccer ball into a goal

Jumping rope continuously

Standing long jump for distance

Medicine ball throw

---

## Closure and Assessment

### Written and Oral

- Ask which activities used muscular strength, which used muscular endurance, and which used both, and why.
- Have students write a short definition of muscular strength and give two examples of physical activities that require muscular strength.
- Have students write a short definition of muscular endurance and give two examples of physical activities that require muscular endurance.

### Project

- Provide students with a list of physical activities and have them identify skills that require muscular strength and endurance (see examples).

| Activity | Muscular strength | Muscular endurance |
|---|---|---|
| Baseball and softball | Throwing ball from center field | Pitching for an inning |
| Horseback riding | Placing western saddle on horse | Carrying saddle to horse |

## Extending the Lesson

- Have the students look at a famous sports figure and discuss the types of training and skills they went through to make them a successful athlete. Discuss the kinds of workouts that they would need to perform to improve the sport that they enjoy performing.
- Construct a bulletin board showing that proteins are essential foods for building muscle mass. Assert that building muscle mass helps build strong bones. Show the kinds of foods that need to be consumed to get the correct amount of minerals, vitamins, and protein needed for strong muscles.

# 11    Checkup

## Intermediate Level

Being physically active and developing muscular strength and endurance are directly related to health. Feeling good, having strong bones and good posture, and doing your daily chores and tasks without difficulty are all **benefits of muscular strength and endurance**.

## Purpose

Students will (1) identify how muscular strength and muscular endurance are important to everyday life choices; (2) understand how muscular strength and endurance maintain an ideal body mass; and (3) identify muscular strength and endurance activities that help develop the ability to do daily activities with greater ease.

## Equipment Needed

- Hanging ropes for climbing (preferably 3)
- Scooters
- 3 long ropes
- Mat for climbing stations
- Basketball or weighted ball
- Cones
- Tape to mark the floor or a long rope
- Station signs with health benefits on them

## Relationship to National Standards

**Physical Education Standard 4:** Student achieves and maintains a health-enhancing level of physical fitness—Student will identify several activities related to the components of physical fitness.

## Set Induction

Explain that today's activities will help students recognize the health benefits of having good muscular strength and endurance. Brainstorm a list of these health benefits, including the following:

a. Being better able to maintain good posture and strong bones
b. Being able to perform well in fitness assessments
c. Feeling competent to pursue a variety of physical activities without fear of failure
d. Being able to successfully complete daily chores
e. Being able to participate in leisure activities
f. Being able to meet physical demands that may arise in an emergency
g. Being able to participate in activity without injury

## Procedure

The activities are stations in which the groups rotate. Do you have the muscle strength and endurance to . . .

1. Swing into the river—Student uses a hanging rope to swing from point A, jumps off, and lands on a mat (jumps into the river). Remind students of benefits e and f.

2. Jump over the creek—Student performs a standing or running long jump over a tape or rope placed on the floor. The tape or rope can be in the shape of a "V" to provide for different abilities. Remind students of benefits e and f.

3. Climb up the mountain—Student climbs a hanging rope. (Identify different levels as reaching different mountain peaks, e.g., Mt. Everest as the highest.) Remind students of benefits d and e.

4. Push-ups or curl-ups—Be in the health standard zone for *FITNESSGRAM* muscular strength and endurance assessments by performing the push-up test and/or curl-up test. Remind students of benefits a, b, and c.

5. Pull in a big fish—Student A (the big fish) sits on a scooter some distance from student B (the fisherman). Using a long rope, student B pulls (reels in) partner A to the beach. Remind students of benefit e.

6. Carry out the trash—Student chooses a number of cones to carry as he walks laps around the gym. Remind students of benefit d.

7. Make the shot—Student performs a shot put or a chest shot with a weighted ball to a spot on the floor from a designated spot. Remind students of benefit e.

8. Airlift rescue—Student A (the rescuer) gently swings a hanging rope to student B (person being rescued). Student B jumps to catch it and holds onto the rope as she swings over to safety. Remind students of benefit f.

## Teaching Hints

Substitute or add activities specific to your school, region of the country, and student needs (e.g., javelin throw, medicine ball throw, using weights or equipment from an exercise room).

## Closure and Assessment

### Written and Oral

- Select two benefits and list two situations that illustrate the importance of each benefit.

### Project

- Share with your group the two most important benefits for you and discuss why.

## Extending the Lesson

- Have students bring in or draw pictures of community members involved in muscular strength and endurance activities in daily life.
- Describe an occupation requiring muscular strength and endurance. Specify whether the occupation is more related to strength or endurance.
- Have a strength trainer come to a class and discuss their role in improving muscular strength and muscular endurance in their clients.

# 12 Flip Card File

## Intermediate Level

**Frequency** is how many days per week you should perform muscular strength and endurance exercise to improve your health. You should participate in strength and endurance activities one to three times a week. Leave a day of rest in between each exercise period. Daily activities such as carrying groceries, a backpack, or raking leaves also develop muscular strength and endurance.

## Purpose

Students will (1) design a personal muscular strength and endurance activity file and participate in muscular strength and endurance activities at least three times a week; (2) understand that frequency is one component of the FITT principle to improving strength and endurance; and (3) understand that a diet sufficient in proteins and fuels (carbohydrates and fats) helps improve muscular strength and endurance.

## Equipment Needed

- Four or five 3 x 5 index cards for each student
- Yarn, string, or a metal ring to connect cards for each student (if file not already started)
- Class chart to record student's frequency of practice (optional)
- Equipment needed for stations (see Procedure)
- Hole punch (one per station or prepunch cards)

## Relationship to National Standards

**Physical Education Standard 3:** Student exhibits a physically active lifestyle—Student will engage in moderate to vigorous physical activity outside of physical education class.

## Set Induction

Review the importance of muscular strength and endurance. Explain that today students will make a personalized muscular strength and endurance activity flip card file (to add to file begun already, if appropriate). Instruct students to perform muscular strength and endurance activities three times a week with at least a day of rest in between sessions. If a student wants to do some muscle activities every day, she should alternate muscle groups. For example, day one do upper body and abdominals and day two do quadriceps and lower legs. Brainstorm times that may be appropriate for this activity (e.g., at the beginning of class, during physical education fitness activities, during any free time at school, such as, in class [with teacher's permission] or during breaks, or at home).

## Procedure

1. Set up stations, each with choices of muscular strength and endurance activities. The following are some suggestions:
   - Upper body
     - Crab walk
     - Knee push-ups
     - Triceps push-ups

- Abdominals and lower back
  - *FITNESSGRAM* curl-ups
  - Four-count curl-ups
  - *FITNESSGRAM* curl-ups held in "up" position for eight counts
- Quadriceps
  - Wall sit
  - Split lunges
  - Quad sets (holding isometric contraction for five seconds)
- Lower leg
  - Toe raises
  - Heel raises
  - Rope jumping

| Days | Curl-Ups |
| --- | --- |
| Monday | |
| Tuesday | |
| Wednesday | |
| Thursday | |
| Friday | |

2. Have students rotate through each station, selecting and copying a muscular endurance activity onto a 3 x 5 card. When finished with the stations, each student will have several cards for the personalized flip card file.

3. If cards are not prepunched, have students punch a hole in the corner of each card and connect cards with yarn, string, or a metal ring (or add cards to an already existing card file).

4. Explain how to record the frequency of muscular strength and endurance activities. To record frequency, have students check it off on a class chart or record it in a personal physical education portfolio.

## Teaching Hints

Have students write their names on their flip cards, and brainstorm with them ways to be responsible for keeping track of their cards. You may wish to establish a lost and found spot for them. Note that not every student will be self-motivated to use the cards. Therefore, your encouragement and a system of accountability, such as recording frequency, will be necessary.

## Closure and Assessment

### Written and Oral

- Write a short definition of frequency as it relates to muscular strength and endurance.

### Project

- Design an additional muscular strength and endurance fitness file entry for each of the following: upper body, abdominals or lower back, quadriceps, and lower legs. You may use a sport or an activity you enjoy to develop your fitness file entries. Use your fitness file entries for one week.

## Extending the Lesson

- Bring or have students bring in pictures of types of activities that increase muscular strength and muscular endurance.
- Develop a bulletin board showing the muscular system.

# 13 Parachute Power Lift

## Intermediate Level

**Intensity** is defined as the amount of weight or resistance (load) you must move to make your muscles stronger without injuring yourself. The weight or resistance can be your body, tubes, groceries, hand weights, or machines. As you move the resistance, your muscles should become more tired. Your muscles become tired for many reasons, including lack of fuel, lack of oxygen, and the production of a substance that prevents the muscle from contracting (lactic acid), causing muscle fatigue. Attention to good nutrition—eating adequate amounts of carbohydrates, proteins, and fats as well as drinking enough fluids—will reduce the chances of muscle fatigue.

## Purpose

Students will (1) demonstrate the principle of intensity by participating in an activity that requires them to increase resistance; (2) understand the types of resistance to improve muscular strength and endurance; (3) learn that intensity is individual based on interests and goals; and (4) recognize that muscles become tired for many reasons, including poor diet and lactic acid buildup.

## Equipment Needed

- Parachute
- Weighted balls or other weights for resistance

## Relationship to National Standards

**Physical Education Standard 3:** Student exhibits a physically active lifestyle—Student will engage in moderate to vigorous physical activity outside of physical education class.

## Set Induction

Define *intensity* as it relates to muscular strength and endurance. Assert that like the other components of health-related fitness, muscular strength and endurance are individual—each varies from person to person based on various factors. Explain that fatigue, or tiredness, results from making poor food choices (or being hungry, that is, low on fuel) or from lactic acid buildup (define). Explain methods for varying intensity with resistance. Tell students that proper training can give them the muscular strength and endurance to do more with less fatigue.

## Procedure

1. Have students spread out evenly around a parachute that is rolled up to a smaller size than normal.

2. Introduce intensity for muscular strength and endurance by having students perform the ocean wave easy lift, above head and back to knees in four counts.

3. To change the intensity of the force of the pull, have students pull the chute together by stepping back before the lift or lift the chute with one arm while the other arm is touching the deltoid.

4. Place objects (balls) in the chute to add weight, or resistance, to the lifting.

## Teaching Hints

Discuss how the muscles should feel and how the muscles do feel while working. Point out how the activity varies with intensity.

## Closure and Assessment

### Written and Oral

- Write a short definition of intensity as it relates to muscular strength and endurance. List methods a person could use to vary intensity.

### Project

- Students select a physical activity they enjoy and then design an intensity sequence from low intensity (easy) to high intensity (hard) for the selected activity.

## Extending the Lesson

- Have students give examples of ways intensity can be changed to increase strength or endurance and place the ideas on the FITT bulletin board next to the "I" (see chapter 8, Activities 12 through 15).

- Have each student list variations that increase the intensity of activities requiring muscular strength and endurance that he or she likes to do, for example, swimming—add fins or hand paddles.

- Have each student choose an exercise and modify it to increase its intensity.

# 14 Rep and Set Workout

## Intermediate Level

**Time** (duration) is how many repetitions and sets you perform to improve or maintain your muscular strength and endurance. A **repetition** is one complete movement of one exercise. A **set** is a fixed number of repetitions of one exercise. **Rest** occurs between each set. To start with, experts recommend you do one set of 8 to 12 repetitions.

## Purpose

Students will define time (duration) using repetition and set concepts as they relate to muscular strength and endurance, and will learn that time depends on the goal and purpose of the activity.

## Equipment Needed

- Tumbling mats or carpet squares
- Equipment necessary for activities selected

## Relationship to National Standards

**Physical Education Standard 4:** Student achieves and maintains a health-enhancing level of physical fitness—Student will engage in appropriate activity that results in the development of muscular strength.

## Set Induction

Define *time, repetitions,* and *sets* as they relate to muscular strength and endurance activities. Brainstorm how the goal and purpose of an activity can affect time. Explain that one set of 8 to 12 reps is sufficient for beginning physical education class purposes.

## Procedure

1. Design a rep and set workout for any of the *FITNESSGRAM* muscular strength and endurance assessments. For example, for curl-ups, you can use the curl-up strips or tape lines or let the students walk their fingers up three or four steps.

2. Divide students into groups of three and assign each group to a mat.
3. Have one student in each group begin with one set of eight repetitions.
4. Have two students in the group check the form of the student performing the curl-ups: feet must stay on the floor, fingers must slide across the strip, tape, or floor on each curl-up, and head must be lowered back to mat to complete each curl-up.
5. Rotate so all three students have the opportunity to do curl-ups.

## Teaching Hints

Remember, a sensible guide for children is one set of 8 to 12 repetitions. So when first training, children should perform one set until they can demonstrate proper form in the muscular strength and endurance activities you have selected. Design a poster to help students understand the repetition and set definitions. Use a picture of the exercise as one rep and then eight pictures of the exercise to represent sets.

## Closure and Assessment

### Written and Oral

- Write a short definition of time (duration) as it relates to muscular strength and endurance. Explain the difference between a set and a repetition.

### Project

- Have each student select one muscular strength and endurance activity and demonstrate the ability to perform 8 to 12 repetitions using proper form.

## Extending the Lesson

- Explain that time for muscular strength and endurance is not minutes, but repetitions and sets. Place the definitions of the repetitions and sets on the FITT bulletin board (see chapter 8, Activities 12 through 15).
- Have each student perform the class activities outside of class and record repetitions in an activity log.

# 15  Muscle Magic

## Intermediate Level

**Type** means what kind of activity you participate in to improve or maintain muscular strength and endurance. You develop muscular strength and endurance by doing specific exercises and activities for specific muscles and muscle groups. The type of muscular strength and endurance activities you do should depend on your personal goals and interests.

## Purpose

Students will identify specific exercises that improve muscular strength and endurance in specific muscles and muscle groups, and understand that the correct type of strength training they perform depends on the activity or sport for which they are training.

## Equipment Needed

- Muscle Magic signs (listing muscle or muscle group name, a picture, and one or more exercises and activities that develop muscular strength and muscular endurance for that particular muscle or muscle group, for example, triceps—push-ups, dips; gastrocnemius—toe raises, jump rope; and so on)
- Equipment for activities: jump ropes, dyna bands, bike tubes, and so on
- Music (optional)

## Relationship to National Standards

**Physical Education Standard 4:** Student achieves and maintains a health-enhancing level of physical fitness—Student will identify several activities that relate to a component of physical fitness.

## Set Induction

Define *type* as it relates to muscular strength and endurance. Offer some examples and ask students to share more examples. Introduce the activity or activities you have planned for today, stressing safety and correct technique.

## Procedure

There are many ways to play Muscle Magic.
1. Introduce a "Muscle of the Week."
   a. Discuss where the muscle is; what it does; and how it helps in daily work, play, and sports.
   b. Teach various exercises that work the muscle or muscle group.
2. Play Muscle Magic by setting up stations.
   a. Post each Muscle Magic sign at a station.
   b. Rotate small groups of students from station to station until everyone has participated in all the activities.

## Teaching Hints

Be sure to stress safety and proper form at stations where students are using dyna bands or bike tubes. Add music to enhance motivation and increase participation.

## Closure and Assessment

### Written and Oral

- Write a short definition of type as it relates to muscular strength and endurance. Briefly explain specificity of training.

### Project

- Have student design a set of Muscle Magic cards for a physical activity in which he or she has an interest.

## Extending the Lesson

- Collect pictures of people using muscles in various activities, work, play, sports, and so on.
- Develop a "Muscle of the Month" bulletin board. Each month feature a muscle used in your *Physical Best* activities.
- Create a board game using specific muscles and their anatomical name.

# 16 On Your Way

## Intermediate Level

**Progression:** The goal of improving muscular strength and muscular endurance (demonstrating progress) requires your muscles to do more than usual (more often, increased intensity, and more time). Doing more than usual is another way of saying **overload**.

## Purpose

Students will demonstrate progression from baseline toward a realistic goal selected by the student with help from the teacher.

## Equipment Needed

- Record sheets for the assessment
- Goal-setting worksheet
- Select, depending on assessment items selected:
  - Curl-up—curl-strips and cadence tape
  - Push-up—cadence tape
  - Modified pull-up—modified pull-up bar
  - Pull-up—pull-up bar
  - Flexed-arm hang—pull-up bar

## Relationship to National Standards

**Physical Education Standard 4:** Student achieves and maintains a health-enhancing level of fitness—Student will meet the health-related fitness standards as defined by *FITNESSGRAM*.

## Set Induction

Explain that today students will participate in assessments that will measure their baseline (current) muscular strength and endurance. (Choices from *FITNESSGRAM* include curl-ups, push-ups, modified push-ups, pull-ups, flexed-arm hang, and trunk lift.) Demonstrate the procedures for each assessment you wish to use in this lesson. Explain the principle of progression means that working on each FITT component should—over time—lead to progress, that is, increased strength. State that today they'll be measuring their current muscular strength and endurance so they can measure their progress later in the school year.

## Procedure

1. Choose which assessment you are going to practice.
2. Have students practice the assessment tasks you have selected.
3. Explain that over time and with practice, muscular strength and endurance will increase. State that later each student will repeat the assessment tasks to see if he or she is improving.
4. Help each student set a personal goal.
5. Students can write their goals down on record sheets.

## Teaching Hints

You can introduce formal goal-setting process at this age (see chapter 2). Samples are found in the Appendix.

## Closure and Assessment

### Written and Oral

- Review the process for goal setting and the goals each student sets. Each student should be able to report improved or maintained muscular strength and endurance upon reassessment.

### Project

- Have students develop a long-range goal for the specific muscular strength and muscular endurance test. After a long-range goal is established, have students write four small (stepping-stone) goals to help accomplish reaching the long-range goal. This shows progression for activities for muscular strength and muscular endurance and progression for goal setting. Provide gold stars or popular stickers for accomplishing each stepping-stone goal. Examples: Goal is to do 15 pull-ups at the end of the school year—Stepping-stone goals: three more pull-ups every two months.

## Extending the Lesson

Develop a progression bulletin board (see chapter 8, Activity 12), adjusting for this component (e.g., intensity is resistance and time is reps and sets).

# 17 Push-Up–Curl-Up Fun

## Intermediate Level

The goal of increasing muscular endurance (**progression**) requires doing more than usual. Time, type, intensity, and frequency all depend on one another.

## Purpose

Students will explain one example of progression in a muscular strength or muscular endurance activity and understand that frequency, intensity, time, and type are all related and affect the overall performance of the body.

## Equipment Needed

- Challenge poster (see sidebar)
- Segmented music tapes (15-15 tape, 20-15 tape, 30-15 tape, and so on; first one for today, others for future lessons)
- Beanbags
- Small plastic bucket
- Mat

---

**Challenge Poster Ideas**

*Note*: Add pictures if desired.

Push-Up Fun—assume push-up position and move hands to the cadence: over, over, back, back.

Beanbag Push-Up—assume a push-up position, then pick up a beanbag with one hand and place it in the bucket. Repeat with the other hand and pick up a second beanbag; continue this pattern until all the beanbags are in the bucket. Continue longer by then taking the beanbags out of the buckets. (If you do not have buckets, students can place beanbags over a line and back.)

Triceps push-up—in a crab position, lower the body while flexing (bending) elbows, and return to starting position by extending arms.

Regular push-up

Elevated push-up—assume the push-up position but raise feet off the floor by resting on a folded mat, a bench, or the like.

Four-count curl-up—in a curl-up position, knees bent, come up to touch knees, toes, knees, then return to floor.

Reverse curl-up—start in the up position, knees bent, and lower self slowly in four counts.

Arms-folded curl-up—do a curl-up, knees bent with arms folded across the chest.

One-legged curl-up—do a regular curl-up with one leg bent and the other raised off the floor and hooked around the opposite ankle.

---

## Relationship to National Standards

**Physical Education Standard 3:** Student exhibits a physically active lifestyle—Student will select and participate regularly in physical activities for the purpose of improving skill and health.

## Set Induction

Define *progression* as it relates to frequency, intensity, time, and type. Teach and allow students to practice the push-up and curl-up positions to ensure correct technique. Remind students that each individual must work from his or her current abilities to gradually and safely progress to better and better performance. It is important to remind students that they are each improving, and not competing with one another.

## Procedure

1. Display the challenge poster and begin a segmented music tape to manage the activity.
2. Direct each student to work in a self-space. Remind them to warm up and stretch before beginning.
3. Have each student choose one challenge (push-up or curl-up variation) from the poster and, beginning slowly, perform the exercise while the music is playing.
4. Direct students to rest when the music is off.
5. Repeat the same exercise challenge for a second set, then a third set (depending on individual abilities).
6. After the third set, have each student choose another exercise challenge from the poster.
7. Continue the challenges at your discretion.

## Teaching Hints

Be sure to have students warm up and cool down properly. When revisiting this activity, increase the workload by having the students perform the challenges with a new music tape (more time spent on activity, less on rest).

## Closure and Assessment

### Written and Oral

- Write a short definition of progression as it relates to muscular strength and endurance.

### Project

- Discuss with your partner(s) the improvement you have made through the hard work and goal-setting process. Discuss what you did well and what you could improve. Share with the class those suggestions.

## Extending the Lesson

- Take students to visit the high school weight training room or a health club.
- Bring in an orthopedic surgeon or physical therapist to discuss muscular strength and muscular endurance and their importance in overall health.

# 18 Hot Stuff and Cool Moves

## Intermediate Level

The purpose of a **warm-up** is to increase the temperature of the muscles, allowing them to move easier. Warm-up activities get the muscles ready to perform work, helping reduce the risk of muscle injury. The purpose of a **cool-down** is to stretch the muscles that have been asked to tighten during an activity.

## Purpose

Students will experience and then explain the importance of a warm-up and cool-down related to muscular strength and endurance.

## Equipment Needed

- Get Fit Exercise routines in *You Stay Active* book
- Mats

## Relationship to National Standards

**Physical Education Standard 4:** Student achieves and maintains a health-enhancing level of physical fitness—Students will learn about the importance of maintaining fitness in relationship to being healthy.

## Set Induction

Discuss and make sure students understand the importance of properly warming up before an activity and cooling down gradually.

## Procedure

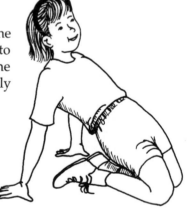

1. Teach students or let them design a warm-up routine appropriate for the main activity. Remind students to be sure to focus on large muscle movement, work the full range of motion, breathe easily, and work slowly and steadily.

2. Proceed with the day's activities.

3. Design and teach a cool-down routine. Include an easy stretch for those muscles used during the day's activities.

## Teaching Hints

Make sure that the students see the relationship of the warm-up to the day's physical education class activities.

## Closure and Assessment

### Written and Oral

- Explain why warming up and cooling down are important for muscular strength and endurance exercises.

### Project

- Ask the students to share with their group or partner(s) warm-ups that they know.

## Extending the Lesson

- Research the importance of muscular strength and endurance and stretching. Write a paragraph discussing activities or exercises that improve muscular strength and endurance and how stretching enhances the strength and endurance activities required by daily life.
- Construct a bulletin board showing specific warm-up and cool-down exercises for specific sports.

# Chapter 10

# Flexibility

# 1 Human Alphabet Stretch

## Primary Level

**Flexibility** is the ability to bend, stretch, and twist with ease, moving through a full **range of motion**.

## Purpose

The student will recognize that the body is capable of a wide range of movement, requiring bending, stretching, and twisting at many joints. The range of motion depends on your muscles' ability to stretch. In addition, students will explore a variety of stretching positions while learning where joints bend.

## Equipment Needed

- Laminated alphabet letters (optional)
- Music (optional)

## Relationship to National Standards

**Physical Education Standard 4:** Student achieves and maintains a health-enhancing level of physical fitness—Student will identify the components of health-related physical fitness.

## Set Induction

Define *flexibility* and explain what *range of motion* means. Bring in pictures of activities that need flexibility in order to perform the activity properly, or brainstorm a list with students. This activity will challenge students to perform a stretch in the form of an alphabet letter for at least 8 counts. Doing several letters and increasing the number of counts will increase their flexibility during the activity.

## Procedure

1. Have each student find a self-space. The students will move around the activity area until a signal to stop.
2. Explain that students will stop on a signal and form the letter you show with their bodies. An option is to play music while the students are moving, and stop the music as the signal to stop and stretch.
3. Repeat as often as desired.

## Teaching Hints

This activity assumes that the students are at least somewhat familiar with the alphabet. Most children may be able to form the letter. Children with physical disabilities will make shapes of the letters with the most appropriate body parts in light of their specific disabilities. Extend the activity by having small groups work together to form cooperative group letter shapes.

## Closure and Assessment

### Written and Oral

- Tell me one thing you are able to do when you are flexible.
- Tell me two alphabet letters that use a lot of flexibility when playing the Human Alphabet Stretch game.

### Project

- Cut out or draw a picture of an activity that uses good flexibility.

## Extending the Lesson

- Ask students to bring their spelling lists from the classroom. Use these lists to spell words to reinforce memorization or spelling.
- Have the children spell in upper and lower case letters.
- Set a time limit on making the letters.

# 2   Flexibility on Stage

## Primary Level

**Flexibility** helps us to do our daily activities without risk of injury from muscle strain or torn tendons. Good **range of motion** in all joints allows us to enjoy a wide variety of physical activities that can, in turn, contribute to a healthful life.

## Purpose

Students will identify the need for flexibility to pursue or maintain a healthy, active life.

## Equipment Needed

- Active People Cards (see sidebar)

---

### Active People Card Ideas

To create cards, look for pictures in magazines or computer clip art sources. Some popular ideas include the following:

- Changing a lightbulb
- Throwing a softball
- Raking the leaves
- Kicking a football
- Washing the windows
- Swimming
- Painting the house
- Rowing a boat
- Picking apples
- Long-jumping

---

## Relationship to National Standards

**Physical Education Standard 3:** Student exhibits a physically active lifestyle—Student will identify at least one activity associated with each component of health-related physical activity.

## Set Induction

Bring in pictures from magazines depicting active people in different roles. Explain that in this activity, students will role-play a variety of daily living tasks (e.g., brushing teeth), sport activities (e.g., gymnastics), or job related tasks (e.g., sweeping with a broom). Have a few students try to demonstrate the moves involved in specific activities.

## Procedure

1. Select or have a student select an Active People Card.
2. Give the cue "You're on stage" to signal the children to demonstrate the activity suggested on the card.
3. On the next cue, "Cut that scene," direct the children to freeze as if a movie camera stopped on an action frame.

4. Select two or three students to remain frozen while the class examines their poses, identifying which joints are bent. (You could also inquire of the "models" as to which muscles feel stretched.)

5. Choose another Active People Card.

6. Continue selecting new cards as long as desired.

## Teaching Hints

Make sure the students hold each pose for a period of time before they discuss the joints they use.

## Closure and Assessment

### Written and Oral

• Tell or write two benefits of being flexible.

### Project

• Have each student design an Active People Card, demonstrating flexibility.

## Extending the Lesson

Have each student make a collage using magazine clippings of active people engaged in tasks that show the need for good flexibility.

# 3 Parachute Flexibility

## Primary Level

**Flexibility** helps us do our daily activities without risk of injury from muscle strain or torn tendons. Adequate **range of motion** in all joints allows us to enjoy a wide variety of physical activities that can, in turn, contribute to a healthful life.

## Purpose

Students will identify the need for flexibility to pursue or maintain a healthy, active life.

## Equipment Needed

- Parachute
- Active People Cards (see Activity 2)

## Relationship to National Standards

**Physical Education Standard 3:** Student exhibits a physically active lifestyle—Student will identify at least one activity associated with each component of health-related physical activity.

## Set Induction

Review *flexibility* and *range of motion*. Explain that today's activity will help students see how important flexibility is.

## Procedure

1. Arrange students around the parachute with the Active People Cards on the floor under the center of the parachute.

2. Have students grasp the edges of the parachute (the stage "curtain") firmly and lift it up overhead. Have students practice raising and lowering the parachute safely.

3. When ready to begin, have the students raise the parachute overhead and send four or five students into the center (the "stage").

4. Have the remaining students safely pull the parachute down ("Close the curtain").

5. Direct the students on the stage to select an Active People Card and prepare to perform when you signal them.

6. Signal the remaining students to raise the curtain ("Curtain up"). Have them hold it up as long as possible while the students on stage perform.

7. Students should exit after the teacher calls "Hold pose" and counts "1-2-3." The parachute should be held up until they come off the stage.

## Teaching Hints

Be sure to have students practice the parachute skills of lifting the chute and pulling it down safely before placing students inside (on stage). Use the Active People Cards students made in the previous activity.

## Closure and Assessment

### Written and Oral

- Tell or write two benefits of being flexible.

### Project

- Make a pipe cleaner (chenille rod) person and bend it into an active pose.

## Extending the Lesson

- Have each student finish collages started in Activity 2.
- Encourage the children to play with the Active People Cards during recess.
- Have students interview their parents and/or senior citizens to ask about their flexibility as they have grown older, and then write a few sentences about the interview.

# 4 Commercial Stretch Break

## Primary Level

**Frequency** is the number of times per week you need to stretch to make muscles flexible. Experts recommend that to make and keep your muscles flexible, you should stretch at least three times a week.

## Purpose

Students will participate in stretching activities and tasks at least three times a week.

## Equipment Needed

- None

## Relationship to National Standards

**Physical Education Standard 3:** Student exhibits a physically active lifestyle—Student will identify at least one activity associated with each component of health-related physical activity.

## Set Induction

Discuss with students the differences between physically active and sedentary lifestyles. Explain that today they will be practicing (role-playing) a way to turn an activity that is not good for their bodies into a healthful one. Explain that upon the signal they are to stop, pretend you (the teacher) are a commercial on TV, and perform the stretches that you model.

## Procedure

1. After warming up, begin the main class activity.
2. At some point in the lesson, interrupt the activity by signaling and saying "commercial stretch break."
3. Lead the students in several stretching tasks as they pretend to be watching you as a commercial on TV.
4. Stretch for 2-3 minutes, and then resume the main activity lesson after the commercial stretch break is over.
5. Interrupt three times during the class period, telling students they should stretch at least three times a week. Encourage them to try stretching during TV commercials at home.

## Teaching Hints

Make sure the students stretch the muscles that are used in the lesson that you are teaching. This way, students see a specific relationship between the activity and stretching.

## Closure and Assessment

### Written and Oral

- Write or tell the number of days per week you should perform flexibility activities. Name a flexibility activity you could do for each day.

### Project

- Have students complete a Commercial Stretch Break activity sheet on their own for one week, recording stretching frequency and activities. Collect at the end of the week and check for appropriateness of frequency and activities.

## Extending the Lesson

- Send home a "Stretching Score Sheet" to record stretching exercises that are done at home. Have students keep a record of the stretching frequency and return the sheets to the teacher for homework (e.g., three weeks).
- Share the idea with classroom teachers. Ask them to "have commercial stretch breaks" on the days of the week that students do not have physical education class.
- Construct a bulletin board to represent the FITT formula. Use the caption "To Be Fit, You Must Think FITT." List the FITT acronym down the left side of the bulletin board. Explain to students that the "F" stands for frequency. Display a calendar on the board to visually represent the concept that stretching activities should be performed at least three days per week.

# 5 Safety Stretches

## Primary Level

**Intensity** is how far you need to stretch to improve or maintain flexibility. Adequate **range of motion** in all joints allows us to enjoy a wide variety of physical activities that can, in turn, contribute to a healthful life.

## Purpose

Students will practice stretching as far as they can *without* feeling pain.

## Equipment Needed

- Signs with name and picture of each stretch and safety stretch hint. (*Tip*: Take pictures of students practicing each stretch to add to signs.)
  - Don't bounce
  - Inhale/exhale
  - Don't lock joints
  - Don't hyperextend joints
  - Hold the stretch
  - The stretch should not hurt
  - Don't pull on joints

## Relationship to National Standards

**Physical Education Standard 4:** Student achieves and maintains a health-enhancing level of physical fitness—Student will identify the components of health-related physical fitness.

## Set Induction

Define or review what range of motion is and describe its benefits. Explain that everyone has different ranges of motion and, today, students are going to learn (or review) how to perform stretches safely so that each individual can increase his or her range of motion.

Discuss the concept of intensity: To make a muscle more flexible, stretch it so it feels tight, but doesn't hurt. If you don't stretch it to that point, your flexibility won't improve. But if you stretch too far and your muscle hurts, you could injure it. Listen to the messages your body gives you.

Use a rubber band or Silly Putty to illustrate what happens when you stretch a muscle too far. It may pull and break. Have the children gradually stretch it and feel how tight it can go before it starts to break. Compare this to the way a muscle stretches.

## Procedure

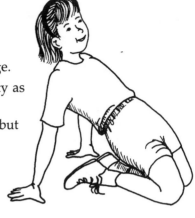

1. Have each student find a self-space.
2. Display a stretch sign for students to perform.
3. At the end of the stretch, repeat the safety message.
4. Show another stretch sign, continuing the activity as long as desired.
5. Remind students to stretch until they feel a pull, but not pain.

Stretch suggestions include the following:

- Back-saver sit-and-reach
- Calf stretch
- Straddle stretch
- Bent-elbow stretch
- Reverse hurdler
- Cross-chest stretch
- Butterfly stretch

## Closure and Assessment

### Written and Oral

- Discuss the question "How does your body let you know when you are using too much intensity while stretching?"

### Project

- During class have the students demonstrate the concept of intensity by participating in stretching activities and counting as they stretch.

## Extending the Lesson

Explain to students that the "I" in FITT stands for intensity. Turn the "I" on the FITT bulletin board (see Activity 4) into "Intensity = How Far!"

# 6 At Least 10 Alligators

## Primary Level

**Time** is how long you need to hold a stretch to improve or maintain flexibility. Experts recommend you hold each stretch, without bouncing or jerking, for 10 seconds (progressing to 30 seconds). Repeat each stretch a minimum of three times.

## Purpose

Students will demonstrate an understanding that safe stretches are done without bouncing and are held for a period of 10 seconds or longer to improve or maintain flexibility.

## Equipment Needed

- Make a sign with "10 Alligators" written on it. If desired, decorate the sign with pictures of alligators.

## Relationship to National Standards

**Physical Education Standard 3:** Student exhibits a physically active lifestyle—Student will identify at least one activity associated with each component of health-related physical activity.

## Set Induction

Instruct students as to the importance of not bouncing or jerking as they perform each stretch. Remind them that everyone is different in how much flexibility they have, and that they should not stretch to a point of undue discomfort. Tell them that today they will practice holding stretches for at least 10 seconds.

## Procedure

1. Have students find a personal space in an activity area. On a signal they move in general space using a locomotor pattern.

2. On the signal "Stop!" students freeze. Then ask "What do you see?" They respond with "at least 10 alligators."

3. Immediately after they say "at least 10 alligators" the teacher assumes a stretch position for the students to imitate. The teacher then cues the students to count them, "One alligator, two alligators, three alligators . . ." until they reach ten.

4. Repeat the lesson choosing another locomotor pattern, calling "Stop," and asking "What do you see?"

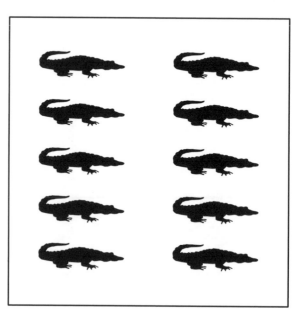

5. Continue, using the same stretch at least three times as the class moves across the activity area.

6. Take as many trips across the activity area as desired, using a different stretching position for each trip.

## Teaching Hints

Monitor students closely to ensure they do not bounce or jerk when stretching. Invite students who are stretching correctly to demonstrate for others.

## Closure and Assessment

### Written and Oral

- How long should you hold a stretch position to keep flexible?
- How long should you hold a stretch position to improve your flexibility?

### Project

- Have students demonstrate other stretches. Each stretch should last for at least 10 seconds and be free of bouncing and jerking.

## Extending the Lesson

- Create a bulletin board depicting pictures of various stretch poses. The title of the board could be "At Least Ten Alligators" and numbers one through ten could connect the pictures.
- Explain to the students that the first "T" in FITT stands for time. Remind them to hold stretching activities for at least 10 seconds, gradually working up to 30 seconds. Turn the first "T" on the FITT bulletin board into "Time = How Long!" Place a clock on the bulletin board next to the "T" for time.

# Muscle Galaxy

## Primary Level

**Type** means that only certain types of exercise affect the flexibility of muscles, and **specificity** means that only those muscles that are being stretched will become more flexible.

## Purpose

Students will demonstrate the concept of specificity by naming a muscle and doing a task that stretches that muscle.

## Equipment Needed

- None

## Relationship to National Standards

**Physical Education Standard 3:** Student exhibits a physically active lifestyle—Student will identify at least one activity associated with each component of health-related physical activity.

## Set Induction

Explain what *specificity*, or *type*, means. State that different stretches stretch different muscles. So, for example, if you wish to increase your leg muscles' flexibility, you must do stretches that focus on this area of the body, and so on. Ask students to name different stretches or show them a few, discussing which muscles they stretch. Explain that today they will imagine they are traveling through outer space while practicing different types of stretches, which stretch different, specific muscles.

## Procedure

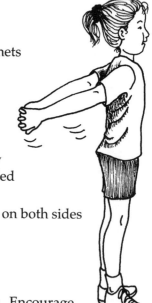

1. Select a muscle on which to focus.
2. The students are pretending to visit several imaginary planets that bear the name of the selected muscles (see sidebar).
3. The teacher chooses a locomotor pattern for the students to travel through "space."
4. The teacher signals when the students arrive at a planet and indicate that greetings are in order. The greeting consists of rhythmically saying the muscle name slowly and simultaneously doing a task that stretches the identified muscle.
5. If appropriate, repeat stretches that should be performed on both sides of the body.
6. Continue game as long as desired.

## Teaching Hints

Demonstrate the "greeting" and action for proper technique. Encourage students to perform each stretch with quality and in a safe position.

| Muscle Galaxy Examples | | |
|---|---|---|
| **Planet** | **Greeting** | **Action** |
| Deltoid | "Del Toid" | Deltoid stretch |
| Gastrocnemius | "Gas Troc" | Gastrocnemius stretch |
| Biceps | "Bi Ceps" | Biceps stretch |
| Hamstring | "Ham String" | Hamstring stretch |
| Triceps | "Tri Ceps" | Triceps stretch |

## Closure and Assessment

### Written and Oral

- Name a muscle and have students demonstrate the appropriate stretching activity.

### Project

- Give students a picture of a person and the muscles. Have students draw an "X" on the muscles they stretched.
- Match the name of the muscle on the side of the picture to the muscles in the picture.
- Have students draw pictures of other activities that stretch the various muscles identified in the Muscle Galaxy activity.

## Extending the Lesson

- Have students help label muscle locations on a poster picture of a child.
- Explain to the students that the second "T" stands for type. Turn the second "T" on the FITT bulletin board into "Type = Which Exercise!"

# 8 Getting Started

## Primary Level

The goal of improving flexibility (demonstrating **progression**) requires doing more than usual. Practicing the habit of regular stretching at least three times a week every week will help you maintain or improve flexibility over time.

## Purpose

Students will demonstrate progression from baseline fitness performance toward a realistic goal selected by each student with help from the teacher.

## Equipment Needed

- Sit-and-reach box
- Ruler or measuring tape
- Record sheets (see below)

## Relationship to National Standards

**Physical Education Standard 4:** Student achieves and maintains a health-enhancing level of physical fitness—Student will identify the components of health-related physical fitness.

## Set Induction

Explain that today students will participate in assessments that will measure their baseline (current) flexibility. (Choices from *FITNESSGRAM* include back-saver sit-and-reach, shoulder stretch, and trunk lift.) Demonstrate the procedures for each assessment you wish to use in this lesson. Explain that the principle of progression means that working on each FITT component should—over time—lead to progress, that is, increased flexibility. State that today they'll be measuring their current flexibility so they can measure their progress later in the school year.

## Procedure

1. Choose which flexibility assessment you are going to practice: sit-and-reach, trunk lift, shoulder stretch, and so on.

2. Have students practice the assessment tasks you have selected.

3. Explain that over time and with practice, flexibility will increase. State that later each student will repeat the assessment tasks to see if he or she is increasing flexibility.

4. Help each student set a personal goal.

5. Students can write their goals down on record sheets.

| Days | Stretches |
|------|-----------|
| Monday | |
| Tuesday | |
| Wednesday | |
| Thursday | |
| Friday | |

## Teaching Hints

Ensure students practice and warm up before doing the assessment stretch. Monitor the stretching assessments to make sure students do not bounce or jerk. Have students practice flexibility activities over time. Reassess and identify progress as individuals or as a whole class.

## Closure and Assessment

### Written and Oral

- Discuss the following with students: How much should you stretch to improve the progression of a particular stretch (e.g., sit-and-reach)? To show flexibility progression you need to (1) stretch the same amount (2) stretch less than usual (3) stretch more than usual.

### Project

- Have students develop a colorful calendar showing flexibility progression.

## Extending the Lesson

- Encourage self-testing by having a sit-and-reach box available for students to informally measure themselves before, after, or during classes.
- Construct a progression bulletin board:

  Progression = Progress

  F = Stretch more often

  I = Stretch with increased intensity

  T = Increase time for stretch

  T= Type of stretches (which ones for which muscles)

# 9 Warm-Up–Cool-Down

## Primary Level

A **warm-up** gets your body ready for activity. Slow and steady stretching is an important part of a proper warm-up, helping to prevent strains by increasing the elasticity of the muscles and tendons. A **cool-down** helps the body slow down gradually following activity. Slow and steady stretching is also an important part of a proper cool-down, reducing the chances of suffering tight, sore muscles.

## Purpose

Students will identify stretching as an important part of a proper warm-up and cool-down.

## Equipment Needed

- Stretching Idea Cards (resources: Alter 1998; Virgilio 1997; Corbin & Lindsey 1993)
- Pictures of students stretching to use on Stretching Idea Cards

## Relationship to National Standards

**Physical Education Standard 3:** Student exhibits a physically active lifestyle—Student will identify at least one activity associated with each component of health-related physical activity.

## Set Induction

Bring in spaghetti (cooked and uncooked). Let students try to bend the uncooked spaghetti. What happens? Now let them bend, stretch, and twist the cooked spaghetti. Does it bend, twist, and stretch with ease?

Ask if anyone can explain what a warm-up and a cool-down are. Explain the importance of these activities and why stretching should be part of both. State that today students will be practicing some stretches that are helpful parts of effective warm-ups and cool-downs. The teacher should choose several Stretching Idea Cards before the class so the children can share a variety of stretches during the activity.

## Procedure

1. Have students walk slowly throughout the activity area, and after giving a stop signal, select a student to lead the class in stretching. Students select a card with a stretch on it from a deck of Stretching Idea Cards.
2. Continue by asking several more students to share a stretch.
3. After an adequate warm-up, proceed with the main activity you have planned.
4. Right before class ends, have students repeat the Stretching Idea Cards activity as a cool-down.

## Teaching Hints

Be sure you spend adequate time reviewing flexibility tasks during the Set Induction phase of the lesson so the students you select during the activity can choose from a variety of stretches.

## Closure and Assessment

### Written and Oral

• Remind students of the important role stretching plays in a safe approach to being physically active. Ask questions such as the following: "Why do you stretch to warm up?" and "Why do you stretch to cool down?" Encourage students to make a habit of stretching before and after physical activity.

### Project

• List stretches that students could use for warm-ups and for cool-downs.

• Have students teach a family member two of the stretches they learned in class and report on this experience.

## Extending the Lesson

• Make a "Healthy Habits" bulletin board, highlighting stretching.

• Have students draw a list of stretches and be able to explain them; then give that list to adults or teachers to be used as a break in their teaching.

# 10 Maintenance Checkup

## Primary Level

When you stretch your muscles regularly, they stay long and flexible. We call this **use**. When you don't make stretching a regular habit, they become tight and stiff because of what we call **disuse**.

## Purpose

Students will understand the need for regular stretching to maintain good flexibility.

## Equipment Needed

- None

## Relationship to National Standards

**Physical Education Standard 4:** Student achieves and maintains a health-enhancing level of physical fitness—Student will identify the components of health-related physical fitness.

## Set Induction

Explain that like a car, our bodies also need regular maintenance to keep them in good working order. State that today students will be pretending they are cars, and they will perform flexibility exercises (stretches) to help maintain their bodies in good working order.

## Procedure

1. Lead students through activities that represent the maintenance tasks needed to take care of a car, ensuring it will perform well for many years. Have students "drive" around town, doing locomotor skills you select.

2. Upon your cue, have students "stop for maintenance."

3. Call out the maintenance activity and model the stretching task that represents it. Examples of maintenance checkup activities:

   - Checking the windshield wiper—triceps stretch

     Raise right arm across the front of body, and with opposite hand, push elbow gently to stretch the triceps for 10 seconds. Repeat with other arm.

   - Rotating the tires—spinal stretch

     Rotate body to right and hold for 10 seconds. Repeat to left.

   - Checking the brakes—gastrocnemius stretch

     Lunge on right foot, lock the back knee, and drop the heel to the floor. Push back with the bent leg; hold for 10 seconds. Repeat with left leg.

   - Checking the shock absorbers—quadriceps stretch

     With support of hand on wall, stand on one leg and lift other leg with knee bent behind; pull the leg back to safely stretch quadriceps; hold for 10 seconds. Repeat with other leg.

- Checking the fan belts—hamstring stretch

  Sit in straddle position, reach down right leg, and hold for 10 seconds. Repeat with left leg.

- Checking the head- and taillights—abdominal stretch and the like

  Lying on floor on back, stretch as long as possible, pointing toes (taillights) and fingers (headlights) to make your body extra long; hold for 10 seconds. Relax, then repeat several times.

## Closure and Assessment

### Written and Oral

- Ask "What must you do to maintain flexibility? How do you continually maintain and check flexibility?"

### Project

- Have students keep an activity calendar, recording the days they do flexibility activities. Give stickers to students who report stretching three or four days a week.

## Extending the Lesson

Bring to school pictures of physical activities that need particular muscles to be flexible, to be used on the bulletin board.

# 11 Flexibility Flash Cards

## Intermediate Level

**Flexibility** is the ability to bend, stretch, and twist with ease, moving through a full **range of motion** at many joints.

## Purpose

Students will become aware and demonstrate that we need flexibility in a number of joints to accomplish all the movements we ask our bodies to perform.

## Equipment Needed

- Flexibility Flash Cards (resources: Alter 1998; Virgilio 1997; Corbin & Lindsey 1993). Flash cards should be done on 8-1/2 x 11 paper—large enough for the whole class to see. The number of cards depends on the length of activity: at least six stretches are recommended. Be sure to include one stretch from each major body part (arms, shoulders, torso, legs, and back).
- Pictures of stretches for cards

## Relationship to National Standards

**Physical Education Standard 4:** Student achieves and maintains a health-enhancing level of physical fitness—Student will identify several activities related to each component of physical fitness.

## Set Induction

Review the definition of *flexibility*. Explain that today students will be using Flexibility Flash Cards and doing stretches to enhance flexibility. Tell students that everyone has a different flexibility potential. Emphasize that they should not feel pain when stretching and we do not compete in stretching exercises.

## Procedure

1. Have students each find a self-space.
2. Have everyone warm up with some movement (e.g., jog, skip, slide, carioca, and so on).
3. Give a stop signal. Then, as you flash a card, have students assume the stretching position and hold it for 10 to 30 seconds.
4. Have students resume locomotion.
5. Use as many Flexibility Flash Cards as desired before proceeding to your main activity.
6. Use the cards to help students cool down at the end of the lesson.

## Teaching Hints

Remind students as often as necessary that we do not compete when stretching; we simply each try to increase our own flexibility. Monitor students closely to ensure they are not bouncing or jerking while stretching.

## Closure and Assessment

### Written and Oral

- Write a short definition of flexibility. List two reasons why flexibility is important.

### Project

- Have students design and make Flexibility Flash Cards that will help maintain a full range of motion at the joints of the body.

## Extending the Lesson

- Have students perform selected tasks that use a limited range of motion at a critical joint. Examples include the following:

  Long jump—isolate or limit knee bend

  Overhand throw—isolate or limit elbow bend

  Prone lying—isolate or limit spinal flexion and twisting

- Have each student draw a picture of him- or herself playing a favorite sport or activity, then list two or three stretches that will help improve flexibility in the sport or activity.

# 12 Flexibility for Health

## Intermediate Level

Highly flexible people are likely to be healthy and avoid injury (e.g., flexibility in the low back and hamstring muscles minimizes the potential for developing low back pain).

## Purpose

Students will recognize that flexibility is health related.

## Equipment Needed

- 8 flexibility task cards
- 8 Why Stretch? posters based on material in Alter 1998; Virgilio 1997; or Corbin & Lindsey 1993. Sample messages include:
  - Reduce muscle tension and make the body feel more relaxed.
  - Help coordination by allowing for freer and easier movement.
  - Increase range of motion.
  - Prevent injuries such as muscle strains.
  - Prepare you for physical activity by making muscles ready to move.
  - Become more aware of your body.
  - Promote circulation.
  - Feel good.

## Relationship to National Standards

**Physical Education Standard 3:** Student exhibits a physically active lifestyle—Student will select and participate regularly in physical activities for the purpose of improving skill and health and identify the benefits derived from regular physical activity.

## Set Induction

Review the reasons for stretching.

## Procedure

1. Have students start at one of eight flexibility stations. Place a flexibility task card and a Why Stretch? poster at each station.

2. As each student performs a task, direct him or her to also read the message on the poster.

3. After a short time, signal students to rotate to the next station.

4. Continue in this manner until everyone has visited all eight stations.

## Teaching Hints

Use the circuit frequently so students can more readily report why they should stretch. The answers listed are samples; edit their wording, depending on the students' reading abilities. Substitute different flexibility tasks when repeating this activity to give students practice doing a wide variety of stretches.

## Closure and Assessment

### Written and Oral

• Write or tell four reasons why stretching is important.

### Project

• Work in small groups and design new flexibility activities or exercises for each of the eight reasons why stretching is important.

## Extending the Lesson

• Have students bring in pictures of sports and activities that use stretching to enhance performance.

• Develop a flexibility bulletin board. Highlight the significance of stretching for each sport or activity.

# 13 Flexibility Flip Card File

## Intermediate Level

**Frequency** is the number of times per week you need to stretch to make your muscles flexible. Experts recommend that to make and keep your muscles flexible, you should stretch at least three times a week.

## Purpose

Students will each create and then use a personalized flexibility flip card file at least three times a week.

## Equipment Needed

- 8 (9 if one is used for recording frequency) 3 x 5 index cards for each student
- Yarn, string, or a metal ring to connect cards for each student
- Hole punch (one for each station or prepunch index cards)
- Posters or task cards of stretches with instructions (*Tip*: Take pictures ahead of time of students performing each stretching activity to place on these.)
- Class chart to record students' practice frequency (optional)

## Relationship to National Standards

**Physical Education Standard 3:** Student exhibits a physically active lifestyle—Student will select and participate regularly in physical activities for the purpose of improving skill and health and identify opportunities in the school and community for regular participation in physical activity.

**Physical Education Standard 4:** Student achieves and maintains a health-enhancing level of physical fitness—Student will identify several activities related to each component of physical fitness.

## Set Induction

Review the importance of stretching frequently. Explain that today students will make a personalized flexibility flip card file. They will use the flip cards to do stretches at least three times a week. Brainstorm with the students times that may be appropriate for this activity (e.g., at the beginning of class, during physical education fitness activities, during any free time at school, such as, in class [with teacher's permission] or during breaks, or at home).

## Procedure

1. Set up eight stretching stations, each with choices of stretching activities that students can perform.

| Days | Stretches |
|------|-----------|
| Monday | |
| Tuesday | |
| Wednesday | |
| Thursday | |
| Friday | |

2. Have students go to each station and select one stretch to practice and copy onto a 3 x 5 card. When finished with the stations, each student will have eight cards for their personalized flip card file.

3. If cards are not prepunched, have students punch a hole in the corner of each card and connect cards with yarn, string, or a metal ring.

4. Explain how to record the frequency of stretching activities. To record frequency, have students check it off on a class chart or record it on another 3 x 5 card attached to the file.

## Teaching Hints

Have students write their names on their flip cards and brainstorm with them ways to be responsible for keeping track of their cards. You may wish to establish a lost and found spot for them. Note that not every student will be self-motivated to use the cards. Therefore, your encouragement and a system of accountability, such as recording frequency, will be necessary.

## Closure and Assessment

### Written and Oral

- Write a short definition of frequency as it relates to flexibility.

### Project

- Add a personal touch to your file by designing flip cards for the physical activity of your choice. Then record how often you do the activities.

## Extending the Lesson

- Develop a personal fitness portfolio. Add the flexibility flip cards and recorded frequency data to each student's physical education portfolio.

- Construct a bulletin board to represent the FITT formula (see instructions under Extending the Lesson in Activities 4 through 7 earlier in this chapter; adapt board as intermediate activities progress through the FITT acronym).

# 14 Good Stretch Workout

## Intermediate Level

**Intensity** is how far you need to stretch to maintain or improve flexibility. How far must be monitored by personal judgment. In other words, the stretcher must choose to be safe. Muscles should feel tight, but not painful. Stretch slowly; do not bounce.

## Purpose

Students will practice safe stretching techniques, stretching to a point of tightness without feeling pain.

## Equipment Needed

- Stretching Record Sheets
- Measuring equipment, such as, rulers or tape measures
- Pencils

## Relationship to National Standards

**Physical Education Standard 4:** Student achieves and maintains a health-enhancing level of physical fitness—Student will monitor intensity of exercise.

## Set Induction

Review or introduce how to safely increase the intensity of a stretch:

1. Perform the stretch to a point of easy tension (10 to 30 seconds).
2. Relax.
3. Repeat the stretch to mild tension and hold (20 to 30 seconds).
4. Relax.
5. Repeat again and see if you can go a little farther without feeling pain and hold (30 seconds).

Review or introduce the rules for safe stretching: No bouncing or jerking; move slowly and steadily. Do not compete with anyone else. Discuss the meaning of "Pain is no gain." Offer these tips as well: Exhale when moving into the stretch. Breathe normally while holding the stretch. Inhale when releasing.

## Procedure

1. Divide students into partners (or small groups of three at the most) to do the following flexibility tasks, take measurements, and record each student's three trials on a stretching record sheet.

2. Rotate students through flexibility assessment stations.

3. Have students use a stretching record sheet such as the one shown in the Appendix.

## Teaching Hints

Remind students to perform a light warm-up before stretching. As necessary, keep reminding students that flexibility tasks are not competitive activities! Other measurable flexibility tasks might include the straddle sit, measuring the reach forward or the distance between feet from heel to heel, and the shoulder stretch (one of *FITNESSGRAM* test items) measuring how close fingertips come to meeting. This is a sample assessment, not a true assessment. Remember, the concept of intensity is the focus. Note that you do not need a standard sit-and-reach box. Instead, students measure almost to toes, touch toes, reach past toes, and so on.

## Closure and Assessment

### Written and Oral

• Write a short definition of intensity as it relates to flexibility. Explain how you can monitor intensity when stretching.

### Project

• Have each student select four stretches for which to keep a measurement log, for a period of three weeks.

## Extending the Lesson

• Make a collage entitled "Pain Is No Gain." Have students find pictures in sports magazines or newspapers depicting athletes sidelined with pulled muscles.

• Have students write a paragraph, answering the question "Why is pain no gain?" Place samples on the FITT bulletin board.

# 15 Hold That Stretch

## Intermediate Level

**Time** is how long you need to hold a stretch to improve or maintain flexibility. Experts recommend you hold each developmental stretch, without bouncing or jerking for 10 seconds (progressing to 30 seconds). Repeat each stretch a minimum of three times.

## Purpose

Students will practice safe stretching techniques, recognizing that flexibility is improved by slow and steady stretching to a point they can hold without pain for 10 seconds (progressing gradually to 30 seconds).

## Equipment Needed

- None, unless you have a Polaroid or digital camera (the second integrates technology but is optional)

## Relationship to National Standards

**Physical Education Standard 4:** Student achieves and maintains a health-enhancing level of physical fitness—Student will monitor intensity of exercise.

## Set Induction

Review the features of a safe stretch.

## Procedure

Use a Polaroid or digital camera (if technology is present in school) to take pictures of students stretching.

1. Have students walk, jog, or skip through the area.

2. Give the cue of "Slow and steady . . . hold that stretch" to tell students to stop the locomotor task and safely perform the stretching task you're modeling.

3. Have students hold the stretch for at least 10 seconds while you pretend or actually take pictures of two or three students performing the stretch.

4. Repeat the activity using different stretches, each time choosing new students for the pictures.

5. Look at the pictures to see if the stretches were performed correctly.

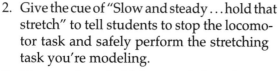

## Teaching Hints

Before attempting this activity, ensure the behavior management and social skills of the class will tolerate the playful atmosphere that photographing students will evoke without losing the focus of the lesson. You can reinforce both the time and the intensity concepts with this activity.

## Closure and Assessment

### Written and Oral

- Write a short definition of time as it relates to flexibility.

### Project

- Have students lead peers through a self-designed flexibility warm-up that focuses on stretches needed for the activity they are performing.

## Extending the Lesson

Add the stretching pictures you took to the FITT board.

# 16  Flex-a-Flavor Cards

## Intermediate Level

**Specificity**, or **type**, means that only the muscle you are stretching will become more flexible (e.g., if you do stretching activities for your arms, your legs will not become more flexible).

## Purpose

Students will understand that to gain flexibility in a certain area, it is necessary to do stretches specific to that area or muscle group.

## Equipment Needed

- Make a set of Flex-a-Flavor Cards in the shape of ice cream cones. The idea of the "flavors" or "colors" helps to reinforce the concept that there is variety in stretching tasks (resources: Alter 1998; Virgilio 1997; Corbin & Lindsey 1993).
- Construction paper for cones
- Pictures of stretches (optional but very helpful)

## Relationship to National Standards

**Physical Education Standard 4:** Student achieves and maintains a health-enhancing level of physical fitness—Student will identify several activities related to each component of physical fitness and begin to develop a strategy for the improvement of selected fitness components.

## Set Induction

Review or introduce the concept of *specificity*, or *type*. Review the features of a safe stretch. Demonstrate and practice stretches unfamiliar to students.

## Procedure

You can use the Flex-a-Flavor Cards in a variety of ways:

1. Use the cards with the whole class performing the same task at once. (This is a good way to introduce the cards if the stretches are unfamiliar to the students.)

2. Randomly draw or have a student draw a task from the "deck." Or if you number the cards, you or a student can pick a number or series of numbers for the class to perform.

3. After each task, identify or have a student identify the specific area or muscle group the stretch stretched.

4. Scatter cards randomly about the floor. Have students travel around them doing locomotor movements until you give a cue to find a card, upon which students go to the nearest card and do the indicated stretch. Repeat the activity until students have explored a number of stretching cards.

5. Reinforce the concept of specificity (type) by helping students recognize that in order to exercise all body areas they must do a variety of different stretching tasks. If desired, ask students to share which task they "felt" stretched a specific body area or muscle identified by you.

6. Organize cards to address specific body areas or muscle groups, such as all lime (green) cards are stretches for legs, all strawberry (pink) cards are stretches for the arms and shoulders, all blueberry (blue) cards are stretches for the back, and all orange cards are for other areas of the body. Have students rotate through all four stations, practicing several tasks at each station.

## Teaching Hints

Be sure to spend enough time teaching the stretches to students before using the cards in more self-directed ways. If possible, on each card, provide a picture as many students in this age group still need the visual cue. For variety, use one way of using the cards listed under Procedure in one lesson and the other ways in future lessons.

## Closure and Assessment

### Written and Oral

• Write a short definition of type as it relates to flexibility.

### Project

• Discuss with students the type of flexibility tasks that are most appropriate for preparing the body to perform different sport tasks:

Swinging a bat—trapezius stretch

Weight lifting curl—biceps stretch

Dribbling a basketball—triceps stretch

Jumping rope—gastrocnemius stretch

Bicycling—hamstring stretch

Then have each student design a set of Flex-a-Flavor cards for a physical activity in which he or she currently has an interest.

## Extending the Lesson

• Talk to the classroom teachers about taking "stretch breaks" during classes. Have each student make a set of stretching cards to use in the classroom when the teacher calls a "stretch break."

• Have the students take the stretch cards home and teach their parents new stretches learned during class.

# 17 On Your Way

## Intermediate Level

The goal of improving flexibility (demonstrating **progression**) requires doing more than usual. Practicing regular stretching every week will help you maintain or improve flexibility over a period of time.

## Purpose

Student will demonstrate progression from baseline fitness performance toward a realistic goal selected by the student with help from the teacher.

## Equipment Needed

- Sit-and-reach box
- Ruler or measuring tape
- Recordkeeping sheets (see the Appendix)

## Relationship to National Standards

**Physical Education Standard 4:** Student achieves and maintains a health-enhancing level of physical fitness—Student will identify the components of health-related physical fitness.

## Set Induction

Explain that today students will participate in assessments that will measure their baseline (current) flexibility. (Choices from *FITNESSGRAM* include back-saver sit-and-reach, shoulder stretch, and trunk lift.) Demonstrate the procedures for each assessment you wish to use in this lesson. Explain that the principle of progression means that working on each FITT component should—over time—lead to progress, that is, increased flexibility. State that today they'll be measuring their current flexibility so they can measure their progress later in the school year.

## Procedure

1. Choose which flexibility assessment you are going to practice: sit and reach, trunk lift, shoulder stretch, and so on.
2. Have students practice the assessment tasks you have selected.
3. Explain that over time and with practice, flexibility will increase. State that later each student will repeat the assessment tasks to see if he or she is increasing flexibility.
4. Help each student set a personal goal.
5. Students can write their goals down on record sheets.

## Teaching Hints

Ensure students practice and warm up before doing the assessment stretch. Monitor the stretching assessments to make sure students do not bounce or jerk. Have students practice flexibility activities over time. Reassess and identify progress as individuals or as a whole class.

## Closure and Assessment

### Written and Oral

- Write a short definition of progression as it relates to flexibility.

### Project

- Show progression in a FITT workout to meet the personal goal you established on your flexibility fitness assessment.

## Extending the Lesson

- Encourage self-testing by having a sit-and-reach box available for students to informally measure themselves before, after, or during classes.
- Construct a progression bulletin board:

  Progression = Progress

  F = Stretch more often

  I = Stretch with increased intensity

  T = Increase time for stretch

  T= Type of stretches (which ones for which muscles)

# 18 Squad Follow

## Intermediate Level

A **warm-up** gets your body ready for activity. Slow and steady stretching is an important part of a proper warm-up, helping to prevent strains by increasing the elasticity of the muscles and tendons. A **cool-down** helps the body slow down gradually following activity. Slow and steady stretching is an important part of a proper cool-down, reducing the chances of tight, sore muscles.

## Purpose

Students will identify stretching as an important part of a proper warm-up and cool-down and demonstrate a short routine they can use in both situations.

## Equipment Needed

- Music (optional)

## Relationship to National Standards

**Physical Education Standard 3:** Student exhibits a physically active lifestyle—Student will select and participate regularly in physical activities for the purpose of improving skill and health.

## Set Induction

Discuss the importance of warming up and cooling down properly before and after strenuous physical activity. Review the important elements of stretching (e.g., safety, FITT).

## Procedure

1. Divide students into small groups (squads).
2. Teach the students a short routine of stretching tasks that will serve as a good warm-up or cool-down activity.
3. Then have students create a short routine in their small groups, encouraging each member to contribute a stretching task. If desired, play appropriate music (something that would lend to slow and steady stretching) to accompany the routines.

## Teaching Hints

Once the small groups have developed and practiced their short routines and you have ensured they are adequate, have each squad share the responsibility of leading the class in warm-ups or cool-downs over the course of several lessons.

## Closure and Assessment

### Written and Oral

- List two important things you should remember when stretching to warm up or cool down.

### Project

- Design a personal warm-up and cool-down routine that demonstrates the important elements of stretching.

## Extending the Lesson

- Encourage volunteers to come visit another class and lead them in their Squad Follow warm-up and cool-down routine.
- Portfolio assignment: Think about a particular sport or activity and design a stretching routine for that sport or activity.

# 19 Watching Out

## Intermediate Level

Pay attention to the way your body feels when you do flexibility activities. The muscle you are stretching should feel tight, but you should not feel pain. Do stretches slowly. Don't bounce or jerk.

## Purpose

Students will perform stretching activities safely and recognize that some traditional stretching exercises can be harmful.

## Equipment Needed

- Pictures of contraindicated stretches (Alter 1998, pp. 25-28)

## Relationship to National Standards

**Physical Education Standard 5:** Student demonstrates responsible personal and social behavior in physical activity settings—Student will utilize safety principles in activity situations.

## Set Induction

Explain that new information (research) is always coming our way. If the new findings suggest that what used to be OK is now something that may be unsafe, we have to make changes. This is what has happened with some traditional stretching exercises. State that today students will be learning about certain stretches the experts say they should avoid for safety reasons.

## Procedure

Find pictures of stretches that have been found to cause injury in some people and explain why people should avoid doing them. Some examples include:

- Plough—puts a lot of pressure on spine, promoting forward head and humped back. There is no appropriate variation for children.
- Hurdler stretch—the knee is placed in an unnatural position causing stress in the knee cartilage. This stretch can be made safer by sitting sideways on a bench and allowing the leg that the traditional hurdler stretch bends underneath the body to hang free (Alter 1998, p. 102).
- Standing toe touch—puts a lot of stress on the muscles of the back. A safe alternative is the back-saver sit-and-reach (demonstrate, then have students practice).

## Teaching Hints

Be sure to use pictures to show the contraindicated stretches. Do *not* demonstrate the unsafe tasks.

## Closure and Assessment

### Written and Oral

- Ask the students to explain how they can change the stretches that cause injury into stretches that provide a safe way to become flexible.

### Project

- Have students make a poster that depicts the unsafe stretches and corresponding safe alternatives.

## Extending the Lesson

- Show students several examples of research resources in physical education.
- Discuss whether the students have ever been asked to do stretches that are unsafe for them and role-play how to politely refuse to do these stretches if someone else asks them to (coaches, classroom teachers, parents).

# Chapter 11
# Body Composition

# 1 Body Works Tag

## Primary Level

**Body composition** is what your body is made up of. Your body is made of several components: muscles, bones, tissues, water, and fat cells. The health of your body composition depends on two things: nutrition and physical activity. Nutrients are the building blocks needed by your body to create your body composition.

## Purpose

Students will understand that the body is composed of muscles, bones, tissues, water, and fat cells and that foods and physical activity affect body composition.

## Equipment Needed

- Cards with individual components of body composition written on them (muscle, fat, and so on)
- Poster showing and describing the functions of the body composition components
- Five or more poly-spots
- Music (optional)

## Relationship to National Standards

**Physical Education Standard 3:** Student exhibits a physically active lifestyle—Student will identify at least one activity associated with each component of health.

**Health Education Standard 1:** Student will comprehend concepts related to health promotion and disease prevention—Student will describe the basic structure and functions of the human body systems.

## Set Induction

Define body composition and discuss how physical activity and nutrition affect it. Discuss the poster showing the different components of body composition. Explain that today students will be playing a tag game that includes physical activity to improve their body compositions as they review the body composition component terms.

## Procedure

1. Scatter the poly-spots about the activity area.
2. Have students line up on the end line of the activity area.
3. Tell or whisper to each student what component of body composition they are going to be, or if they can read give them a card with a body composition component on it. Then collect the cards.
4. Choose one to three students to be "Body Catchers." They stand in the middle of the playing area

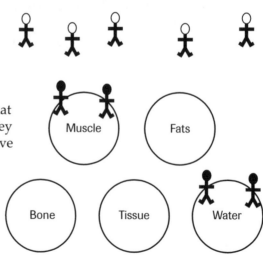

and their job is to loudly call out one of the body's components, thereby signaling the students who represent that component to travel across the activity area. The "Body Catchers" try to tag students before they reach the far end line.

5. If a student is tagged, he or she must stand on a base (poly-spot) and try to help tag others.
6. Continue playing the game, calling out each component in turn.
7. Call "body composition" to signal those representing any component to move across the activity area.

## Teaching Hints

The students who are waiting to be called out can be performing an activity that improves other fitness components (e.g., pretend step aerobics routine, pretend jump rope routine, multiple kinds of push-ups, multiple kinds of curl-ups, dribbling basketball in place, or a line dance routine). The activities could be included on the cards—for instance, fat could be knee push-ups, and water could be pretend jump rope. This way they would know ahead of time what they are going to do when they wait at both ends of the gym. Remember, never play out a tag game until the last student is caught. Change taggers often so all students enjoy physical activity.

Use music and only play the music during the tagging time. This allows the waiting students to perform to music, and gives the other children only so much time to get across the room or they are caught.

## Closure and Assessment

### Written and Oral

- Thumbs-up or thumbs-down: Muscles, bones, tissue, water, and fat cells make up your body. This is known as your body composition. Ask who were what parts of the body.
- Hold up a model or picture representing the components of body composition (muscles, bones, tissues, water, and fat cells). Have students identify each of the components.

### Project

- The health of your body composition depends on two things: nutrition and physical activity. Cut out or draw a picture of a physical activity and of a food item important for maintaining a healthy body composition.

## Extending the Lesson

Have the students make a poster that depicts "Body Composition = Bones + Muscles + Water + Tissues + Fat."

# 2 | Body Composition

## Primary Level

Having a healthy amount of lean body mass and fat mass (a **healthy body composition**) helps you play and work better. If you eat too little food, you will not have the energy to work, learn, or play. If you eat too much food, your body will store the energy it does not use as fat, which might lead to overfatness.

## Purpose

Students will identify several benefits of a healthy body composition.

## Equipment Needed

- White and blue Body Composition Benefit Cards (see sidebar)

---

### Body Composition Benefit Cards

White Cards—Benefits of Fat

- Helps body adjust to heat and cold
- Protects organs and bones from injury
- Source of energy

Blue Cards—Benefits of Lean Body Mass

- Reduces chances of diseases
- Helps heart do its job
- Helps your body do the best job of using the foods you eat

---

## Relationship to National Standards

**Physical Education Standard 4:** Student achieves and maintains a health-enhancing level of physical fitness—Student will sustain activity for longer periods of time while participating in chasing and fleeing activities.

**Health Education Standard 3:** Student will demonstrate the ability to practice health-enhancing behaviors and reduce health risks—Student will demonstrate strategies to improve or maintain personal health.

## Set Induction

Discuss how too little and too much food may affect a person. Brainstorm a list of possible benefits of a healthy body composition with students. Accept all answers without evaluation. Explain that today's activity will help them see if they were correct and thorough in their list. This freeze tag game will also help them learn the importance of having a healthy balance of lean body mass (defined as "weight" at this age) and fat.

## Procedure

1. Tell the students to spread out and find a space in the activity area. Designate two taggers and two rescuers.
2. Signal everyone but the taggers to begin moving using a locomotor skill you select. On a signal send the taggers out to tag all the players except the rescuers.
3. When tagged, the fleeing student must "freeze" (or strike a balance pose or do anything else you designate) and wait to be rescued.
4. The rescuers travel through the group giving benefit cards to frozen students, allowing them to travel again. One rescuer gives out white cards and the other rescuer gives out blue cards.
5. Students must get both a white card and a blue card to become unfrozen. Allow students to keep their cards.
6. Continue for a short time.
7. At the end of each round, read or have students read the benefits on the cards that have been distributed.

## Teaching Hints

Understand the reading level of your students. If they can not read, discuss the benefits of having both lean body mass and fat.

## Closure and Assessment

### Written and Oral

- Write or tell if both lean mass and fat provide benefits.
- List one benefit for body fat and two benefits for lean mass.

### Project

- Have students cut out or draw a picture representing one benefit of body fat and one benefit of lean body mass.

## Extending the Lesson

- Continue to use the body composition poster. List more of the benefits of lean body mass under "Muscles + Bones + Tissues + Nutrients + Water" and the benefits of fat under "Fat."
- Discuss what happens to the body when there is not a good balance of lean body tissue to fat.
- Discuss the diseases of bulemia and anorexia nervosa as well as obesity in children.
- Design a bulletin board that demonstrates balance, moderation, and variety in a healthy diet. (See chapter 7.)

# 3 My Body

## Primary Level

**Growth and developmental influences on body composition**: Your body is made of billions of cells that need all type of foods to live. Your body shape, type, and size are influenced by many factors, some of which you can control and some which you cannot control. The uncontrollable factors are your genetics (family history), age, and gender. Controllable factors are how much you eat, what you eat, and how much physical activity you do.

## Purpose

Students will understand the factors that influence their body shape, type, and size and understand the uniqueness of each person and how each person is different in his or her nutrient and physical activity requirements.

## Equipment Needed

- Variety of balls, such as, playground, Nerf, tennis
- Hula hoops

## Relationship to National Standards

**Physical Education Standard 3:** Student exhibits a physically active lifestyle—Student will identify the benefits derived from regular physical activity.

**Health Education Standard 1:** Student will comprehend concepts related to health promotion and disease prevention—Student will describe relationships between personal health behaviors and individual well-being.

## Set Induction

If time allows, use an ink pad and fingerprint each child. Have student compare the fingerprint with everyone else's to show how everyone is different. The fingerprints are all different just like the bodies are all different and come in all different sizes, colors, and shapes.

Explain that each student will choose the ball they will use for this activity. Explain that their choices are similar to their fingerprints and bodies, in that everyone has their own and that they are not always the same as the other classmates.

## Procedure

1. Place a variety of types and sizes of balls about the activity area in hoops and allow students to use any size ball they are comfortable with.

2. Take students through a series of manipulative skills (e.g., toss and catch, ball handling, bounce and catch, roll and catch, dribbling, partner skills, and so on), offering students two or three challenges in each of the skill categories.

3. Explain that we are not all the same size. Many factors influence our size and shape, such as what we do and eat and the family we come from (our parents).

## Teaching Hints

Be sure to allow each student to select the ball he or she is comfortable with. Add claps, turns, and so on to the skills you're using to increase the level of challenge.

Make sure that there are more than enough balls for every student in order that the majority get their choice.

## Closure and Assessment

### Written and Oral

- Ask "What lesson did I want you to learn about body composition by participating in today's activity?"

### Project

- Direct students to do the following: "Ask your mom or dad for the following recent photos: of you, of your mom or dad, and of that parent's parents. Try to get photos that are of each person's whole body. Paste the photos side by side on a sheet of paper. Compare body shapes, types, and sizes of the people in the photos. Make a list of at least four things you see related to body shape, type, and size." (*Note*: You may choose to make a sample photo array to use for comparison, rather than having all students bring in photos.)

## Extending the Lesson

- Have each student draw a picture of her family involved in physical activity.
- Have each student draw a picture of himself doing his favorite activity or something he likes about himself.
- Have the students create a menu that they would eat for a school lunch. Discuss the types of food that make their lean body mass healthy and the types of foods that increase fat content. (See chapter 7.)

# 4 A Balancing Act

## Primary Level

Food is the fuel and building blocks your body needs to perform well. Food gives energy that helps you learn better, be active, and enjoy life. A variety of foods from each food group gives us the nutrients such as fats, carbohydrates, and proteins that are needed for **appropriate nutrition**. The Food Guide Pyramid helps us decide what kinds of foods and how many servings to eat each day for a **healthy body composition**.

## Purpose

Students will (1) understand that nutrients such as fats, carbohydrates, and proteins come from the foods we eat; (2) identify the food groups the nutrients fall under and the number of servings needed for good nutrition; and (3) identify the nutrients and what sources of foods are rich in these nutrients.

## Equipment Needed

- Poster of the Food Guide Pyramid

## Relationship to National Standards

**Physical Education Standard 3:** Student exhibits a physically active lifestyle—Student will recognize that physical activity is good for personal well-being.

**Health Education Standard 1:** Student will comprehend concepts related to health promotion and disease prevention—Student will describe relationships between personal health behaviors and individual well-being.

## Set Induction

Introduce or review the Food Guide Pyramid. Discuss the three aspects of the Purpose statement. Explain that today students will use the recommended serving numbers to guide how they do the activities. Remind them that both physical activity and sound nutritional practices are body composition factors a person can control.

## Procedure

1. Use the Food Guide Pyramid to develop balance challenges for the students to perform:

   Example 1: Balance on the number of body parts that represent the number of servings of fruit you should eat each day.

   Example 2: Balance on the number of parts that represent the number of servings of vegetables you should eat each day.

2. Continue the activity as long as desired, using other food groups' serving numbers and offering other challenges.

3. To increase the difficulty of this activity, have the students perform balances with a partner.

## Teaching Hints

Encourage problem solving. Ask students to work with partners or in groups to make creative shapes. Ask questions that allow students to give the range of servings recommended per day for each of the food groups. Review which foods are in each of the food groups as you proceed through the lesson. The idea of balance also means balancing the types of foods that people choose for a daily diet.

Use food serving samples to demonstrate exactly how much one serving amounts to, either with plastic food or equipment in the gym that is the same size as the serving (e.g., tennis ball equals one orange).

## Closure and Assessment

### Written and Oral

- We see and hear a lot of nutritional information every day. Which of these sources is most likely to give reliable information to help build a healthy diet? Circle your choice (offer pictures or do verbally for younger students):

  **Advertising**        **Food Guide Pyramid**        **Restaurant Menu**

- Name a food group and have students signal the number of servings they should have each day from that group by holding up the correct number of fingers.

### Project

- Have the students share with a partner(s) the types of food that they eat and the food group on the pyramid to which they belong.

## Extending the Lesson

- Have students draw pictures of appropriate breakfast foods on paper plates and display them with the corresponding caption and information from the modified Food Guide Pyramid. Have them cut pictures from old magazines and paste them in the correct places on the Pyramid.

Concentrated fats, oils, & refined sugars
Use sparingly

Milk, yogurt, & cheese group
2–3 servings

Meat, poultry, fish, dry beans, eggs, & nuts group
2–3 servings

Vegetable group
3–5 servings

Fruit group
2–4 servings

Bread, cereal, rice, & pasta group
6–11 servings

Liquids
2–3 quarts

- Have students list or draw their 10 favorite foods. Describe the taste of each. Why do you like them? Where do they fit in the Food Guide Pyramid?

- Have the students check their kitchen cupboard at home and find foods that match all the letters of the alphabet, A to Z. Discuss the nutritional value of the foods in class.

- Have students make a breakfast poster entitled "Break the Fast" with the information "Remember that breakfast is one of the most important meals of the day. Your body has gone all night without energy and needs to be refueled." Photocopy the text for younger students.

# 5 It Comes—and Goes

## Primary Level

A process called **metabolism** controls the way your body uses food. Everyone has a different metabolism rate, but we all use the same nutrients to make the body run. The rate (fast or slow) of your metabolism is affected by your genetics (family history), age, and level of physical activity. These factors influence the rate in which your body uses food (how fast or slow). A metabolism that is too slow results in excessive weight gain and poor body composition, because the body doesn't use up nutrients fast enough. A metabolism that is too fast results in excessive weight loss and poor body composition, because the body uses up nutrients too fast.

## Purpose

Students will understand the meaning of the word *metabolism*, that everyone's body functions are unique, that each person requires the same nutrients but in different amounts, and that each person's body uses the nutrients a little differently.

## Equipment Needed

- Approximately 20-30 balls (yarn, if possible) for a class of 30 (one ball per pair of students, with a few spares)
- Traffic arrow signs (optional)

## Relationship to National Standards

**Physical Education Standard 4:** Student achieves and maintains a health-enhancing level of physical fitness—Student will participate in moderate to vigorous physical activity in a variety of settings.

**Health Education Standard 1:** Student will comprehend concepts related to health promotion and disease prevention—Student will explain how health is influenced by the interaction of body systems.

## Set Induction

Define *metabolism* and how it relates to body composition. Explain that although everyone needs the same nutrients, everyone's metabolism is different. State that today students will play a game to show how metabolism affects body composition.

## Procedure

1. To play this simple throwing game, pair off students, then separate pairs to form two groups divided by a boundary line. Designate one side as "A" and one side as "B." Give all of the "B" students one ball.

2. On a signal, each student throws the ball over to the other side.

3. The first time the teacher tells the students to throw the balls underhand and slowly. The teacher uses a stopwatch and times them to see how long it takes them to throw them slowly.

4. The second time the teacher asks them to throw them overhand quickly. The teacher times them and lets them know how how long it takes to throw them quickly.

5. Connect the activity to the lesson on metabolism by saying the following:

   "Sometimes your metabolism uses food slowly and it takes longer to use it up, like when you threw the balls slowly. Sometimes your metabolism uses food up more quickly and it takes a shorter time to use it up, like when you threw the balls quickly. Each of us is different in how fast or slow we burn 'food' fuel, just like the different times it took each of you to throw the balls."

## Teaching Hints

You can use traffic arrow signs to show the direction in which the ball should move next. To help students stop immediately upon the signal, give them a warning count: "Five, four, three, two, one, throw!!!"

The same activity can be done with kicking, or striking with floor hockey sticks, and so on.

## Closure and Assessment

### Written and Oral

- The way the body processes food into fuel is called metabolism—yes or no.
- Everyone's metabolism is the same—yes or no.

### Project

- Using the letters of the word metabolism, during class write the word METABOLISM on the board and have students identify a body composition component word for each letter: M = muscles, E = energy, B = bones, and so on.

## Extending the Lesson

Use one of these bulletin board ideas:

- Use the theme "Start the Day Off Right."
- Use the theme "Fuel for the Day."
- Show how food is used as energy in the body. List the nutrients—carbohydrates, fats, and proteins.
- Have students draw or bring pictures of why each person is different. Place on a bulletin board with each student's name, pictures, and reasons why they are different from others.

# 6 Moderate to Vigorous Fun A

### Primary Level

Physical activity, strength training, daily tasks, chores, continuous activity, and nutrition are the key factors in maintaining or improving your **body composition**. Daily physical activity and sound nutritional practices will allow you to enjoy life and be active for a lifetime. The more intense the activity, the greater its effect on body composition.

## Purpose

Students will begin to recognize that moderate and vigorous physical activities affect body composition and, to obtain the same benefit, a person has to perform some activities longer.

## Equipment Needed

- 10 Activity Cards with an activity on one side of the card and numbers 1 through 10 marked on the other side.
- Red and green paper; container

## Relationship to National Standards

**Physical Education Standard 4:** Student achieves and maintains a health-enhancing level of physical fitness—Student will recognize the physiological indicators that accompany moderate to vigorous physical activity.

**Health Education Standard 3:** Student will demonstrate the ability to practice health-enhancing behaviors and reduce risks—Student will demonstrate strategies to improve or maintain personal health.

## Set Induction

Discuss the differences between moderate and vigorous activity. Explain that even household chores can count as physical activity and, along with appropriate nutritional practices, can contribute to a healthy body composition. Brainstorm a list of key factors affecting body composition. Explain that today students will be role-playing various activities and deciding which are moderate and which are vigorous in intensity.

## Procedure

1. Have a student pick a number at random between 1 to 10.

2. Read the instructions for the activity corresponding to the number the student selected.

3. Have students role-play the action for the number of seconds listed, explaining that this corresponds to what the *Surgeon General's Report on Physical Activity and Health* (1996) suggests is the number of minutes of each activity needed to burn 150 calories.

4. Repeat by having another student choose a number.
5. Continue until you have touched upon each activity.

   **More vigorous:**

   1. Bicycling 4 miles in 15 minutes—15 seconds
   2. Jumping rope—15
   3. Shoveling snow—15
   4. Stair-walking—15
   5. Running—15

   **Moderate:**

   6. Raking leaves—30 seconds
   7. Walking—30
   8. Basketball shooting—30
   9. Bicycling 5 miles in 30 minutes—30
   10. Volleyball—45

## Teaching Hints

Help students begin to recognize that to obtain the benefit it takes more or less time, depending on how vigorous the activity is. Be sure to help students identify which activities are considered moderate and which ones vigorous.

## Closure and Assessment

### Written and Oral

- Ask "What factors that influence body composition will help you be active for a lifetime?"
- Conduct an exit poll, answering the statement "Physical activity is important for healthy body composition." Have students drop a red piece of paper into a container if they think the answer is "no" and a green piece of paper if they think the answer is "yes."

### Project

- Have students make a "Calorie Machine" diagram, drawing a gadget that shows a list of foods eaten during a day going into the machine. Have students draw a variety of physical activity choices that send calories out. Explain that the body is this calorie machine and if more calories go in than out, it can lead to obesity.

## Extending the Lesson

As homework, have students write down what they ate for one day and the physical activity they did for that day.

# 7    Artist, Clay, Model

### Primary Level

**Issues in our society** that affect body composition: You cannot look at a person's appearance and judge their health level. There are a lot of factors that determine if a person is healthy (e.g., activity level, appropriate nutritional practices, age, family history, smoking, illness, and so on).

## Purpose

Students will understand that a person's appearance does not indicate his or her health level.

## Equipment Needed

- Magazine pictures
- 1 blindfold for each group of three (optional)

## Relationship to National Standards

**Physical Education Standard 3:** Student exhibits a physically active lifestyle—Student will identify the benefits derived from regular physical activity.

**Health Education Standard 1:** Student will comprehend concepts related to health promotion and disease prevention—Student will describe the relationships between personal health behaviors and individual well-being.

## Set Induction

Discuss how what we think we are seeing is not always a true picture. Explain that today students will be trying to make judgments when they don't have all the clues. The same is true for health—you can't tell if a person is healthy or not just by looking.

## Procedure

1. Divide students into groups of three:

   Artist—Student closes eyes or wears a blindfold.

   Clay—Student who will be molded to mirror the model.

   Model—Assumes a pose.

2. Explain that the "artist" must feel how the model is posed and attempt to mold the "clay" into the same shape as the "model." After a few tries, the artist may look and see how closely the other two students' shapes are alike.

3. Repeat until each student has assumed each role.

## Teaching Hints

Remind students that things are not always what they seem to be and the same is true about health: We can't always tell about someone's health without a lot of information.

## Closure and Assessment

### Written and Oral

- As a class, brainstorm a list of factors that determine if a person is healthy. Have each student show which factor he will work on in the coming week with a show of hands.

### Project

- Show students a picture of a "healthy"-looking model. Have each student list things that may be unhealthy about the model that you can't see looking at the picture.

- As a class, create a jingle for a TV commercial called "Factors That Make People Healthy."

## Extending the Lesson

Have pairs of students make several clay sculptures, trying to duplicate a different model each time. Each student should try both making the sculpture while blindfolded and describing the model to his or her partner. This can be a cooperative project with the art teacher.

# 8    Balancing the Body

## Intermediate Level

Carbohydrates, fats, and proteins, as well as water and minerals, are the principal building blocks of **body composition**. One measure of body composition is the ratio of lean body mass (bones, muscles, tissues, nutrients, and water) to fat. Because lean body mass weighs more than fat, using a scale to determine your ideal body composition does not work. A person who is overweight on a scale, may actually be in good shape. It is just as important to avoid having too much fat. Your body needs both lean body mass and fat to function properly.

## Purpose

Students will (1) identify that lean body mass weighs more than body fat; (2) learn how to maintain an ideal body mass; and (3) understand how body composition is determined.

## Equipment Needed

- 1 hula hoop per small group
- 6 foam balls per small group
- 6 beanbags per small group
- Music

## Relationship to National Standards

**Physical Education Standard 4:** Student achieves and maintains a health-enhancing level of physical fitness—Student will maintain continuous aerobic activity for specified time and for activity.

**Health Education Standard 1:** Student will comprehend concepts related to health promotion and disease prevention—Student will describe the basic structure and functions of the human body and systems.

## Set Induction

Use two objects that are the same size but weigh different amounts to demonstrate that lean mass and fat mass can take up the same space but have different weights (a tennis ball and a solid rubber ball the same size work well). Pass the two balls around and explain how our total body weight does not indicate whether or not our body composition is healthy. Explain that today's activity will help students learn more about healthy body composition using foam balls for fat weight and beanbags for lean weight.

## Procedure

1. Divide students into small groups.
2. Give group of four or five students a hoop and six foam balls, and put six beanbags for each group in the middle of the gym.

3. Have two or three students in each group jog twice around the perimeter of the gym to take one foam ball to the center of the gym.

4. At the same time, have the other students in each group sprint back and forth to the center of the gym to pick up one beanbag on each trip until the group has four beanbags.

5. Explain that the beanbags represent lean mass and the foam balls represent fat weight. To reinforce to students that lean mass weighs more than fat, have students hold the pieces of equipment to experience the weight difference.

6. Reverse roles and repeat.

## Teaching Hints

Provide some basic safety rules before beginning, including the need to stay in self-space. Stress the importance of working and cooperating as a team. Stress the importance of having more lean body mass on your body compared to fat mass, but fat mass is just as important in the functioning of the body. Emphasize that the level of activity in this game helps them maintain or reach a healthy ratio. You can vary this game to demonstrate the balance of carbohydrates, fats, and proteins needed as building blocks for a healthy body composition.

## Closure and Assessment

### Written and Oral

Ask several questions, such as the following:

- What is the ratio of lean mass to fat called?
- Which weighs more?     **Lean mass**        **Fat**
- What are the components of lean mass?
- What can you do to maintain a health body composition?

### Project

- Design a project (shadow box, bulletin board, HyperCard stack on the computer) that illustrates the definition of body composition and the fact that physical activity helps you reach and maintain a healthy body composition.

## Extending the Lesson

- Tie in math and science by asking the classroom teacher to teach students the difference between weight and mass and to explore the concept of ratios.

- Provide a variety of pictures of individuals, including everyday people, athletes, celebrities, and models. Have the students arrange the pictures from most healthy-looking to most unhealthy-looking. Through guided discussion, have students discover that appearance does not always indicate good health. Guided discovery discussion questions could include the following:

  - How did you decide which people look the healthiest? Why?
  - Discuss healthy and unhealthy behaviors practiced by sports heroes or other media celebrities, using pictures of specific people.
  - Discuss how deceptive appearances can be in judging good health.

# 9 Maintaining Balance

## Intermediate Level

**Healthy body composition**: Food provides the fuel and building blocks that keep your body functioning. The energy that food gives your body contributes to your body composition. Maintaining a healthy ratio of lean body mass to fat mass allows you to enjoy life, be active, have energy to spare, and grow and develop.

## Purpose

The student will learn the benefits of body fat and lean body mass and gain an awareness of concerns associated with anorexia and obesity.

## Equipment Needed

- 20 plastic bowling pins or 2-liter soda bottles
- Body Composition Benefit Cards (see sidebar)

---

### Body Composition Benefit Cards

Construct with illustrations or use a poster as well.

**Benefits of fat:**

- Acts as an insulator, helping the body adapt to heat and cold
- Acts as a shock absorber, helping protect internal organs and bones from injury
- Helps body use vitamins effectively
- Acts as stored energy when the body needs energy

**Benefits of lean body mass:**

- Helps in burning calories
- Provides structure for the body
- Helps the body move effectively

---

## Relationship to National Standards

**Physical Education Standard 3:** Student exhibits a physically active lifestyle—Student will identify the critical aspects of a healthy lifestyle.

**Health Education Standard 3:** Student will demonstrate the ability to practice health-enhancing behaviors and reduce health risks—Student will demonstrate strategies to improve or maintain personal health.

## Set Induction

Explain or review the fact that a healthy ratio of lean body mass to fat mass is about four or five to one. State that both too little fat and too much are unhealthy. Briefly describe anorexia and obesity. Explain that, today, students will be playing a game that will provide the physical activity they need to reach or maintain a healthy body composition. The game will also demonstrate a healthy ratio of lean to fat mass. Review safety rules that apply to this game (e.g., stay in self-space, move with control, and so on).

## Procedure

1. Divide the class into two teams.

2. Have teams stand on opposite sides of the playing area in which you have scattered the 20 pins.

3. Assign the following tasks: Team A sets pins down; Team B sets pins up, but everyone on the team must perform five jumping jacks after setting down a pin. Explain that the pins down represent fat, and the pins up represent lean mass. The object of the game is to have only two, three, or four pins down at a time.

4. Before giving the start signal for each round, read a Benefit Card statement. Alternate reading a health benefit for body fat and one for lean body mass.

5. Signal students to begin to hustle safely through the playing area either setting pins down or up, depending on their team's assignment.

6. After one or two minutes, signal students to freeze and count the number of pins down to determine if a good balance of body mass to fat mass remains. Remind students that to maintain a good balance in this game— only two, three, or four pins can be down. Then remind students that maintaining a healthy balance is not always easy and requires good nutritional habits and physical activity most days of the week.

7. To begin each new round, have teams switch jobs (i.e., Team A sets pins up and Team B sets pins down).

8. Continue for as many rounds as desired, reading a Benefit Card before each round.

## Teaching Hints

Demand safety. If a student is recklessly knocking pins down a significant consequence should occur. Benefit statements are best remembered if they are visual. Add rest (safe) areas into the game so that those who need a rest can do so.

## Closure and Assessment

### Written and Oral

- Ask "Why is it important to have both lean mass and body fat?"

### Project

- Design a health-related TV commercial, highlighting the benefits of both body fat and lean mass, and act it out.

## Extending the Lesson

Have a school cafeteria worker talk to the class to discover how the nutritionist plans nutritionally appropriate meals.

# 10 Ease on Down the Road

## Intermediate Level

**Growth and developmental influences** on body composition: There are many factors that influence your body composition. The role of nutrients, how much energy you take in (food), and how much energy you use (working, playing, growing, and learning) influence your body composition and are controlled by you. Factors you cannot control, such as your age, gender, and genetics, food sensitivities, and lifestyles, also play an important role in your body size, type, and shape.

## Purpose

Students will identify variables that may affect their growth and development in relation to body composition, and will understand that each person is unique in physical activity and nutrition requirements.

## Equipment Needed

- Influence signs (showing factors that influence body composition—see Procedure)
- Cones

## Relationship to National Standards

**Physical Education Standard 3:** Student exhibits a physically active lifestyle—Student will identify the benefits derived from regular physical activity.

**Health Education Standard 1:** Student will comprehend concepts related to health promotion and disease prevention.

## Set Induction

Discuss how growth and development, as well as other factors, can affect body composition. Remind students that these are all individual. Ask students to identify which factors a person can control and which they cannot control. Explain that today's activity will help each student reach or maintain a healthy body composition through physical activity. Encourage students to be physically active outside of physical education as well.

## Procedure

1. Using cones, create a highway for students to travel through. Also create signs within the area of the highway that state the factors that affect body composition. Place a tagger along each of the pathways within each of the identified zones.

2. Explain that each zone represents a variable that influences your body composition, such as age, heredity, physical activity, gender, and nutrition habits.

3. Designate a locomotor movement to travel with along the road.

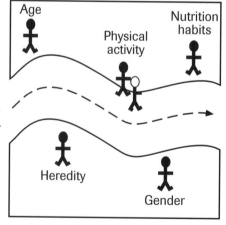

Healthy highway

4. Signal students to move down the highway passing through each zone, trying to avoid being tagged.

5. Have tagged students move to the sides of the road, read the factor listed on the highway sign, perform the activity that is on the sign and then return to the start to begin again.

6. Send students along the highway several times, changing taggers each time.

## Teaching Hints

Begin the game with a slow-paced locomotor movement (walk, hop, skip, and so on). One tagger could be in each zone on the highway. You can create two kinds of zones: controllable factors (nutrition and physical activity) and uncontrollable factors (heredity, age, gender). On the other hand, you could put each of the five factors in its own zone.

## Closure and Assessment

### Written and Oral

- List two factors you can control and two you cannot that influence body composition.

### Project

- Discuss with your partner(s) factors that influence your eating habits and body composition. As a group, choose a favorite restaurant and discuss the kinds of foods that your group consumes there. Look up the calories and nutrients in those foods.

## Extending the Lesson

- Pretend to travel a famous road or highway in your area of the country and integrate history or geography. Create signs that tell others about factors that influence body composition.

- Collect pictures of people from different countries and cultures and point out similarities and differences in the nutritional practices of various cultures, such as the kinds of foods they eat and how they are prepared (be sure to avoid making biased statements and attitudes).

# 11 Nutrient Tag

## Intermediate Level

Food is important as a source of **nutrients** that are grouped into carbohydrates, proteins, and fats as well as minerals, vitamins, and water. These nutrients give the body energy to support growth, repair body parts, and regulate body processes. It is important to have a well-balanced nutritional plan and physical activity in your life to develop and maintain a healthy body composition.

## Purpose

Students will learn the roles of carbohydrates, fats, proteins, vitamins, minerals, and water in relation to healthy body composition as well as the roles of balance, variety, and moderation.

## Equipment Needed

- Pictures of foods that have the 6 nutrients (list roles of the nutrients)
- Several cards with 1 of each of the 6 nutrients listed on them (enough for at least one per student)
- Poly-spots for home bases

## Relationship to National Standards

**Physical Education Standard 4:** Student exhibits a physically active lifestyle—Student will describe healthful benefits that result from regular and appropriate participation in physical activity.

**Health Education Standard 3:** Student will demonstrate the ability to practice health-enhancing behaviors and reduce health risks—Student will demonstrate strategies to improve or maintain personal health.

## Set Induction

Discuss the importance of a well-balanced nutritional plan and incorporating physical activity into your daily life. These are essential to maintaining a healthy body composition. List or have students list the six nutrients. Then state that carbohydrates and fats are the main energy sources and proteins are important for building muscle mass. The daily nutritional plan should include foods with the six essential nutrients, which students will review in the game today.

## Procedure

1. Scatter the poly-spots about the activity area.
2. Have students line up on the end line of the activity area.
3. Tell or whisper to each student what nutrient they are going to be, or if they can read give them a card with a nutrient on it. Then collect the cards.
4. Choose one to three students to be "Nutrient Catchers." They stand in the middle of the playing area and their job is to loudly call out one nutrient, thereby signaling the students who represent that nutrient to travel across the activity area. The "Nutrient Catchers" try to tag students before they reach the far end line.

5. If a student is tagged, he or she must stand on a base (poly-spot) and try to help tag others.

6. Continue playing the game, calling out each nutrient in turn.

7. To increase cognitive learning, each time you prepare to play, ask a student to tell the class a food that is high in carbohydrates, fats, proteins, and so on.

8. For a fun variation, call "balanced nutrients" to signal the whole class—all six nutrients—to move across the activity area using a controlled locomotor movement.

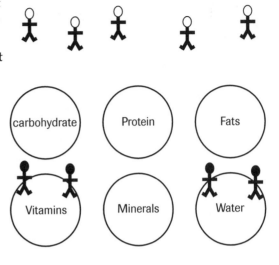

## Teaching Hints

Beyond the fun of the tag game, be sure students focus on the content of the lesson as stated under Purpose and Set Induction. To bring the cognitive domain further into play, give each student a card that has a picture of a food and a list of the essential nutrients found in the food. Ask students to bring in pictures of foods to make the cards. Remember, never play out a tag game until the last student is caught. Change taggers often so all students enjoy physical activity.

## Closure and Assessment

### Written and Oral

- List five of the six essential nutrients that come from food.
- List three reasons why the body needs all six essential nutrients.

### Project

- See how many kinds of foods your group can come up with that have one or two of the nutrients in them such as vitamins—oranges, apples, lettuce, cereal; carbohydrates—rice, ice cream, and so on.
- Have the students write out their breakfast, lunch, and dinner, compare nutrients in the foods, and then analyze the menus. How does each food contribute to a healthy diet?
- Have each student analyze the nutrients that come from her food choices. Then direct each to write a short summary of her findings. The summary should reflect information learned through the food analysis and any changes in food choices a student might wish to make.

## Extending the Lesson

- Ask the classroom teacher to have students learn to spell the nutrients played in the game and key foods that provide these nutrients.
- Make a bulletin board entitled "Diet Myths."

# 12 Pyramid Power

### Intermediate Level

**Metabolism** refers to the sum of chemical reactions that occur in the body to keep us alive. To maintain a healthy body composition, the energy (food) that goes in the body must equal the energy (activity) used. Everyone metabolizes food differently according to genetics, age, and physical activity level. A higher physical activity level leads to a higher metabolic rate, which in turn helps the body use food for fuel instead of creating excess fat.

## Purpose

Students will understand that (1) the different amounts and kinds of food you eat provide different amounts of energy in processing the food for fuel; (2) "calories in" (those eaten) must equal "energy out" (those spent) to have a healthy body composition; and (3) each person's metabolism is unique.

## Equipment Needed

- Pyramid Cards (triangular shapes, on each with a food item listed, the calories, the energy needed to process the food, and the number of walls to touch for physical activity)
- 4 wall signs that have 2 numbers on each of them (1 and 5, 2 and 6, 3 and 7, and 4 and 8). They are placed on the walls or on the back of a chair.
- Music (fun and continuous)

## Relationship to National Standards

**Physical Education Standard 4:** Student achieves and maintains a health-enhancing level of physical fitness—Student will identify several activities related to each component of physical fitness.

**Health Education Standard 3:** Student will demonstrate the ability to practice health-enhancing behaviors and reduce health risks—Student will demonstrate strategies to improve or maintain personal health.

## Set Induction

Introduce or review the definition of *metabolism* and the factors that influence it. Explain that today's activity will help students achieve a balance of calories in and out by involving them in vigorous physical activity while they learn about different foods, their calories, and the activity required to process those calories. Review safety rules (staying in self-space and so on).

## Procedure

1. Choose whether you want students to work individually or in small (two or three students) groups. If using small groups, one member goes out to pick up the food pyramid and brings back the information to the group. The whole group then follows the one that picked up the food pyramid jogging to each wall.
2. Place the Pyramid Cards in the center of the room.
3. Have each student find a personal space in the activity area to use as a home base.

4. Have each student pick one card and take the card back to his or her home base, read it, then perform the listed activity (number of walls to touch). Have students keep each card until the end of the game. Some Pyramid Cards have the message "0" walls, which indicates that the student must draw another card.

5. Walls must be touched in the correct (numeric) order.

6. Continue the activity for five to seven minutes.

## Teaching Hints

Play some fun, continuous music during the activity. Remind students to be careful when moving through open spaces. Working in partners or small groups, students could skip to slow down the movement. When working alone, students can use different locomotor skills when moving from wall to wall, or integrate skill themes (dribbling, tossing and catching, and so on) instead of traveling from wall to wall. To enhance cooperative learning skills, have small groups stay connected while they travel from wall to wall. You might also choose to have students return chosen cards to the card pile immediately instead of keeping them.

## Closure and Assessment

### Written and Oral

- Write a short definition of metabolism. List two factors that influence the rate of metabolism.

### Project

- Have students create a collage showing a train ("metabolism") that goes slow or fast, depending on what students put in the storage cars. Choose from pictures and cards with various physical activities and foods from various food groups. For example, more vigorous physical activities tend to increase the metabolic rate, and foods with more calories will take longer to process as fuel.

## Extending the Lesson

- Have students arrange the Pyramid Cards they collected into food groups in the shape of the Food Guide Pyramid. Let them discuss their nutritional plans for the day. This is a great way to integrate a nutrition lesson in physical education. Ask "Did they have enough servings of [a specific nutrient, such as carbohydrates]?"

- Ask the classroom teacher to introduce or review how to read food labels for calories and integrate math by figuring out how much activity will metabolize each serving.

# 13  Activity and Health

## Intermediate Level

**Physical activity** and healthy **nutrition** are the keys to maintaining a healthy body composition. Being physically active helps you control your weight, tone your muscles, and balance the calories in and out. You should try to participate in moderate physical activity most days of the week; daily is better.

## Purpose

Students will learn about a variety of activities they can enjoy that are moderate to vigorous and participate in a number of moderate to vigorous physical activities.

## Equipment Needed

- Using the *Surgeon General's Report on Physical Activity and Health* (1996), set up a physical activity circuit with a variety of activities such as touch football, basketball shooting, dancing fast, jump rope, and so on. On each station card, list the physical activity the students will perform, plus one other example (raking leaves, gardening, washing windows, shoveling snow, and the like).

## Relationship to National Standards

**Physical Education Standard 3:** Student exhibits a physically active lifestyle—Student will identify several moderate to vigorous physical activities that provide personal pleasure and participate daily in some form of health-enhancing physical activity.

**Health Education Standard 3:** Student will demonstrate the ability to practice health-enhancing behaviors and reduce health risks—Student will demonstrate strategies to improve or maintain personal health.

## Set Induction

Explain to the students that the objective of this activity is to understand that many different types of physical activity are good for the body and that each contributes to an active, healthy lifestyle.

## Procedure

1. Divide students into small groups and assign one group to each station.
2. Give students two minutes to participate in the station's physical activity, then have them rotate to the next station.
3. Repeat the activity until everyone has visited all stations.

## Teaching Hints

As a variation, allow each student the opportunity to choose one or more activities he enjoys during the allotted time, rather than having everyone rotate through all the stations. You may wish to use this activity at the end of the body composition unit so students have activity choices after learning the roles of nutrition and physical activity.

## Closure and Assessment

### Written and Oral

- Explain why physical activity is important to maintaining a healthy body composition.

### Project

- Using the principles discussed in this book, design a Daily Activity Calendar to implement for one month. Keep track of how well you implemented the activities you selected for the month.

## Extending the Lesson

Develop a bulletin board entitled "Physical Activity—A 'Key' to a Healthy Lifestyle." Place a number of construction paper "keys" on the bulletin board, which list a wide variety of physical activities. Place pictures of people (students or magazine and newspaper clippings) as well as of a variety of activities. Examples of activities for keys include the following: washing and waxing the car; washing windows or floors; volleyball; touch football; gardening; wheeling self in wheelchair; walking, basketball, bicycling; dancing fast; raking leaves; water aerobics; running fast; jogging; shoveling snow.

# 14 Insides Count

## Intermediate Level

**Issues in society** that affect body composition: Healthy body composition is not always well understood. Indeed, a person's appearance does not indicate his or her health level. Judging people—especially by what they look like—is not a good practice. Several factors influence each person's body composition: culture, peer pressure, advertising, and lifestyle choices.

## Purpose

Students will identify social issues related to culture, peer pressure, advertising, and lifestyle that influence body composition and demonstrate respect for all people, recognizing that healthy body composition is found in people of many different sizes and shapes.

## Equipment Needed

- Soft taggers, such as tennis balls or yellow foam balls

## Relationship to National Standards

**Physical Education Standard 3:** Student exhibits a physically active lifestyle—Student will identify the benefits derived from regular physical activity.

**Health Education Standard 1:** Student will comprehend concepts related to health promotion and disease prevention—Student will describe the relationships between personal health behaviors and individual well-being.

## Set Induction

Define *cholesterol*. Discuss the different factors that influence body composition. List foods that are high in cholesterol. Remind students that you can't tell if someone is unhealthy simply by looking at her. Explain that today's activity allows you to see how difficult it is to get around if cholesterol starts blocking the way—even if things look fine on the outside.

## Procedure

1. Have students start at each end line of the activity area and try to run into the area designated as the heart. This area should be large enough for about half of the class to stand in.
2. Give the first signal, "Veins!" Have two students on the sidelines hold soft taggers (yellow foam balls or tennis balls). Direct these students to try to tag the runners as they go to the heart.
3. If a runner is tagged, that runner becomes a tagger (give him a soft tagger).
4. Once the runners have reached the heart, they listen for the signal "Arteries!" which sends them away from the heart and back to the end lines. Again, if tagged, runners assume the tagging role. All taggers must stay on the sidelines.

5. Stop the game when there are only three or four runners left. Explain that as the game continued and more "cholesterol taggers" joined the sides, it became more and more difficult to travel in and out of the heart as happens in real life if our arteries become too full of cholesterol.

6. If time permits, play the game again.

## Teaching Hints

Emphasize that outside packaging does not always give us a clue as to what is on the inside. What is inside is more important. Any body type, size, or shape is subject to accumulating too much cholesterol inside if the person does not practice good physical activity and nutrition habits. Demand safety. Sliding and diving are not okay ways to get in or out of the heart. Mandate that falling is the same as being tagged.

## Closure and Assessment

### Written and Oral

- Define cholesterol, arteries, and veins.

### Project

- Create a restaurant menu that depicts Healthy Heart Foods or foods that are low in cholesterol or fat content.

## Extending the Lesson

- Have each student develop a collage, illustrating the issues related to culture, peer pressures, advertising, and lifestyle that influence his or her body composition. Have each student place a photo of herself in the center and place pictures of the issues she is dealing with around the photo.

- Have a physician come to the class to discuss how heart disease affects the heart and overall health.

# References _____

Alter, Michael J. 1998. *Sport Stretch*. 2d ed. Champaign, IL: Human Kinetics.

Biddle, Stuart and Marios Goudas. 1996. "Analysis of Children's Physical Activity and Its Association With Adult Encouragement and Social Cognitive Values." *Journal of School Health* 66(2):75-78.

Bouchard, Claude, et al., eds. 1993. *Physical Activity, Fitness, and Health Consensus Statement*. Champaign, IL: Human Kinetics.

Centers for Disease Control (CDC). 1999. *Promoting Physical Activity: A Guide for Community Action*. Champaign, IL: Human Kinetics.

Cheung, Lilian W.Y., and Julius B. Richmond, eds. 1995. *Child Health, Nutrition, and Physical Activity*. Champaign, IL: Human Kinetics.

Corbin, Charles B. 1987. "Physical Fitness in the K-12 Curriculum: Some Defensible Solutions to Perennial Problems." *Journal of Physical Education, Recreation and Dance* 58(7):49-54.

———— and R. Lindsey. 1997. *Fitness for Life*. 4th ed. Glenview, IL: Scott, Foresman.

Council on Physical Education for Children (COPEC). 1992. *Developmentally Appropriate Physical Education Practices for Children*. Reston, VA: National Association for Sport and Physical Education (NASPE).

Craft, Diane H. 1996. "A Focus on Inclusion in Physical Education." In *Physical Education Sourcebook,* ed. Betty F. Hennessy. Champaign, IL: Human Kinetics.

Davison, Bev. 1998. *Creative Physical Activities and Equipment*. Champaign, IL: Human Kinetics.

Desmond, Sharon M., et al. 1986. "The Etiology of Adolescents' Perceptions of Their Weight." *Journal of Youth & Adolescence* 15(6):461-474.

Graham, George. 1992. *Teaching Children Physical Education: Becoming a Master Teacher*. Champaign, IL: Human Kinetics.

Harris, Jo, and Jill Elbourn. 1997. *Teaching Health-Related Exercise at Key Stages 1 and 2*. Champaign, IL: Human Kinetics.

Hennessy, Betty F., ed. 1996. *Physical Education Sourcebook*. Champaign, IL: Human Kinetics.

Hichwa, John. 1998. *Right Fielders Are People Too: An Inclusive Approach to Teaching Middle School Physical Education*. Champaign, IL: Human Kinetics.

Hill, James O., and John C. Peters. 1998. "Environmental Contributions to the Obesity Epidemic." *Science* 280 (May 29):1371-74.

Hinson, Curt. 1995. *Fitness for Children*. Champaign, IL: Human Kinetics.

Hopper, Christine J., et al. 1997a. *Health-Related Fitness for Grades 1 and 2*. Champaign, IL: Human Kinetics.

———. 1997b. *Health-Related Fitness for Grades 3 and 4*. Champaign, IL: Human Kinetics.

———. 1997c. *Health-Related Fitness for Grades 5 and 6*. Champaign, IL: Human Kinetics.

———. 1995. *Teaching for Outcomes in Elementary Physical Education*. Champaign, IL: Human Kinetics.

Individuals With Disabilities Education Act. 20 U.S.C. §§ 1400 *et seq.*, 84 Stat. 175, Pub. L. 91-230 (1970 as amended).

Kraemer, William J. and Steven J. Fleck. 1993. *Strength Training for Young Athletes*. Champaign, IL: Human Kinetics.

Lavay, Barry W., et al. 1997. *Positive Behavior Management Strategies for Physical Educators*. Champaign, IL: Human Kinetics.

Leadly, Kathleen. 1994. "Physical Education Homework." *Teaching Elementary Physical Education* (March):13.

McGinnis, J.M., and W.H. Foege. 1993. "Actual Causes of Death in the United States." *JAMA* 270(18):2207-12.

McSwegin, P.J., et al. 1989. "Fitting in Fitness." *Journal of Physical Education, Recreation and Dance* 60(1):30-45.

Melograno, Vincent J. 1998. *Professional and Student Portfolios for Physical Education*. Champaign, IL: Human Kinetics.

Mosston, Muska, and Sara Ashworth. 1990. *The Spectrum of Teaching Styles: From Command to Discovery*. New York: Longman.

———. 1994. *Teaching Physical Education*. 4th ed. New York: Macmillan.

National Association for Sport and Physical Education (NASPE). 1995. *Moving Into the Future: National Standards for Physical Education, a Guide to Content and Assessment*. St. Louis: Mosby.

National Consortium for Physical Education and Recreation for Individuals With Disabilities (NCPERID). 1995. *Adapted Physical Education National Standards*. Champaign, IL: Human Kinetics.

Nieman, David C. 1998. *The Exercise-Health Connection*. Champaign, IL: Human Kinetics.

Ormrod, J.E. 1995. *Educational Psychology Principles and Applications*. Columbus, OH: Merrill.

Paffenbarger, Ralph S., Jr., and Eric Olsen. 1996. *LifeFit: An Effective Exercise Program for Optimal Health and a Longer Life*. Champaign, IL: Human Kinetics.

Pate, Russell R., and Richard C. Hohn. 1994. *Health and Fitness Through Physical Education*. Champaign, IL: Human Kinetics.

Raffini, James P. 1993. *Winners Without Losers: Structures and Strategies for Increasing Student Motivation to Learn*. Needham Heights, MA: Allyn & Bacon.

Rainey, Don L. & Murray, Tinker D. 1997. *Foundations of Personal Fitness: Any Body Can... Be Fit!* St. Paul, MN: West.

Ratliffe, Thomas, and Laraine M. Ratliffe. 1994. *Teaching Children Fitness: Becoming a Master Teacher.* Champaign, IL: Human Kinetics.

Rink, Judith R., and Larry D. Hensley. 1996. "Assessment in the School Physical Education Program." In *Physical Education Sourcebook*, ed. Betty F. Hennessy, 39-55. Champaign, IL: Human Kinetics.

Rowland, Thomas W. 1990. *Exercise and Children's Health.* Champaign, IL: Human Kinetics.

Safrit, Margaret J. 1995. *Complete Guide to Youth Fitness Testing.* Champaign, IL: Human Kinetics.

Sallis, James F. 1991. "Self-Report Measures of Children's Physical Activity." *Journal of School Health* 61(5):215-219.

Saltman, Paul, Joel Gurin, and Ira Mothner. 1993. *The University of California at San Diego Nutrition Book.* Boston: Little, Brown.

Schiemer, Suzanne. 1996. "A Positive Learning Experience: Self-Assessment Sheets Let Students Take an Active Role in Learning." *Teaching Elementary Physical Education* (March):4-6

Sharkey, Brian J. 1997. *Fitness and Health.* 4th ed. Champaign, IL: Human Kinetics..

Siedentop, Daryl. 1991. *Developing Teaching Skills in Physical Education.* 3rd ed. Mountain View, CA: Mayfield.

Strand, Bradford N., et al. 1997. *Fitness Education: Teaching Concepts-Based Fitness in the Schools.* Scottsdale, AZ: Gorsuch Scarisbrick.

Surgeon General of the United States. 1996. *Physical Activity and Health at a Glance: A Report of the Surgeon General.* Washington, DC: U.S. Government Printing Office.

Taubes, Gary. 1998. "As Obesity Rates Rise, Experts Struggle to Explain Why." *Science* 280 (May 29):1367-68.

Virgilio, Stephen J. 1997. *Fitness Education for Children.* Champaign, IL: Human Kinetics.

Walsh, B. Timothy, and Michael J. Devlin. 1998. "Eating Disorders: Progress and Problems." *Science* 280 (May 29):1387-90.

Wickelgren, Ingrid. 1998. "Obesity: How Big a Problem?" *Science* 280 (May 29):1364-67.

# Appendix

# Worksheets

# Activity Goals Contract

Week of _____     My plans are to do:

|  | Activity I plan to do | Time of day | Friend(s) who will be active with me |
|---|---|---|---|
| **Monday** | | | |
| **Tuesday** | | | |
| **Wednesday** | | | |
| **Thursday** | | | |
| **Friday** | | | |
| **Saturday** | | | |
| **Sunday** | | | |

Student:_____ Date:_____ Teacher:_____

# Fitness Goals Contract

To improve my personal fitness level, I, with the help of my teacher, have set the following fitness goals. I will participate in the activities outlined in this plan to achieve improved physical fitness. Based on my current level of fitness, I believe that these goals are reasonable.

| Fitness component test item Circle appropriate item | Score Date: _____ | My goal | Activities to improve physical fitness | Follow-up score Date: _____ |
|---|---|---|---|---|
| **Aerobic capacity** *One-mile walk/run* *The PACER* | | | | |
| **Body composition** *Percent body fat* *Body mass index* | | | | |
| **Muscle Strength, Endurance & Flexibility** *Curl-up* | | | | |
| *Trunk lift* | | | | |
| *Push-ups* *Modified pull-ups* *Pull-ups* *Flexed-arm hang* | | | | |
| *Back-saver sit-and-reach* *Shoulder stretch* | | | | |

Student:_____ Date:_____ Teacher:_____

# Heart Rate Task Sheet

Name: _____     Date: _____

| Station number | Task | Beginning pulse | Pulse after _____ seconds |
|---|---|---|---|
| 1 | | | |
| 2 | | | |
| 3 | | | |
| 4 | | | |
| 5 | | | |
| 6 | | | |
| 7 | | | |
| 8 | | | |

# Stretching Record Sheet

Name: _____     Date: _____

| Stretch | Trial 1 | Trial 2 | Trial 3 |
|---|---|---|---|
| Triceps stretch | | | |
| Spinal stretch | | | |
| Gastrocnemius stretch | | | |
| Quadriceps stretch | | | |
| Hamstring stretch | | | |
| Abdominal stretch | | | |
| | | | |
| | | | |
| | | | |
| | | | |
| | | | |
| | | | |
| | | | |
| | | | |
| | | | |

# Heart Obstacle Course Worksheet

Make signs labeling the parts of the heart, telling students what activity to do, and listing a benefit of aerobic activity:

❏ **Vena cava** (blue sign)—Using blue beanbags, toss and catch the bags between one another or practice your favorite tossing and catching skills. The blue beanbags mean the blood has no oxygen and needs to return to the lungs to pick up the oxygen and drop off waste products. Benefit: Strong heartbeat.

❏ **Right atrium** (blue sign)—Use scooter boards through cones to show the blood flow through the heart. Benefit: Increased blood flow.

❏ **Right ventricle** (blue sign)—Log roll down a mat. Benefit: Better circulation to fight disease and increase immune system.

❏ **Lungs** (blue sign)—Use a small parachute and have the students move in a counter-clockwise direction, making waves as they keep the parachute in the air. Stop and then have the students perform a cloud depicting the lungs filling with air and providing the cells of the body with fresh oxygen. Benefit: Have fun, enjoy life.

❏ **Left atrium** (red sign)—Pick up the red playground ball and practice your favorite basketball or soccer dribbling skills under control. The red equipment symbolizes oxygenated, fresh blood that has returned to the heart from the lungs. Benefit: Less risk of heart disease.

❏ **Left ventricle** (red sign)—Have the students perform their favorite jump rope skill. Benefit: Less risk of obesity.

❏ **Aorta** (red sign)—Blood leaves the heart and goes out to the body. Choose your favorite aerobic activity to participate in (step aerobics, jump rope, PACER, jog around the gym). Benefit: More oxygen to the muscles throughout the body.

Use red and blue chalk to draw the blood pathway along the circuit. To relate lack of physical activity and nutrition to health, place warning sign activities along the blood's pathway. Label each of these "Risk Factor." For example, direct students to do the following:

❏ **Heart attack**—Stop and stretch, symbolizing no movement of blood through the heart.

❏ **Cholesterol clog**—Crawl through a tunnel instead of over a mat, symbolizing restricted movement of blood through the arteries.

❏ **Smoking**—Walk instead of run to show a lack of oxygen getting to the muscles due to a coughing attack caused by the lungs and clogged arteries.

❏ **Obesity**—Carry weights during the circuit to show how extra weight can slow you down.

## More About Physical Best, the Program, and the American Fitness Alliance

Physical Best is the educational component of a comprehensive health-related physical education program. It's designed to support existing curriculums and enable teachers to help students meet NASPE's health-related fitness standards. Physical Best resources include:

- *Physical Best Activity Guide—Elementary Level*
- *Physical Best Activity Guide—Secondary Level*
- The teacher's guide, *Physical Education for Lifelong Fitness*
- Educational workshops available through AAHPERD, which enable teachers to become certified as Physical Best Health-Fitness Specialists

The Physical Best program is offered through The American Fitness Alliance (AFA), a collaborative effort of AAHPERD, the Cooper Institute for Aerobics Research (CIAR), and Human Kinetics. AFA also offers assessment resources, which can be combined with Physical Best to create a complete health-related physical education program:

- The *FITNESSGRAM* test for evaluating students' physical fitness, developed by CIAR
- *The Brockport Physical Fitness Test*, a national test developed specifically for youths with disabilities
- *FitSmart*, the first national test designed to assess high school students' knowledge of concepts and principles of physical fitness

Additional AFA support resources are available and even more are in development, such as a physical activity text for high school students and a middle school version of FitSmart. All AFA resources are designed to foster the development of quality health-related physical education programs that promote the benefits of lifelong physical activity and health in young people.

*Sponsorship for Physical Best is provided by Gopher Sport and Mars, Incorporated.*